SHAPING THE WOLF WITHIN YOUR DOG

Janella Sanders!

Note for Librarians: A cataloguing record for this book
that includes the U.S. Library of Congress Classification
number, the Library of Congress Call number and the
Dewey Decimal cataloguing code is available from
the Library and Archives of Canada. The complete
cataloguing record can be obtained from the National
Library's online database at:
www.collectionscanada.ca/amicus/index-e.html
ISBN 1-4120-1213-9

TRAFFORD

**This book was published *on-demand* in cooperation with
Trafford Publishing.**
On-demand publishing is a unique process and service
of making a book available for retail sale to the public
taking advantage of on-demand manufacturing and Internet
marketing. **On-demand publishing** includes promotions,
retail sales, manufacturing, order fulfilment, accounting and
collecting royalties on behalf of the author.

Suite 6E, 2333 Government St.,
Victoria, B.C. V8T 4P4, CANADA
Phone   250-383-6864
Toll-free   1-888-232-4444
Fax   250-383-6804
E-mail   sales@trafford.com
www.trafford.com/robots/03-1591.html

10   9   8   7   6   5   4   3   2

SHAPING THE WOLF WITHIN YOUR DOG

NATHAN B. CHILDS

Trafford Publishing   *Victoria, B.C. Canada*

ALSO BY NATHAN CHILDS

Leader of the Pack: Shaping Dog Instincts Through Pack Training

SHAPING THE WOLF WITHIN YOUR DOG

Table of Contents

ACKNOWLEDGEMENTS

SPECIAL THANKS goes out to everyone who has supported this effort: my children, parents, brother and sisters, and friends who have given encouragement and proof read countless manuscripts; to Joanne McCormick, Lynn Seefurth, Cathy Peek, Linda Caron, Billie Gordon, Cynthia and Wayne Watkins, Cathy and Steve Simpson, Candace Hoffman, Lahoma Fox, Cecilia DeSonia, Victor and Malinda Wilkes, Maggie Louie, and Mark Bazlove for their support, photography, artwork, editing, and computer expertise. And special thanks goes to my father, Walt Childs, for the opportunity to learn this wonderful trade.

And to all those great dogs that have walked the trails with me.

Back cover photography by Sue Farias: collars@knology.net

Photography in Chapter 12 by Joanne McCormick

Photography in Chapter 22 by Wayne and Cynthia Watkins

Introduction

At the age of fourteen, I began a dog-training career that would span four decades. Being the kennel boy at my father's gun-dog kennel did not give me the opportunity to be schooled in the trade. I don't know if there were any schools for dog trainers in 1964. In those days, people would emulate those who had well-trained dogs by imitating their training techniques. This is how information was commonly shared before the Information Age.

Even though accessible information has increased today, there seems to be much confusion about the subject of dog training. At the present time there are three methods being used to train dogs. Positive-reinforcement trainers believe that dogs respond best when food rewards are included with their training. Force trainers believe that dogs respond best to a heavy hand. As a result, these trainers constrain their dogs' rebellious nature with excessive force and traumatic discipline. A growing number of trainers are proclaiming the virtues of clicker training. Clicker training includes rewarding a dog with food when he is doing what the trainer wants. With a clicker in one hand and a treat in the other, clicker trainers are offshoots of the positive-reinforcement camp.

For those who understand that dogs are intelligent animals, this book is dedicated to you. For everyone else, this book is written for you. With an understanding that dogs are complex and cunning creatures that express and feel emotions, you will see why force trainers and positive-reinforcement trainers are missing the boat. For me, and a growing number of enthusiasts, the only sure way to train a dog is to connect with the animal on its level. When we make this connection, we will induce in our dogs the desire to gain our favor.

The majority of dog trainers are positive-reinforcement trainers. And most of the rest will strike their dogs or use electronic training devices (shock collars) and prong collars to validate their authority. These are the force trainers. Clicker trainers use a clicking device to hold their dogs' attention. Nicole Wilde writes in her book, *So You Want to be a Dog Trainer*: "A small device called a clicker is used to mark the exact moment the dog is doing what we'd like. The click is then followed by a treat."

Which method of training dogs is best: force training, positive-reinforcement training, clicker training, or none of the above? Obedience training is only a means of validating leadership with a dog. If you haven't established your alpha position, teaching your dog to execute a few obedience commands will not change his attitude or behavior. In order for your dog to respect you, he must accept your alpha status. A dog will respect your leadership when you are able to communicate as an alpha leader. He will not respect your leadership when you use force or food rewards during his training. You can train seals and dolphins to perform for food, and you can force wild horses to accept a saddle if you inflict enough fear upon them; but in both examples, you have not "connected" with these animals. You have only conditioned or controlled them.

When you connect with intelligent animals, they are responsive to their training because it is their nature to follow a leader. The key to training a dog is making this connection. Making a psychological connection with a dog is what I call pack training. I have used pack-training techniques with over 3000 dogs. My students have included gun dogs, obedience trial dogs, field trial dogs, wolf dogs, guard dogs, family protection dogs, and over 70 breeds of family pets. Whether you own a pampered toy breed or a hardened working dog, they are basically the same pack animal.

Pack training is a means of establishing social order with a dog. By communicating your leadership in your dog's language, you can establish your alpha position and shape your dog's instincts to your advantage. When you know how to shape your dog's instincts, you can instill in your dog the will of a pack member. When your dog believes that he is your pack member, he will be the loving pet that you desire.

Being a pack member is the best possible life for a dog. Pack members have all of the perks (e.g., eat, sleep, and play) and few of the responsibilities. On the other hand, the job description of a pack leader includes maintaining order, supervising family and social activities, marking territory, and protecting the pack from all outside threats. And it's a long day! Pack members live a comparatively stress-free life because they do not have the burden of these responsibilities.

When you communicate with your dog as an alpha leader, your dog will respond as a pack member. In order to communicate your leadership to a dog, you must be able to speak his language. You can learn how to speak Dog by studying wolf behavior or learning from those who have. What do wolves have to do with our dogs? It is an accepted fact that the ancestors of our dogs were wolves. In order to understand the nature of your dog, you need to go to the source. When you study wolf behavior you will discover the following traits of your dog:

The natural behavior of canines
How canines communicate
How alphas lead their packs
How canines submit to authority
How alphas discipline and show affection
The hierarchy of the wolf social order
The natural friendliness, loyalty, and devotion of pack animals

When wolves are compared to dogs, you will see that wolves are basically wild dogs. Wolves and dogs have the same means of communication, and both exhibit the same behavior—but do they also have the same instincts? Do the laws of Nature apply equally to both?

Shaping the Wolf Within Your Dog is a study of wolf and dog behavior. With an understanding of how wolves and dogs communicate and establish social order, you can establish social order in your pack-family and live in harmony with your dog. By communicating your love, will, and authority in your dog's language, you will not have to resort to bribery or violence.

Because you will be employing the same techniques of an alpha wolf and speaking a common language, your dog will accept your alpha status. As a pack trainer, you will be shaping the wolf instincts that are intact and engaged in each of our dogs. Dogs are eager to have a pack leader who listens to them and speaks their language. When you can be that leader, your dog will want to follow your lead.

With few exceptions to the rule, great companion dogs are pack members, and problem dogs are pack leaders. A great dog is a family asset, but an alpha dog in your home is a distinct nuisance and a possible liability. When you become your dog's leader, you will experience what it means to be the leader of the pack.

In The Beginning

Even though I had a fear of large dogs, two small dogs left a mark on my early childhood. Buster was a six-week-old terrier mix. Our time together was cut short, for he died of distemper soon after he came home with me. I remember holding him as he labored to breathe. The other dog was a courageous and loyal Welsh corgi named Hansel. Hansel always accompanied me when I walked aimlessly in the neighborhood or fished in the lake near our home. He never wandered away, and always took a defensive attitude when approached by a strange dog or someone he didn't know.

As a fighter, Hansel was a gladiator, even when the odds were stacked against him. Like all superheroes, Hansel had an archenemy that was bigger than life—in the form of a seventy-pound pointer named Ruff. Whenever he and Hansel had the opportunity, they would engage one another in battle. Even though Ruff was never vanquished, Hansel never submitted to the neighbor's dog. Following one of their battles, the frustrated pointer would walk away, leaving Hansel posturing as the bloody victor.

Hansel was always dominant and aggressive with the neighborhood dogs, so he didn't make many friends. His strategy during a confrontation was to attack his adversary's belly and throat by going under the dog's legs and fighting on his back. Hansel taught me about the character of dogs by demonstrating his loyalty, courage, cunning, and protectiveness.

At the age of fourteen, I moved from my grandmother's Central Florida home to my father's home in the Florida Panhandle. My father managed 10,000 acres of timberland along the banks of the Chipola River in Calhoun County. His tree farm became my backyard and private hunting ground. Being a kid who loved to hike, and having a kennel full of hunting dogs, I did what any kid would have done – I went hiking and hunting with the dogs.

As children, we knew our dogs would not wander away when we hiked in the woods. Kids have always understood the dynamics of a pack hierarchy. When kids gang up, there will always be a leader and followers. When a pack of dogs run or hunt together, there will always be a leader and followers. By hiking and hunting with my father's dogs, I had taken on the responsibility of a pack leader providing leadership and pack activities to a pack of dogs. As a result, I created a pack hierarchy and established social order. The breeds of dogs that we kept were golden retrievers, pointers, English setters, Brittany spaniels, and beagles.

Then along came a pup named Wink. My father had a good reason to believe in the pup's potential. Wink was from the same pedigree that he had established over the years. The pup's mother was a Field Trial Champion golden retriever, and his grandmother was also an excellent gun dog and our family pet. Dad knew he had a special bloodline of golden retriever, and it paid off big with this pup.

It has been said that a professional dog trainer is someone who has owned an incredibly special dog, and is actively and earnestly searching for another. A special dog is a physically sound animal with high intelligence, undying loyalty, a strong desire to please, a sound temperament, and a winning disposition. In addition to these characteristics, Wink was extremely cunning as well. He especially enjoyed problem-solving games, such as retrieving in high grass or heavy brush. One of his favorite games was the shell game where I hid one of his toys under one of three cans. After shuffling the cans, I would say, "Okay," and he would turn over the can with the prize.

Wink's temperament was dominant-aggressive, but he wasn't dog aggressive. While he never started a fight with the other dogs on the property, he did put down a few rebellions. Even though golden retrievers are rarely dog aggressive, Wink was still able to be the dog of rank in our gun-dog kennel. He earned his high social status by posturing his dominance and disciplining the other dogs whenever they tested his authority.

What had set Wink apart from the other dogs was his exuberant disposition. He was always eager to hunt, swim, and hike the trails; and should those activities not be slated, he would initiate games of retrieve the pinecone and play as long as someone kept throwing. He never tired of playing this repetitive game, yet during hunting season, Wink was more interested in retrieving birds than pinecones.

Wink was the first dog that I attempted to train. In the 1960s many dog trainers would strike their dogs with their hands or beat them when they misbehaved. Others would use heavy-handed techniques to teach their obedience commands. Even though I had rejected the idea of force training, an alternative method of training dogs was not known. I knew the bond between me and my pup was strong, and Wink was always eager to follow my lead. He always came when I called and ranged close when he was running off lead. Without knowing the term at the time, I had connected with my pup.

To have a loyal and happy companion dog, you must make this pack connection. When your dog feels connected to you, he will see you as his leader and himself as your pack member. By taking Wink for daily hikes, I established social order by communicating my alpha status with my friendship, leadership, and pack activities. During his puppy development, I taught him to solve problems and overcome obstacles (e.g., walking across log bridges, crossing shallow creeks and train trestles, and climbing riverbanks). He always showed courage and resolve when undertaking something new or difficult. In the same manner, I taught him to swim by allowing him to wade in shallow water until his desire to swim surfaced on its own. In the past, pups were commonly taught to swim by throwing them into deep water.

By his third month of life, Wink was inquisitive and courageous during our hikes, but his cautious nature prevented him from exploring on his own. As his confidence grew, however, so did his curiosity. This was manifested when Wink ran down the trail without me for the first time. At that moment I had two options, but instead of running after him or calling him back to me, I hid behind a tree – and then I called him. What I witnessed next is something I have experienced with every pup that has played this game with me. When I called him, Wink glanced back in my direction, and when he realized that I had vanished, he urgently ran back to find me. Upon his discovery, we celebrated his success before continuing our hike, but whenever he gave me the opportunity, I would play another game of hide-and-seek.

Wink learned to love this game as well. Even as an adult dog, he would initiate the game by either pretending not to be paying attention as he trotted down the trail or running ahead in an excited manner. But I never won the game. Even when I sent him out for retrieves across the river and hid downwind before he returned, Wink would confidently and nonchalantly find me.

The childhood game of hide-and-seek is a powerful pack-training technique. Not only does the game create an incentive for pups to come on command, it also teaches them to follow our lead. As a five-month-old pup, Wink was ranging close when he was running free in the woods and coming when I called him.

When it came time to teach Wink his obedience commands, Dad showed me a trick to teach a dog to heel by your side. He used a switch to swat a pup on the nose when he forged ahead. When I tried it with Wink, his expression communicated that he didn't understand why I was swatting him, so I decided to try something else. By this time I already knew that Wink wanted to follow my lead. I also knew he had the ability to solve problems, so I used this understanding to teach him to heel. By producing a natural consequence for his inattentiveness, I knew Wink would have no problem learning to heel by my side. I discovered that bumping him with my leg, when he forged ahead, produced a natural and positive consequence. Whereas the switch caused Wink some concern and confusion, he took no offense at being bumped in the head when I made a sudden left turn. By making sharp left turns and bumping his head when he tried to walk ahead of me, I produced a consequence without causing any confusion or trauma. After one fifteen-minute lesson, Wink had an understanding of the game of Heel and the consequence of his inattentiveness. In a few days, Wink was heeling with enthusiasm and confidence.

Wink was my mentor, for he taught me far more than I taught him. Most of all, he taught me how rewarding a relationship with a dog could be. Wink also gave me the confidence and motivation to train other dogs, so I asked my father if I could train the dogs he contracted for training—and my journey with dogs began! My first client was a gun-shy one-year-old black Lab named Coal. His owner believed that Coal was gun-shy because he would run away from gunfire. Instead of coming across as a typical anxious gun-shy dog, Coal was very outgoing and dominant tempered. However, when Dad rubbed his ears, Coal lowered his head and moaned. Upon a closer inspection, it was apparent that he had an infestation of ear mites. Once treated for the parasites, he no longer showed any signs of gun-shyness because it was no longer a painful experience. Coal taught me that the ability to read a dog could mean the difference between success and failure when it came to training dogs.

By the time I got my driver's license, I had already trained several Labs, golden retrievers, and bird dogs – and I had trained them without using food rewards or excessive force. Instead of bribing or beating my dogs, I had established a pack hierarchy by taking the lead position. Each time I did this, the result was the same. I produced pack members that were eager to please me and less likely to test my authority. This "eagerness to please" was expressed by a dog's attitude when he worked for me.

By this time in my life, it was apparent that force-trained dogs often appeared nervous or anxious, or even worse, depressed or scared. Off lead training was usually difficult for these dogs, but the dogs I had pack trained would eagerly and confidently work off lead. In the years to come, I would discover that pack training is an effective means of training dogs of every description. Stubborn and strong-willed dogs become less dogged and more submissive to authority. Submissive and shy pups gain confidence in themselves and their owners. In the summer of 1964, I had no way of knowing how other dog trainers were training their dogs. I assumed that other dog trainers were using pack-training techniques, but, as it turned out, I belonged to a select minority.

In the '60s the majority of dog trainers were force trainers. Today the majority of dog trainers are positive-reinforcement trainers, or lure-reward trainers. Whereas force trainers emphasize harsh discipline, positive-reinforcement trainers take the opposite approach by emphasizing rewards. Superficially, positive-reinforcement training appears to be the antithesis of force training, yet both are extreme philosophies that are not based on pack behavior or the natural laws. They are both unsound training strategies because dogs neither bribe nor traumatize their subordinates. Instead of leading their dogs, these trainers use bribes or traumatic force to obtain obedient and good behavior. Dogs use neither method to establish order with other dogs—so why do we think these techniques are the best means of training a dog?

Truth can be an elusive reality. While truth is always present, it is not always seen or understood. For some people, truth is a forgotten awareness. This would seem to be the case with many dog owners. As kids, we knew how to communicate with our dogs. As adults, we either have forgotten this skill or have decided to learn a new way of relating to our dogs. People don't understand their dogs' behavior because they don't know the language and nature of dogs. However, a growing number of people understand dog behavior and the importance of establishing and maintaining social order. The establishment of social order produces pack harmony and an obedient demeanor in dogs. It is just that simple. Either you are the alpha leader or most assuredly you are not.

Good dogs are a pleasure. My job is to teach people how they can have the best dog possible. The time invested during a pup's development will pay huge dividends over the lifetime of your dog. You will never have a better friend than your dog. Dogs freely give their loyalty and devotion to their leaders, expecting little in return other than remaining pack members in good standing.

Adolescent children typically make the best pack trainers, and they usually learn my techniques faster than their parents. While many adults resist changing their behavior or breaking their habits, children can incorporate new information with excellent results, because kids do not have the history of beating or bribing their dogs.

If you have never experienced a strong relationship with a dog, or have had little success with conventional dog training classes, this pack-training course can teach you how to establish order in your pack-family. By establishing social order, you will attain a higher level of friendship with your dog. If you can allocate an hour a day during a puppy's first year of life, using my pack-training techniques, you will have the dog you want. And your dog will have the leader he desires.

1

What is Pack Training?

Dogs and wolves are pack animals, and both species acquiesce to the natural law: For any animal grouping to coexist, there must be social order and communication among its members. With this in mind, we should learn as much as we can about pack animals and utilize this knowledge with our dogs. When we understand canine communication and speak their language, we can communicate with our dogs in a positive, coherent manner. When we know how wolves and dogs establish social order, we can learn to live in harmony with our dogs.

Communication and Social Order

By expressing your love, friendship, and leadership to a pup, you will establish social order. When your pup understands your communication, he will feel connected to you. Dogs communicate their leadership and friendship with their behavior, body language, facial expressions, vocalizations, and pack activities. It is not hard to identify the alpha pack leaders, whether you watch wild wolves in Yellowstone National Park or neighborhood dogs in the backyard. The alphas are the animals that appear to be in charge. They express their friendliness and authority to their pack members by showing affection and giving discipline at the appropriate times. Canine discipline usually begins with a fixed stare. A fixed stare is a warning to submit. If the warning doesn't elicit a submissive response, the discipline will escalate with an orderly sequence of events.

Initially, a dog will growl and stare at an offending subordinate. If the offender does not submit, the dominant dog will grip the animal with its teeth. The purpose of the "gripping" is to restore order without causing physical harm. Should submission not be expressed during the gripping, the dominant dog will restrain the subordinate on the ground until he submits. When submission is expressed, order will be restored and forgiveness will be granted.

When you understand how wolves and dogs establish and maintain social order, you can communicate the same messages to your dog. When social order is established, your dog will become your pack member.

Socialization and Leadership

Discipline is one means of expressing leadership to dogs, but it is only part of the process. In addition to giving discipline, we must also satisfy our dogs' other needs by giving love, praise, exercise, companionship, pack activities, and opportunities to explore their world.

Most people are showing affection to their dogs and allowing them to be companion animals. Pack animals want and need companionship. Solitude is rarely chosen, and most dogs will be emotionally damaged by their solitude. Pups also need physical and mental exercise during their development, and they must be socialized in order to feel confident and secure when exposed to the world as adults.

Socialization includes taking pups for rides in the car, play dates with pups and good-natured dogs, meeting friends and strangers in public and at home, and lots of hikes and outdoor activities. If you plan to travel with your dog, you must socialize your pup to every aspect of your travel habits, e.g., airports, sky kennels, boarding kennels, and road trips. When socialized as young pups, dogs will enjoy these activities throughout their lives without becoming overly stressed or anxious.

Pack training establishes social order and creates a bond of friendship between a pup and its owner. By studying wolf behavior, we can learn what it takes to be a pack leader. Alpha wolves neither strike with their legs when they discipline nor do they bribe for good behavior, but they do allow their pups to explore their world; they express love to their pack members; and they discipline their subordinates whenever they are tested. Therefore, if you can satisfy these basic needs, your pup will accept your leadership status.

Hiking with your pup on nature trails will satisfy many of your pup's needs. His need for physical and mental exercise as well as his need for socialization to the outdoors will be satisfied during these hikes. But even more, he will be learning what it takes to follow your lead. You can teach your pup to follow your lead by playing hide-and-seek when he strays. Playing hide-and-seek, when your pup is running down the trail, will produce a meaningful consequence for the behavior. When you play hide-and-seek, there is no need to hide too well—simply step off the trail and kneel down behind some cover before you call your pup. If he runs past your hiding spot, you can call him again. As a result of playing games of hide-and-seek, your pup will want to range close, even when he is busy having fun.

One of your pups' strongest instincts is to stay close to their pack when they are in strange territory. When you hide before you call a runaway pup, he will look back and see that you have disappeared. This will trigger the thought, "I need to find my pack leader!" At that moment, your pup's greatest desire will be to find you. You can reinforce the pup's decision to come on command by heartily praising him when he locates you.

After a couple of hikes and a few games of hide-and-seek, your pup's behavior and attitude will begin to change. Instead of expecting you to follow his lead, your pup will be keeping track of you. This will be evident when your pup frequently looks back to check on your whereabouts. Until this attentiveness is demonstrated, you should continue to look for opportunities to play the game. By taking your pup for frequent hikes, he will be shaped to think and behave as a pack member wanting to follow his leader. As a result, he will want to come when you call and range close when he is running off lead. He will also be getting the physical and mental exercise (i.e., stress management and problem solving) that all developing pups need.

Exercise provides pups with an outlet for their pent-up energy. Following a thirty to forty-five minute run, your pup will want to take a long nap. Your pup will have had fun exploring his world, but you will have begun your walk on the wild side. In Nature, instincts serve to protect wolves and wild dogs. With an understanding of wolf behavior and instincts, you can begin shaping the wolf within your dog.

Dogs utilize various means of communication.

Once social order is established, the bond of friendship is strong and everlasting.

2

Pack Training: an Alternative
To Conventional Wisdom

Do not go where the path may lead. Go instead where there is no path, and leave a trail.
                                                    -- Ralph Waldo Emerson

I grew up living the Huck Finn lifestyle with a variety of hunting dogs. My great-grandfather, grandfather, and father trained hunting dogs. My great-grandfather, George Fortner, was a victim of the Civil War. Following the Union army's burning of their home and barns, he moved his family from Southern Georgia to the Gulf Coast of Central Florida. The Fortner family settled near Tampa in time for the spring planting, but they had no money for seed. For seed money, George captured two red wolves and trained them for a man in town.

My grandfather was held in high esteem for his prized gun dogs in Central Florida. My grandmother loved to tell stories about Burt and his dogs. There was one dog in particular that stood out from the rest. He was a Field Trial Champion English setter named Joe. Being a cunning dog with wanderlust, keeping Joe at home became a personal challenge for my grandfather. When a six-foot fence had no effect on Joe's travel habits, my grandfather added two parallel strands of barbed wire to the top of the fence in the manner of a prison compound. The following morning at the breakfast table, he was telling the story of how he outwitted his favorite dog when his wife told him to look out the kitchen window. Joe was walking on top of the barbed wire.

When I became interested in training dogs, I read all of the books and outdoor magazine articles that were available to me. In one of those books, the author suggested something that I was not willing to do. In order to "gain a dog's respect," this best-selling author was advising his readers to beat a stubborn or defiant dog into submission. Even though I knew of no alternative means of training a dog, I didn't take the author's advice.

Prior to 1970 it was a customary practice to discipline dogs with corporal punishment. Even though there are alternative methods of training dogs today, many people continue to discipline their dogs in this abusive manner. Around 1970 many force trainers were acknowledging the negative effects of their techniques. They realized that shy and timid pups were often traumatized and emotionally scarred by the use of excessive force, so with the intention of correcting the error of their way, they took the opposite approach to training a dog. They became positive-reinforcement trainers. Instead of giving traumatic discipline for bad behavior, these trainers would repetitively offer food rewards as inducements for good behavior.

Discipline administered by positive-reinforcement trainers ranges from mild verbal corrections to raps on a dog's muzzle with the trainer's fingers. Some trainers ignore bad behavior altogether, and others attempt to distract a dog by offering a toy or giving a command when he misbehaves. Even though pups are more motivated by food rewards than adult dogs, this fact does not sway these trainers' belief system—not when they can choose to work with dogs that love repetitious activities and condition them with food rewards. Perhaps this is why many professional dog trainers use golden retrievers, Labrador retrievers, German shepherds, Shetland sheepdogs, border collies, and Australian shepherds for their demo dogs. These sporting and herding breeds thrive on repetitive work and therefore appear eager and attentive when they work for their trainers.

Positive-reinforcement training and force training are not the most effective means of training dogs. Even though force training and positive-reinforcement training are distinctly different disciplines, both have the same flaw. Dogs neither beat nor bribe their pack members—but my, how they lead!

As a boy living with a pack of hunting dogs, I learned how to make a pack connection with dogs. I began my study by watching our hunting dogs and mimicking the behavior of the dominant dogs. I saw how the highest-ranking dog took charge when he was in the company of other dogs. Pack leaders expect their pack members to submit to their authority. They also expect to receive the respect of their subordinates when it comes to their leadership. You can observe this proclivity when you walk your dog in your neighborhood. When there is more than one barking dog behind a neighborhood fence, you may notice one dog disciplining his companion when he gets in the way. The dominant dog is communicating to his subordinate, "I'm in charge and you should stand down!" The leader disciplined his companion because the low-ranking dog was trying to usurp his authority to defend his territory. Maintaining social order is paramount in the mind of a pack leader.

Off lead hikes on nature trails is a great way to establish social order with young pups. You may think your pup will run away from you in the woods, because you have experienced your pup running unconcerned through your neighborhood with you in hot pursuit. And you are partly right. Your pup will likely run away in your neighborhood, and he will not be concerned when you play hide-and-seek in familiar territory. He knows your neighborhood, and will not feel lost when you hide there, but this will not be the case in strange territory.

Pups will be as nervous in the woods as a wild wolf pup would be running free in your neighborhood. Consequently, your pup will not want to be alone in the woods, and he will want to come when you call. By producing a significant consequence for his inattentiveness, you will soon see a dramatic change in your pup's attitude. Instead of your pup expecting you to follow his lead, he will be routinely looking back to check on you. Each time he wants to know your whereabouts, he will be training himself to follow your lead. By communicating your leadership and teaching him to follow your lead, your pup will become your pack member. As a pack member, he will naturally be subservient to your

14

leadership. When your pup has accepted your alpha status, obedience training becomes a simple process of teaching him the meanings of particular commands.

Pack training begins the day your pup comes home with you. Bonding with a pup and socialization are the first steps of pack training. You don't have to wait until your pup has completed his vaccinations to take him for hikes, but the hiking trails should be away from neighborhoods and roads. Pups could be exposed to viruses where non-vaccinated dogs congregate.

In order to communicate leadership to a pup, you must speak his language and understand the nature of dogs. We can learn how to communicate with our pups by studying wolf behavior. Adolph Murie and David Mech, both respected authorities on the subject, describe wolves as highly efficient and intelligent creatures, yet it's their loving and nurturing nature that distinguishes a wolf pack from other animal groupings. Murie noted that a pack of wolves is comparable to a human family, with the entire pack taking responsibility for the care of the alphas' pups.

As a government field biologist, Murie reported in 1944 that some alpha wolves were more like dictators than leaders. He noted that dictators were often killed or ostracized from the pack when they were no longer able to lead. However, benevolent leaders with friendly dispositions were usually allowed to live out their lives with the pack's new leader.

Wolf research has shed light on the mysterious wolf, but there is still much we don't understand. For instance, in a pack of wolves in Alaska, the alpha leaders would not mate. They were brother and sister. When she came in heat, her brother allowed a pack member to breed with his sister, and then the alpha male would raise the pups as his own. I wonder how he knew that breeding with his sister would not be the best course of action for his pup's genetics.

I also wonder what sense is being used when dogs locate their families over long distances. Cheyenne, my high-percentage wolf dog, can sense where I am without having to use her sight, hearing, or smell. Once I had the opportunity to run downwind into the woods, as my five-month-old pup was checking out the bay shoreline a hundred yards away. After climbing a tree, I watched her while she snooped her way down the beach. Then, as always, she looked back to check on me.

What I witnessed next I cannot explain. Because I hadn't called her, I was expecting her to run down the beach until she found my trail leading into the woods. For Cheyenne, that wasn't necessary. When Cheyenne realized that I had hidden, she nonchalantly trotted from the beach, through the woods, and straight to my hiding spot in the tree. If she had seen or heard me running into the woods, she would have come running at that time. And she could not have followed my air-born scent because I had been downwind of her.

You have likely read stories about dogs finding their owners at unknown locations. You may think these stories have been embellished over the years—that is, until you witness one of these events. I was boarding a friend's two-year-old golden retriever-chow mix overnight while she moved into her new house. At daybreak, Dee called to check on Sasha. When I asked why she thought she had to call at the crack of dawn to check on her dog, she informed me that Sasha had just woken her—barking on the front porch of her new home! Sasha had never been there before, and the property was five miles from my home. So how did Sasha know where to look?

At the beginning of the Second World War, the German military were using dogs to track the Allied troops. The U. S. military therefore wanted to know if they could train their troops to avoid detection by these dogs. They tried to destroy a trail in a grassy field by burning the field. They tried to bury the trail by plowing the field. They even tried to camouflage the trail with different masking agents, but no matter what they did, they failed to neutralize a tracking dog's sense of smell. The dogs could track someone's trail in spite of what they did to cover, destroy, or mask the scent. Even when the trail was taken through water, the tracking dogs would follow the scent left on the surface of the water. Tracking dogs could even distinguish an old trail from a fresh trail. Even if the two trails were laid seconds apart, tracking dogs could tell which track was hot.

Dogs can locate drowning victims underwater. Medical researchers are using dogs to detect skin cancer, and they have recently demonstrated that dogs can detect lung cancer before any medical test can duplicate the feat. Dogs can even detect their owners' epileptic fits before they occur. Dogs can also detect drugs and bombs when technology fails to locate them. Are we underestimating our dog's sense of smell when we claim it's 100 times or 1000 times stronger than ours? Are we underestimating the other abilities of our dogs as well?

There is no doubt that dogs are gifted sensory and social animals. While other animals are capable of forming relationships with humans, none compare to the relationships formed between dogs and their owners. In order to optimize these relationships, we should gain as much understanding as we can about these creatures. When you have an understanding of what makes a dog tick, and speak the language of dogs, you can relate to your dogs as a pack leader. When you know how to establish your alpha position, you will not have to physically dominate your dog. When social order is established, you will not have to bribe your dog to behave. Dogs are eager to have pack leaders, but if one is not present, they will likely fill the power vacuum.

When you become a pack trainer, your dog will respond to you as his pack leader.

Because pack members want to follow their pack leaders,
leashes and treats are not necessary for us to have control with our dogs.

Not only are pack-trained dogs obedient,
they are typically happy, relaxed, and confident creatures.

If you have never experienced a special relationship with a dog or have had little
success with conventional dog training classes, this pack-training course will teach
you how to connect with your dog and establish social order.
("Roxanne " and Sylvia Byrd)

3

The Wolf Within

"Before the Spanish came Indians had no horses. Dogs hunted and pulled travois."
--Eugene Rachlis, *Indians of the Plains*

Canis familiaris is the scientific name for the domesticated dog. He is a member of the same genus as the wolf, Canis lupus, and the same family Canidae, or dog family. After decades of controversy, scientists now agree that wolves were domesticated about 12,000 years ago by various native tribes throughout the world. From this wolf stock and various wild dogs came the domesticated dog. Prior to 1967 it was believed that dogs had evolved from jackal ancestry. *King Solomon's Ring* and *Man Meets Dog* (Methuen & Co., Ltd., London), written in the 1950s by Konrad Lorenz, supported this contention. Other biologists have contradicted Lorenz's findings. In the *American Zoologist*, J.P. Scott wrote in 1967: "Wolves are highly social animals, as are dogs, whereas jackals are like coyotes, ordinarily forming groups no larger than a mated pair." He also noted that wolf and dog vocalization patterns were nearly identical, unlike the complex vocal patterns of the jackal.

If dogs are genetically related to the wolf, did they inherit wolf instincts? Canis lupus, also known as the gray wolf, the timber wolf, and the tundra wolf, has always gotten a bad rap. If you took an opinion poll, most people would describe wolves as treacherous and dangerous animals. However, this perception is not supported by the facts.

David Mech, wildlife biologist for the U.S. Department of the Interior, writes in his book, *The Wolf: The Ecology and Behavior of an Endangered Species*: "We will find that wolf society is highly organized and complex, and that expression and communication in the wolf are also well developed." (University of Minnesota Press, 1970)

Adolph Murie, the first biologist to study North American wolves, offered this insight in his 1944 United States government report, *The Wolves of Mount McKinley*: "The strongest impression remaining with me after watching the wolves on numerous occasions was their friendliness towards one another. The adults were friendly toward each other and were amiable towards the pups, at least as late as October. This innate good feeling has been strongly marked in the three captive wolves which I have known." Murie's research also placed emphasis on the importance of a balanced predator-prey relationship in the wilderness.

Even though early wolf research had characterized the wolf as a social and nurturing creature, and even though there were no historical record of a wild wolf attacking a human in the United States, man's persecution of the wolves of North America brought them to the brink of extinction. As a young child, I remember watching television programs with television celebrities hunting Alaskan wolves from airplanes and calling it sport.

After years of government-sponsored wolf bounties, the endangered gray wolves began their stunning comeback around 1970. According to the Timber Wolf Alliance, wolves are found in relatively large numbers in Alaska (8000), British Columbia (6000), and Minnesota (2500), and they are making their presence known in Idaho (284), Montana (108), Maine, Washington, Oregon, Northern California, Utah, Montana, and Wyoming. The average territory of an Alaskan wolf is estimated to be 600 square miles, and the average weight is around 100 pounds. Since 1995 wolves have been released in some U. S. national parks. Today there are dozens of wolf packs in and around Yellowstone National Park. Although surrounded by controversy fueled by the court of public opinion, the wolf is still proving his merit as a survivor.

In order to truly understand your dog's behavior, you must understand the nature of the wolf. The wolf is a highly social animal that lives in groupings called packs. The size of a wolf pack varies: from as few as two, to as many as thirty-seven wolves have been observed in a single pack. A wolf pack will hunt, feed, rest, travel, and sleep together as a cohesive unit, efficiently and amicably. In order for any animal grouping to survive, two conditions must be met: whether we are discussing a school of fish, a pride of lions, a troop of baboons, a nation of men, or a pack of wolves, there must be social order and communication among its members. Wolves and dogs acquiesce to this natural law, which is commonly known as the dominance order.

The Dominance Order

The dominance order, or peck order, was first observed in chickens. Animal behaviorists describe their social order as a social "ladder" in which each chicken occupies a certain rung of social dominance. The top chicken can peck every chicken with immunity from retaliation. The second-highest-ranking chicken can peck every chicken with the exception of the top bird. On down the line, each chicken can peck those below him in ranking, but must accept dominance from those above him. This same pecking order is seen in wolf and dog packs. Each pack member knows its social position in the pack and responds socially according to rank. It was during the '60s that we began to get a better understanding of wolf behavior and their social order. As a result, we have a better understanding of our dogs.

The wolf social order (government) is a hierarchy consisting of two pack leaders and their subordinate pack members. Subordinates are divided into three groups: adults, juveniles, and outcasts. Outcasts are low-ranking wolves that have been relegated to live in the periphery of the pack. Each subordinate attains a distinct level of authority through his or her prowess and determination. Alpha leaders are always the most dominant male and female wolves in the pack.

The alpha male is usually in charge of the entire pack, while the alpha female monitors the female pack members. One of her responsibilities is keeping the estrous females from mating with the alpha male. In wolf packs, the alpha leaders normally have exclusive breeding rights, and both leaders will remain in power until they are too old to lead or defeated in battle by another wolf. On the other hand, juvenile pack members have the drive to acquire as much dominance as they can during their maturation. The quest for power begins the day their eyes open. By the time they are weaned, each pup will know his or her position in the social hierarchy of the litter. With young wolf pups, we can observe the dynamics of the dominance order during their pack activities. As the dominant pups mature, they will continue climbing the social ladder by testing the authority of older pack members. At maturity, if a pup is determined and driven, he or she will either challenge an alpha leader or leave the natal pack to form a new pack with a lone wolf or a neighboring pack.

Wolves use various techniques to attain and demonstrate dominance. "Riding up" is a display of dominance used by wolves and wolf pups. When a wolf rides up, he places his forelegs on the back and shoulders of a subordinate. If the subordinate lowers his head and tail, and accepts the domination, the wolf on top will have validated his authority.

Dominant wolves and pups will also "stand across" a resting subordinate. The wolf on the ground can respond to the domination by escaping, fighting, or expressing submission. Dominant wolves also use their bodies to bump subordinates in a blocking manner as they run past or spin around.

"Game playing" is another means of expressing social status. The game of chase is played when a dominant wolf ambushes and chases a subordinate in a playful but assertive manner. Even though the subordinate enjoys the game, he will exhibit submissive behavior when he is caught. At other times an alpha wolf will lead his subordinates on a carefree and playful run. The games that wolves play are enjoyable, but they are purposeful as well. Game playing demonstrates the social status of one wolf to another.

Another technique used by mid-ranking wolves is the "bite threat." From a safe distance, a wolf will posture dominance at a higher-ranking wolf, as he snaps his jaws together. While it is a display of dominance, its purpose is not to challenge the authority of a superior. A submissive wolf will use the snapping expression as a passive-submissive response to authority. Instead of posturing with pseudo-threatening body language, as the former example, he will snap while crouching low to the ground.

By observing the behavior of wolves in their natural habitat, we will discover the true nature of our dogs. Not only do wolves and dogs behave in the same manner, the behavior of both species communicates the same messages. Understanding how wolves and dogs communicate makes it possible to understand our dogs' behavior. Once we understand what our dogs are communicating, and speak their language, we can respond to them in an appropriate manner.

Dominance

In addition to their dominant behavior, wolves express dominance with their body language and facial expressions, e.g., fixed stares, rigid body posturing, snarling, growling, and a technique known as gripping.

During a gripping, a wolf grips a subordinate with his (or her) teeth. The gripping is a disciplinary measure that does not cause injury. It usually occurs following a fixed stare. During a fixed stare, a dominant wolf's body language is rigid and erect, as he leans toward a subordinate. Should his tail curl over his back and then extend parallel to the ground, increasing levels of agitation are being expressed. The ears will push forward, and the hackles on the back may also rise, when a wolf is extremely agitated.

As it appears, the fixed stare is a warning. The offending subordinate can either submit or resist. Submission can be expressed by lowering the head, tail, and body, as he cautiously approaches his superior. If he resists by ignoring the warning, the discipline will escalate to a gripping. Should submission not be expressed during the gripping, the dominant wolf will force the stubborn wolf to the ground and restrain him until he submits. This is called the alpha roll.

When dominance is countered with submission, the dominant wolf will accept the apology, and life can resume as before. David Mech makes the observation that discretion also comes into play with alpha wolves: "The dominance shown by the alpha animals and other high-ranking wolves can be described as a kind of forceful initiative. When a situation does not require initiative, dominance may not be shown; for example, when a pack is resting. However, when food, favored space, mates, strange wolves, or other stimuli are present, initiative can be seen in the actions of the dominant animals." (*The Wolf: the Ecology and Behavior of an Endangered Species*)

During play and courtship, wolves will also ride-up, grip, and alpha roll one another in a friendly or amorous manner. If the techniques used to express dominance were inherently traumatic, wolves would not incorporate them into their game playing and courtship.

Submission

Pack members are expected to submit to the authority and privilege of higher-ranking wolves. Submission can be expressed in an active or passive manner. Active submission is a friendly expression of respect for the privilege of another wolf. As an expression of active submission, a wolf will repetitively protrude his tongue as he submissively approaches a superior. With his head and wagging tail lowered, the subordinate will then lick the mouth and muzzle of the higher-ranking wolf. This is called the "wolf greeting." As it appears, active submission is a respectful bow to a superior.

Passive submission is a more fearful response to authority. A wolf can express passive submission to a dominant wolf by rolling quickly onto its back or submissively releasing a few drops of urine or tucking the tail between the legs as he crouches passively. While active submission denotes friendliness and acceptance, passive submission expresses fear and helplessness.

Anal presentation is another display of dominance and submission. This technique involves a dominant wolf approaching a subordinate's posterior. His (or her) body language will be expressing dominance by standing tall with his tail held high or horizontal to the ground. The subordinate is expected to remain still, with its tail tucked between the legs, as the dominant wolf sniffs its anal area. If submission is not rendered, a fight may result with the winner expelling the adversary from his territory.

Territoriality

Territoriality is another instinctive wolf behavior. Pack leaders have the responsibility of marking and defending their territory. Their discretionary responses to trespassers will range from acceptance to expulsion. All pack animals use the scents of their urine, feces, and scent glands to mark territory. The leaders will mark new territory and consistently mark existing scent posts throughout their territory. When a strange wolf marks one of their scent posts, it is considered a challenge of their territorial rights. When this occurs, alpha wolves will cover the trespasser's scent with their urine or feces. Alpha wolves are also observed scratching the ground near a scent post. Scratching the ground is another means of marking territory with the scent from the glands between the toes. Scent posts can be anything: trees, rocks, bushes, or even a sharp turn on a trail.

Wolves love to roll in rotting fish, animal wastes, and carrion. There is some difference of opinion as to why wolves roll in smelly or decaying animal matter. Perhaps they are covering the decaying animal's scent with the scent from their body glands, or they just like the stench. Both may be true at different times.

Bonding

Murie and other naturalists have commented extensively on the strong bonds that are formed between wolves. This instinctive bond is best described as a loyal, loving, and respectful friendship. Pack members assisting with the care of the leaders' pups and alpha leaders mating for life are examples of the strong bonds that are formed between wolves. Bonding may well be the strongest of the wolf instincts, and is surely the trait that has endeared the dog to mankind. This caring and devoted nature is found in wild wolves and domesticated dogs.

Wolves and dogs are social creatures. They do not like being solitary animals. Most of us have read and heard stories of a dog's loyalty and devotion to its family. We are filled with admiration and wonder when we hear of dogs saving their families during a crisis or reuniting with their families after a long separation. There is much we can't explain, but we can be certain that dogs and wolves are both loyal and courageous members of the canine family.

Communication

Every grouping of animals must have social order to survive. Thanks to decades of dedicated wolf research, we know how wolves establish and maintain social order. We know that under normal conditions, breeding is an exclusive privilege of pack leaders. As a result of this social order, each pack is ensured to produce genetically superior pups for future packs.

Communication is also necessary for the survival of wolves. Because a lone wolf would have a difficult time taking down elk, moose, or caribou, his chances of survival would be diminished. But when wolves hunt, they are willing and able to communicate and cooperate with one another in a common goal.

Wolves communicate with their behavior, body language, facial expressions, scents, and vocalizations. Vocalizations include squeaks, barks, yips, growls, whimpers, and howls. Howling seems to have different functions: expressing territoriality to neighboring wolf packs, gathering pack members together, and just for the fun of it. Whimpers express joy or concern; growls express aggressiveness; yips, or yelps, express submissiveness; barks are used to sound the alarm when strange wolves are nearby and to challenge or threaten another wolf; and squeaks are comparable to the whines of puppies.

When a wolf sniffs a strange wolf's urine or feces, he is determining the sex, breeding status, and even the emotional state of the wolf at the time of the elimination.

Each vocalization and body posture conveys a different message. Erect ears may be expressing an alerted state, confidence, or dominance. Flattened ears that are pulled back may be expressing joy or submission, depending on the head and tail positioning and accompanying facial expression. Cupped ears are expressing consolation or contentment, while ears extended forward are expressing agitation and the threat of discipline.

A wolf is expressing dominance or social confidence when the tail is positioned over its back. When an erect tail begins to wag excitedly in short, quick strokes, a wolf's agitation or excitement has peaked. When the tail is pulled close to the body or tucked tightly between the legs, varying degrees of submission or fear are being expressed. When the tail is hanging motionless, a relaxed state of mind is being expressed; when the tail begins to rise, the wolf is expressing arousal to a stimulus. When the tail is held straight out and the body is leaning forward, extreme agitation is being expressed. When the tail wags slowly in a lowered position, active submission is being communicated. In general, upright body posturing expresses dominance, while lowered body language expresses submission.

When wolves are compared to dogs, you will see the connection between the two species. When this connection is made, you can begin putting the pieces of the puzzle together. And when the puzzle takes shape, you will see how man has misunderstood the wolf and domesticated dog for many years. You will discover that wolves and dogs have the same genetics, instincts, communication, and behavioral patterns.

Over the last forty years, most biologists and naturalists have come to an agreement about the significance of the wolf's place in the wilderness, and most animal behaviorists have an understanding of wolf temperaments and instincts. It is believed that modern dogs have evolved from wolf ancestry. The breeds of dog that are directly related to wolves are Eskimo dogs, chow, dingo, greyhound, mastiff, shepherds, Spitz, and terriers. All dogs can be genetically traced to one or more of these breeds. Before distinct breed characteristics were established, random cross breeding was widespread throughout the world for thousands of years. As a result, many breeds of dog have several wolf species in their family trees. Because of its direct kinship to a single species of wolf, the dingo is arguably the only true purebred dog.

Canis Familiaris

Since 1970 the behavior of "man's best friend" has raised some eyebrows. In 1971 the Centers for Disease Control (CDC) collected its first data on dog-bite injuries. Prior to 1971 no dog-bite records were kept. In 1970, according to the CDC, there were nearly one million dog-bite cases in the United States. They found that males were twice as likely to be bitten by dogs, and children were more at risk than adults: 40 percent of dog-bite victims were less than ten years old; 28 percent were between ten and nineteen years old; 11 percent were twenty to twenty-nine years old, and 20 percent were thirty years or older. Dr. Michael Callahan, spokesman for Medical Emergency Management in Oakland, California, reported in 1971: "Dog bite is an extremely common problem in the United States. The annual incidence appears to be rising, and dogs bite at least one million persons per year. Dogs account for 80-90% of all animal bites requiring medical attention and almost 1% of all emergency hospital visits."

Thirty-four years later, the number of annual dog-bite cases in the U.S. has risen to 4.7 million. Included in this statistic are three million children under the age of twelve. Since 1970 the number of annual dog-bite victims has increased dramatically. The reported number of dog bites rose 37 percent from 1986 to 1996 (National Center for Injury Prevention and Safety). During the same time span the dog population increased by only 2 percent. The Journal of American Medical Association (JAMA) has reported that dog bite is the second most common childhood injury that receives medical treatment.

Dog bite accounts for one-third of home insurance claims, with insurance companies paying out over $1 billion in annual liability claims (Western Insurance Information Services). Some insurance companies no longer underwrite home insurance policies for families that own certain breeds of dogs: German shepherd, chow, Rottweiler, Doberman pinscher, Akita, Great Dane, pit bull, malamute, mastiff, Siberian husky, wolf hybrid, or wolf dog.

In the '70s the German shepherd, chow, and poodle were the top-three biting breeds in the United States. In the '80s the cocker spaniel was the most likely breed of dog to bite. Today the pit bull and Rottweiler are the two most prolific biters (U.S. Humane Society). In most dog-bite cases, the victim knew the dog that bit him.

Typically, the dog was the victim's family dog. According to the JAMA, 61 percent of all dog bites occur in or near the owner's home, 77 percent of dog-bite victims knew the dog that bit them, 50 percent of dog-bite victims, under the age of four, are bitten by their family dogs.

A number of questions can be raised concerning these statistics:
Why do dogs bite? And why are more dogs biting people today than ever before? Why are young boys twice as likely to be bitten as young girls? If a dog is being territorial or protective when he bites a stranger or a guest in his home, why are children at a higher risk of being bitten than the entire adult population? Do dogs feel most threatened by the children they know? If the territorial or protective instinct is not the issue, is it simply a case of viciousness? If aggressive and vicious temperaments are the problem, why were poodles the third most likely breed of dog to bite during the '70s—and remain one of the most likely breeds to bite? Surely we couldn't argue that poodles are inherently vicious.

There is an honest and logical explanation for aggressive dog behavior. The dog that bites a family member; the dog that attacks the letter carrier; the dog that bites a visitor in his home; the dog that bites a cycling or running child; and the spunky toy breed that sinks his teeth into someone's hand are all communicating the same message. They are communicating their alpha status by disciplining subordinates and outsiders.

Nearly all dog-bite incidents begin with growls and fixed stares. Following the warning, if order isn't restored, an alpha dog will often discipline by gripping the offender with its teeth. We see the same behavior in wolf packs when it comes to discipline. The bite, or gripping, is intended to discipline testing subordinates. The wolf being gripped can either submit or resist the authority of the dominant wolf. By submitting, he will be forgiven; should he resist, there will be a fight for dominance. The fight will end when one wolf submits by rolling submissively onto its back, exposing its belly and throat to the victor. The dingoes of Australia play possum when another wild dog overpowers them.

While alpha dogs discipline with their bites, neurotic dogs bite as a response to fear. But there is another type of dog that will bite for reasons other than discipline or paranoia. While not common, they do exist. I crossed paths with one of these dogs twenty-five years ago in a Washington animal shelter. As I walked through the kennel, I noticed a beautiful German shepherd in a kennel by himself. Unlike the other incarcerated dogs, he wasn't barking or jumping or pacing – he was calmly staring at me with his head held high—but his closed mouth raised a red flag. I wondered what he was thinking as I walked slowly toward his kennel. Was he nervous or only contemplating my presence? If he had been an alpha dog, he would have been posturing his dominance, but he just sat there, resolutely focusing on me without showing any dominance or fear. As I turned to face him, I decided to see how he would respond to a fixed stare.

What happened next caught me completely by surprise. As soon as I postured my dominance, the German shepherd exploded with sudden and tremendous fury, slamming against the kennel door and biting the kennel wire. I had hoped that he would respond with active submission to my fixed stare, because, other than a closed mouth, he wasn't expressing dominance. If he had shown submission to my authority, there was a good home waiting for him, but that was not to be.

The two-year-old German shepherd was not adoptable because he had severely mauled his owner. Then I was told something else about the dog that explained the reaction I provoked in the kennel. The dog's owner had the habit of coming home in a drunken rage, taking out his anger and frustration on the dog. Apparently the German shepherd had decided he had taken his last beating. Unfortunately and unjustly, the dog had to be put down, even though his only crime was biting an abusive drunk.

Physical abuse can produce a fear-biter with one dog, and with another, a defensive-biter. A dog's spirit will be severely oppressed by physical abuse. Frequent beatings will culminate with a dog either fighting back or emotionally breaking down. Most abused dogs will experience the latter. When a dog cowers from his owner's presence, it is likely the dog is a victim of his owner's abuse.

My intention at the humane society wasn't to find a dog that would try to eat his way through kennel wire to get at me or shy away from my fixed stare. I was looking for a stable, confident dog. The shepherd's response, however, had not been triggered by aggression or fear, but self-preservation.

What about dogs that are trained to bite? How do they fit into the pack hierarchy? Are guard dogs actually alpha leaders? Before I offer an answer, let me make a controversial statement: It is possible and natural to have a good-natured dog that will protect its family at the appropriate time. You may be thinking this is a contradiction, especially if you consider guard dogs to be aggressive or vicious. And in many cases you are right.

Teaching a dominant dog to bite is not difficult, but these dogs have no business living in our homes and neighborhoods. Most guard dogs are trained to react aggressively to any sudden movement or dominant behavior. Guard dogs are typically alpha leaders and alpha dictators. Alpha dictators are extremely dangerous because of their earnest desire to demonstrate their authority.

The final type of dog that will bite is unlike all the rest. These are the family protectors. A family protector is a dog that will protect its family in a crisis situation. Their desire is not to bite, but to defend or save their loved ones. There are countless stories of these canine heroes. Here are a few of my favorites:

In 1919 a coastal steamer was floundering offshore in the North Atlantic, dead in the water and unable to be rescued by the other craft in the area. A Newfoundland, with a rope in his mouth, jumped from the rolling ship and towed the steamer to shore.

In 1978 a Seattle, Washington resident fell victim to a massive heart attack while walking his two Dobermans on a public sidewalk. As onlookers approached to help the fallen man, there stood two resolute Dobermans standing guard over their fallen master. While the dogs didn't understand the intent of the Good Samaritans, they knew their master was in trouble and were determined to stand guard until the trouble passed.

In the summer of 2002, I was returning home from my daughter's wedding in Washington State. Cheyenne, my six-year-old wolf dog, and I had been traveling all day and most of the night when I decided it was time to find a motel. In Southern Missouri, motels are few and far between, so when I spied a billboard for the Relax Inn, I disregarded its shabby appearance and pulled off the interstate. The billboard proved to be truthful advertising, for the motel had all the charm of the Bates Motel.

After checking in and entering our room, there was a knock on the door. When I opened it, there stood a bleached-blond girl and a shaved-head young man standing behind her. As I was asking them if I could be of help, Cheyenne came alongside me. Without answering, the girl shrieked and hurriedly walked away with her friend in tow. Ten minutes later there was another knock and a repeat performance once Cheyenne made her presence known. On the third visit, I informed them that whatever they were selling, I wasn't buying, and slammed the door.

By this time I was fully agitated, so I phoned the motel manager for a little assistance. But no one picked up—was the manager's name Norman? As I sat on the bed with a useless phone against my ear, I saw the couple walking past my window; and apparently Cheyenne did as well, for she jumped from the bed, pounded the front door with her front paws, and began growling in no uncertain terms.

Why do dogs protect their families? What produces this sense of loyalty in a dog? The answer can best be illustrated with a hypothetical backyard scene. Neighborhood dogs have converged on your property, and your dog has run out to greet them. The dogs begin sniffing one another and marking the trees and bushes. In short order, one of the dogs takes a position of authority over the others. His (or her) body language is posturing dominance by standing tall with his tail held over his back. The other dogs are expressing submission by lowering their heads and tails when approached by the dominant dog, and licking the dominant dog's mouth, and one dog even rolls onto its back. Yet, all in all, the dogs seem to be enjoying the activity. During encounters such as this, a pack is being formed with the dominant dog taking the lead position. If you watched long enough, you could determine the ranking of each dog, from alpha leader to omega (first to last in social ranking), with no two dogs sharing the same social status. If social order had not been established, the pack would have disbanded or a dogfight would have erupted, with the winner being acknowledged as the alpha.

We have all observed the behavior of dogs in the backyard, so you may be wondering what your dog's behavior in the backyard has to do with his behavior in your home. When two or more dogs come together, whether in the wild or your backyard, a pack is formed with leaders and followers. When you adopt a pup into your family, he does not see a family—he sees a pack. Instinctively it will be a pack he will likely try to dominate as he matures. If he becomes the alpha leader, you will be expected to follow his lead and submit to his authority. On the other hand, if your dog sees you as the alpha leader, he will be a loyal and devoted pet.

Testing Behavior

Practically all dogs have the instinctive desire to rise to a higher social status in their packs. The only exceptions are the extremely shy and submissive dogs, which are too meek to test a pack leader's authority. While testing behavior is more common for male dogs, dominance is not restricted to the male gender. Some dogs test by being smug, stubborn, or antisocial, while others are disruptive, dominant, or aggressive.

Three-month-old puppies typically begin testing their owners. As a pup matures, the tests will increase, both in number and intensity, if he is not disciplined from the start. While most dogs do not become a threat to their families, many pack leaders will use their force to dominate and discipline those who step out of line.

Testing behavior is universal. All dogs and pups test their family members in the same manner. We see the same behavior in wolf packs, so we know that it is instinctive and part of our dogs' psychological make-up. Early testing behavior includes hard mouthing and biting hands, feet, and clothing. Some pups begin testing their owners right away, while others wait a few weeks before testing their owners' resolve. By the time they are four months old, most undisciplined pups will be jumping onto their owners, playing aggressively with family members, not coming when called, and pulling their owners down the street on lead. You will occasionally meet a young pup that will growl at you when you enter his space, e.g., when he's eating, chewing a bone, or playing with a toy. A few of these may even snap at you or sink a tooth in your hand if you continue your advance.

If you read the best-selling books on dog behavior, you will find contradictory explanations for dominant behavior, but the truth remains the truth. The pup that jumps onto his owner's legs and plays aggressively with family members; the pup that doesn't come when called and pulls his owner down the street when he is walked on lead; the pup that growls from his food bowl; the pup that uses hands and feet for chew toys; and the pup that "bites the hand that feeds him" are testing the authority of their family members, as they attempt to rise to a higher position in the social hierarchy.

Most of us have experienced a dog humping our legs, yet the behavior is often misunderstood. Others have had dogs urinate on their legs and have wondered, "What's up with that?" Do dogs think they can breed with our legs or mistake us for a female dog? Do they forget that our legs are not trees or scent posts? Even if we realize that dogs are not dumb animals, we are forced to make rationalizations, such as "the dog has a strong sex drive" or "he sometimes forgets where he is."

Dominant wolves as means of demonstrating dominance use both techniques. It is not forgetfulness when a dog urinates on your leg—he is claiming you as his property. It is not an attempt to breed when a dog humps your leg, or when one male dog humps another dog (dominant female dogs use the same tactic). It is simply a display of dominance. The behavior is saying, "I will do with you as I please, and you must submit."

Contrary to conventional wisdom, there are no homosexual wolves or dogs. How can I make such a blanket statement? If there were cases of homosexual behavior in dogs, we would have photographic evidence of male dogs engaged in the mating process. During a coupling, a male and female dog will be locked in position for up to thirty minutes during the mating process. But there is no penile penetration when a male dog mounts another male dog. It is simply a show of dominance.

Adult alpha dogs utilize more extreme behavioral patterns to express their dominance. Extremely dominant behavior includes the following: chasing cars, bikes, and joggers; destructive behavior in the home; marking the home with urine and feces; and biting family members and visitors. Alpha dogs use these techniques to maintain order and demonstrate their privilege. With the exceptions of fear-biters and defensive-biters, whenever a dog growls, snaps, or bites a family member, friend, or innocent bystander, he is exercising his right to discipline.

We have all seen dogs growling and lunging at people from their owner's arms. Many dog owners think their dogs are being protective when they exhibit this aggressive behavior, but they are not witnessing protective behavior. Stable dogs can discern threats and friendly encounters, so they are not thinking a stranger may suddenly try to harm them or their owners. These dogs are communicating, "I'm in charge, and you should watch your step!" As pack leaders, they are warning strangers with their menacing fixed stares and growls. Claiming that an aggressive dog is being protective is one of the most widespread and illogical misconceptions about dog behavior.

Because wolf pups and outcasts get the bulk of the discipline in a wolf pack, kids and visitors to our homes are at the greatest risk of being bitten—that is, if your dog thinks he is the pack leader. An alpha dog will discipline at his discretion. Today he may ignore a certain behavior, but tomorrow he will discipline the dog or person for the same behavior. Letter carriers know this only too well. Just because a dog allows a postal worker to enter his property today doesn't mean the dog will not try to bite him tomorrow. Dog attacks on letter carriers and meter readers usually occur when the service people are exiting a property.

When we investigate the crime scene, we can determine what triggered the attack:

When a service person enters a property and realizes there is an adult dog in the yard, he is aware of the possible danger and perhaps a little nervous as he performs his duty and exits the yard. A pack member does not interpret this behavior as a transgression. After all, it's not his job to screen visitors. On the other hand, a pack leader sees an apprehensive stranger trespassing and retreating from his territory. An alpha dog interprets this behavior as the cowardly act of a trespasser, and will commonly discipline the intruder as he exits the yard. Wolves utilize the same tactic when it comes to disciplining trespassers and taking down large prey. (The U.S. Humane Society reports that 97 percent of mail carrier dog-bite victims are bitten on the lower extremities.)

While most pack leaders will only intimidate those around them with their dominant body language and unruly behavior, many pack leaders will discipline with their bites. Alpha leaders are typically the dogs that are biting people, and they are responsible for 90 percent of the dog bites in the United States. Fear-biters—dogs that bite as a defensive measure—are credited with the remaining 10 percent of dog-bite cases. While some breeds are more prone to bite than others, every breed of dog is represented in the dog-bite statistics. However, if a dog was disciplined as a pup, he will know his position in the family and will submit to the authority of his owners. If a pup is not disciplined, he may well take charge of your family when he reaches maturity.

The evidence is overwhelming that biting dogs are pack leaders giving discipline: 77 percent of dog-bite victims knew the dog that bit them; 60 percent of dog-bite victims are young children; 77 percent of those children are bitten on the face or head; for every fatal dog bite in the United States, there are 230,000 bites that are not treated by a physician. The same parallel exists in packs of wolves. Wolf pups get the bulk of the discipline, and when they are gripped, it is usually to the head or neck. The bites are not intended to injure. The gripping bite is only meant to discipline a disrespectful or misbehaving subordinate. When wolves and dogs grip their canine subordinates, their thick hides do not tear easily. But when a dog grips a child with its teeth, the skin tears like paper.

With an understanding of the dynamics and purpose of the dominance order, you will know how and why dogs discipline their subordinates. You will also know how and why you should discipline your dog. When you know how dogs communicate their dominance, you will know when your pup is testing your authority. You will understand what is happening when someone is being pulled down the street by his dog, or when a dog stops to sniff and mark scent posts along the way, while his owner waits patiently for him to finish. You will also know why your dog growls at family members and doesn't come when you call. You will know not only what your dog's behavior is communicating but also how to respond.

All aggressive dogs are pack leaders, and all well-mannered dogs are pack members. Pack members are not a threat to their families, but pack leaders often become a liability. Whether you have a toy breed or a giant breed, all dogs behave in the same manner as their ancestor, the wolf. When we realize that discipline is not a negative term, and accept the fact that all dogs need discipline, we can confidently respond to our dogs' testing behavior. Every pup comes equipped with the same instincts, and they all need and want discipline.

When a dog receives love and discipline, he will be a happy and secure family pet. If a dog only receives love, he will be damaged by the omission. He may mature thinking he has the stressful job of being the alpha dog. If a dog only receives discipline, he will be a nervous wreck, not knowing the assurance of his leader's affection. But when a pup receives love and discipline, he will psychologically connect with his owners as a wolf connects with his pack leader.

How do we teach our pups to be respectful pack members? This is the Holy Grail of dog training. When you know how to earn your dog's respect, there is nothing you cannot achieve in your relationship with your dog. When your dog accepts your alpha status, he will respect you. This is the prerequisite needed for higher levels of dog training. If your dog doesn't respect you, he will not be motivated to please you. The same natural law applies to people: If you respect your employer, you will be motivated to work hard; if you do not respect your boss, you will likely do just enough to get by.

Understanding the nature of wolves and dogs also illustrates the need for giving praise and affection to a dog. The best dog trainers are the ones who give consistent discipline and praise. Giving one without the other will be problematical. When praise and discipline are consistently offered at the appropriate times, you will produce confidence and stability in your dog's demeanor. Inconsistent praise and discipline will produce a nervous, anxious dog, as one that doesn't know what to expect.

Dogs thrive on a routine. They love knowing when you come home, when it's time to eat, when it's time to go for a walk, and when it's bedtime. Dogs also want to know how and when discipline will be administered, and they will willingly accept their corrections when your discipline is fair, consistent, and understood. However, if they are slapped or hit for a certain behavior one day and ignored the next, or only mildly corrected, they will feel insecure because of the incoherent and inconsistent discipline.

We see a similar condition with people suffering from post-traumatic stress disorder. It's not so much the shock of a stressful incident but the not knowing when it will happen again that causes the stress. Not knowing what will happen can be far worse than knowing. Most of us have seen dogs suffering from this disorder. Dogs that are disciplined inconsistently, or harshly, will often take on a nervous and timid demeanor. In extreme cases, these dogs will shake uncontrollably in stressful situations. When dogs receive praise and discipline in a consistent and appropriate manner, they will be happy, confident, and obedient pets.

It is no great achievement to train a dog to obey a few commands. The achievement that I want each of you to experience is a dog that obeys because he wants to please his leader. Having a confident, well-mannered dog is possible when you base your relationship upon an understanding of pack animals. Pack training begins the day you bring your pup home with you. All testing behavior must be disciplined in the dog's language, and heartfelt praise should be given for all good behavior. By providing love and leadership, you can shape your pup's instincts and instill in him the will and attitude of a pack member.

By understanding how wolves and dogs establish social order, and taking the initiative to create a healthy pack environment, you can forge a true friendship with your dog. If you can be seen as the pack leader, you will earn your dog's respect. Without respect, you really don't have a positive relationship with your dog. And you will be resigned to become either a force trainer or a treat trainer.

But there is a better way! And it works with every breed of dog, even the so-called hard-to-train dogs, such as hounds, terriers, and Arctic breeds. Pack training is an effective way of training dogs because of the bond that is created between a dog and his owner. It even works with a breed that is supposedly impossible to train—the wolf hybrid, or wolf dog. Conventional wisdom holds that wolf dogs cannot be trained to a high level. Many animal behaviorists claim that wolf dogs do not come on command, and they are nervous and unstable in public. But they haven't met a wolf dog like Cheyenne.

Cheyenne is a high-percentage wolf-malamute cross. She is currently seven years old and my personal demo dog. She is the star of my obedience classes and performs at schools, Boys and Girls Clubs, church events, and nursing homes. She loves children and is social with friends and strangers alike. Cheyenne works as well off lead as she does on lead, and she comes when she's called—always!

High-percentage wolf dogs are extremely intelligent animals whose pack instincts are perhaps more acute than the average dog. For this reason, they do not respond well to force or bribes. In order to train a wolf dog, you must first and foremost be the alpha leader.

Lakota, Cheyenne's sister, expresses her joy in the top photo.
Cheyenne expresses her relaxed state of mind in the bottom photo

.

4

Canine Temperament and Disposition

There seems to be some confusion about the definitions of temperament and disposition. Many people use the words interchangeably. After forty years of training dogs, I am still learning about the temperaments and dispositions of dogs. It is not a black-and-white issue.

In the dictionary, temperament is defined as "the manner of thinking, behaving, or reacting characteristic of an individual," and disposition as "one's customary manner of emotional response; temperament; a tendency or inclination, especially if habitual." For our purposes, the key definition of temperament is "the manner of thinking or behaving," and the key definition of disposition is "the emotional, habitual response."

A dog's temperament is illustrated by his behavior, and his behavior discloses his social status: alpha (dominant-aggressive), mid-ranking subordinate (dominant-submissive), low-ranking subordinate (submissive), or omega (passive). A dog's disposition is characterized by his habitual response to stimuli: aggressiveness, stubbornness, playfulness, eagerness, exuberance, complacency, or timidity.

Using an example of two hunting dogs may help make the point. A pointer is active in the field and loves to hunt for game birds, but his dominant attitude with the other dogs in the hunting party often sparks a dogfight. The other dog, an English setter, gets along well with the other dogs but has little interest in the hunt. His drive to seek out game is weak, leaving him wanting to follow behind his owner or go off on his own adventure. The pointer has a great temperament for hunting and a lousy, dog-aggressive disposition. The setter has a passive temperament and a happy, playful disposition.

Both dogs have character flaws, but the setter's temperament is more problematical. In other words, the pointer could have his attitude changed more easily than the setter could improve his hunting drive. The pointer's dog-aggressive disposition could be the result of failing to socialize him to other dogs when he was a pup, or he was a dominant-aggressive pup that wasn't disciplined appropriately. An aggressive disposition can result from roughhousing with a dominant-tempered pup or playing games of tug-of-war. Dog-aggressive dispositions can be inherited from a pup's parents, and puppies that have been traumatized by dominant dogs may also become dog aggressive.

A dog's disposition is much easier to determine than his temperament. Dispositions range from happy-go-lucky to shy and reserved, and stubborn and short-tempered to eager and playful. A dog's disposition will often be a mirror image of his owner. If you are happy and carefree, your dog will likely reflect this attitude as well. If you are nervous and anxious, your dog may express the same demeanor.

When you know your dog's temperament and disposition, and how he communicates his attitude and feelings, you can determine the motives of your dog's behavior. When you understand your dog's motivation, you will be more likely to respond appropriately to testing and submissive behavior. Failing to respond to testing behavior will only encourage the problem behavior to escalate. Failing to respond to good behavior will be equally detrimental to a pup's development.

Without an understanding of canine motivation, temperament, and disposition, you will be unable to respond appropriately to your dog's behavior. When a dog's bad behavior ultimately turns your resolve to agitation, you will consider giving the dog away, expelling him to the backyard, drugging him, or putting the animal down if the behavior is aggressive. By learning the basics of pack-animal behavior: You can gain a foothold of understanding; with understanding comes confidence; and with confidence you can ascertain your dog's temperament, disposition, and motivation. When you understand pack-animal behavior and speak the canine language, you can respond to your dog's behavior as an alpha leader. Whereas dominant, testing behavior should be disciplined, submissive and obedient behavior should be praised and encouraged.

The basics of pack-animal behavior are as follows:

Alpha pups (and dogs) are extremely dominant, and omega pups (and dogs) are extremely submissive. In every litter of pups, there is an alpha and omega pup. The remaining pups will have varying degrees of dominance and submissiveness. While they all could be considered dominant-submissive, the second highest-ranking pup will be more dominant than the pup ranked a notch higher than the omega pup.

Pups with dominant-submissive temperaments and playful dispositions make the best pets. In their play as well as their work, they are confident, outgoing, and bold, wanting to win every game and solve every problem. While they are competitive and bold, they are not usually stubborn or aggressive, and they readily submit to authority. This combination of traits produces a stable temperament. Dominant-submissive pups will readily submit to authority, whether the authority figure is another dog or their owners. While their play can be dominant, it is not usually intended as a test of authority. When higher-ranking dogs or their owners discipline them for their dominant play, dominant-submissive pups will readily submit.

Dominant-aggressive pups are similar to dominant-submissive pups, only they don't readily submit to authority. They routinely test their owners' authority and require positive leadership from the start. When dominant-aggressive alpha pups are not disciplined, they will become dominant-aggressive alpha dogs.

A submissive-tempered pup with a stubborn disposition is harder to train than a dominant-tempered pup with a stubborn disposition. While his stubbornness will need firm discipline, the pup's submissive temperament may be adversely affected by such discipline. What is needed for these pups is a great amount of patience, the ability to read a dog's emotions and body language, and consistent handling. During their training, submissive-stubborn pups will not progress as quickly as the dominant-submissive or dominant-stubborn pups.

It would seem that dominant-stubborn pups would be difficult to train. However, this is usually not the case for pack trainers. Dominant temperaments are easily shaped with pack-training techniques, and stubborn dispositions will quickly dissipate when social order is established. Dominant-stubborn pups will try their owners' patience, but once they accept their place in the pack order, these pups make excellent pets. Dominant-aggressive and dominant-stubborn pups represent a high percentage of the dogs that become clients. My services are often a family's last resort.

A submissive-tempered pup with a timid disposition is the most difficult pup to train. Submissiveness and timidity are not synonymous terms. While a submissive or shy demeanor is a natural expression of respect for authority, timidity is usually a fearful expression. A timid disposition can be the result of an emotional shock that created substantial and lasting damage to the psychological development of a pup. What is needed for a timid pup is professional handling from someone with patience and understanding. The trainer must also be able to read a dog, because a timid pup can be easily overwhelmed and traumatized.

Timid and extremely shy pups need confidence building more than they need discipline. Whereas verbal corrections will usually be sufficient discipline, praise and encouragement will benefit a timid pup more than his discipline. While building a timid pup's confidence is possible, it will not occur overnight. (Read Chapter 10: Tricks of the Trade)

A dog's social ranking is illustrated by his behavior, and his behavior communicates what he is feeling and thinking. Knowing what your dog is thinking is power. When you know what your dog is thinking, you will know his motivation; when you know how to speak Dog, you can respond to testing and submissive behavior in a coherent and appropriate manner. This is usually when this "connection" with a dog takes place. When your dog knows you know what his behavior is communicating, and knows you will respond to his behavior with appropriate discipline and praise, he will acknowledge your leadership and feel connected to you.

Strong bonds are formed between many members of the animal kingdom. Many mammals, from elephants to dolphins, bond with their mates for life. When a Canadian goose is shot down in flight, her mate will follow her to the ground, even though the hunters continue shooting his way. He wants to be with his mate more than he fears death. Elephants will also come to the rescue of fallen herd members, supporting them with their bodies so they can walk with the herd. In a typical wolf pack, the entire pack functions as a close-knit society, with each pack member caring for the pups, and all behaving with an attitude of friendliness toward one another. Their greatest desire also is to be a family.

We have all heard stories of abandoned dogs locating their owners over long distances. Some of these stories are impossible to explain. For instance, how could a dog follow a trail for over 100 miles—yet a Doberman pinscher did just that in a European tracking trial! And what about the dog that was seen walking down a line of WWI foxholes in France, until he found his master—even though the dog began his search in England!

My favorite story of a dog's loyalty was the dog that walked to an English dock with his master each morning and returned in the afternoon, when his master returned from sea. One day, however, his owner did not return. He had been lost at sea. As the story goes, the dog waited at the docks for his master's return for several years, until he grieved himself to death.

Our journey into the world of pack animals begins with the understanding that dogs are not simple creatures, but complex and wonderful creatures deserving of our time and effort. Being able to read a dog's temperament and disposition will help you shape your dog's behavior and instincts. By being able to freely communicate with your dog, you will be able to establish your alpha status. When there is social order in your pack-family, you will tap a wonderful resource by opening the lines of communication with your canine family member.

And the next time you hear someone refer to a dog as a dumb animal, you can smile, knowing he may be more accurately describing himself.

5

Evaluating a Dog

What you see is what you get.
–Flip Wilson

No two dogs are identical, but we can determine a dog's temperament by identifying the behavioral characteristics associated with dominant-aggressive, dominant-submissive, submissive, and passive temperaments. This is useful information when it comes to choosing a pup from a litter or a kennel, but there is more to consider. A pup's disposition should also be taken into consideration, and early socialization at the breeder's home should be validated as well. Puppies that have been traumatized or socially neglected at the breeder's home will have emotional problems, and many of these pups will become unstable and neurotic dogs.

Neurotic dogs are found in most social circles. We often laugh at these poor souls, not understanding their erratic behavior. Whenever a dog engages in any nonsensical, repetitive behavior (e.g., chasing his tail over and over, biting at imaginary flies, aggressively running up and down a fence line, or pacing in a repetitive manner), he is not just having fun. When a dog growls and snaps from its owner's arms, he is not protecting his owner—he is either demonstrating his dominance or paranoia.

Animals often become neurotic when they are caged. A common neurotic behavior for intelligent animals is pacing. Caged predators commonly pace, but they are never observed pacing in their natural habitat. Caged animals do not behave in the same manner as free animals, and many become neurotic. In order to understand animal behavior, we should observe the animal in its natural habitat.

Fear-aggression is another example of neurotic behavior. Dogs with this psychological disorder may not become fear-biters, but they will posture aggressively when someone approaches or startles them. Other examples of neurotic dogs are the chronic barkers and chewers, and the extremely aggressive dog that is kept on a chain. Conventional obedience training will not change the abnormal behavior of a neurotic dog, but you can relieve a dog of his anxiety and boost his confidence when patience and a never-say-die attitude are two of your virtues.

This brings us to the aggressive dog on a chain. If it were left to me, it would be a crime to keep a dog on a chain or cable. I am not referring to a dog that is tethered on a runner for short periods during the day, but the dog that lives his life chained to a tree. Most intelligent animals will become extremely aggressive when they're chained for extended periods of time. The rest will become chronically depressed.

Around the turn of the twentieth century, my grandfather was arrested for assault and battery. At his preliminary hearing, the judge, who was the defendant's hunting buddy, asked my grandfather, "What in the world made you drag your neighbor off his front porch and tie him to a pine tree?" He was shocked by his friend's behavior. My grandfather replied: "The plaintiff had kept his bird dog chained to the same pine tree for two years, with no doghouse and often without water. When the dog died from heat stroke, my nerves must have snapped because I couldn't stop thinking about showing my neighbor what it felt like to be chained to a tree on a hot summer day in Central Florida." The judge took a long look at both men before dismissing the case for lack of evidence.

A dog's temperament cannot be adequately evaluated in one casual observation. After all, you wouldn't take one casual look at a new car before purchasing it. You would want to evaluate the car's potential and take it for a spin before making the commitment. The same principle should apply when you adopt a pup. You'll be spending more of your life with a dog than you will a new car, so you should evaluate a prospective pup before making the adoption. Making a sound evaluation is possible when you understand canine behavior, posturing, and communication. With this understanding, you can determine whether a pup's temperament and disposition is compatible with your own interests and lifestyle. If you are looking for a family pet, you should adopt a dominant-submissive pup with a playful disposition. If you want a working dog, a pup with a dominant temperament and an exuberant disposition would be a better choice.

Pups express their dominance and submissiveness with their body posturing, facial expressions, and during their play. Dominant-aggressive pups are the most dominant pups in their litters. They like to choose the pack activity, whether it's resting, hunting, or playing; and during play-fights they will always be the most dominant player.

Horses use similar techniques to establish social order in the herd. Secretariat, the 1973 Triple Crown Champion, was known to be the dominant stallion wherever he pastured. It wasn't that he was overtly aggressive with the other horses, yet he still commanded their respect for his privilege. You can often witness the social order of horses at feeding time. When horses return to the barn, a single file is formed with each horse positioned according to rank.

Stubborn pups do not submit readily to authority. A young pup's stubbornness will be expressed during an alpha roll and during playtime with his littermates. Stubborn pups and dogs require many corrections before they submit to authority. Sometimes you won't clearly see a pup's stubborn disposition until you begin his obedience training. While most pups can learn each of the basic obedience commands in a few days, stubborn pups will continue to test their owners' authority long after they understand the meanings of the commands.

Shy pups behave like shy people. They are more standoffish and submissive than dominant-tempered pups, but they are not timid. Timid pups are extremely anxious and the most difficult pups to train. They take longer to train because of the time required to strengthen their confidence. When you own a pup with a combination stubborn-timid disposition, you will be severely challenged. On the one hand, their stubbornness needs to be disciplined, but their timidity will not tolerate firm discipline.

During an evaluation of a client's pup, I will not make any attempt to touch him until he makes physical contact with me. And I will not make hard eye contact until we make this basic connection. The time it takes for a pup to approach me will depend on his or her temperament. Dominant-aggressive pups will approach me much sooner than submissive pups. Omega pups will not approach me without a lot of coaxing.

Pups that express curiosity and cautiousness when meeting a stranger are demonstrating their stable temperaments. The definitive example of a stable temperament is a pup that responds to new experiences with curiosity and caution. The pup that runs away from a stranger, and the pup that runs to a stranger are both displaying unsound tempers. One is showing no curiosity, and the other is showing no restraint. If the pup has not approached me within five minutes, I would consider him to be extremely shy or timid. If he runs to me without hesitation, I would regard him as a dominant or dominant-aggressive pup.

People often tell me their pups picked them out by being the first pup in the litter to approach them. The first pup to approach a stranger is usually the dominant-aggressive pup. His behavior is not communicating that he is picking you to be his owner. He is claiming you as his property. This attitude can also be observed by tossing an object or toy onto the ground in view of a litter of pups. The alpha pup will usually try to claim the prize.

After becoming acquainted with a pup, I will observe his behavior with his family to see if he is dominant (disruptive) or submissive (mannerly) while in their company. As we discuss the puppy's behavior, I will be teaching the owners how to recognize and discipline testing behavior by using the pup as a training prop. I begin by demonstrating how to give a fixed stare. After tossing my car keys on the floor, I will posture dominance to the pup when he takes notice. By leaning toward the pup and growling softly, I will be telling the pup to leave my keys alone. The pup should respond with an active-submissive response to my fixed stare by lowering his head, protruding his tongue, and moving closer to his owner or me. But he should not express fear or dominance to my warning. The pup that shows active submission to a fixed stare will get a high score for a stable temperament. This is typically how stable-tempered pups respond to authority.

When I demonstrate the gripping technique—by gripping the loose skin on the back of his neck—a stubborn or dominant-aggressive pup will struggle to free himself. And when I perform an alpha roll—by restraining him on the floor—he will resist my dominance for several minutes. The submissive and dominant-submissive pups will struggle briefly, if at all, before submitting to an alpha roll. Dominant-submissive and submissive pups will also accept their gripping without resistance. Pups that cry out during a gripping are expressing submission, not pain. These will be the submissive and passive pups. After the preliminary evaluation of a pup's temperament and disposition, I will test his aptitude by taking him for a walk in his neighborhood. Pups will also display their temperaments and dispositions when they walk on lead. Dominant pups are bolder and less attentive, and they pull harder than submissive and passive pups.

Walking a dog is a pack activity, so we should exercise our authority when we walk our pups on lead. You will bring your leadership into focus by producing a consequence for dominant and inattentive behavior. Some dogs are more cunning than others, but every pup, and most adult dogs, can learn to walk mannerly and attentively on lead in two or three thirty-minute lessons. The game that is taught during leash training is follow-the-leader. (Read Chapter 8: A Good Start)

Some pups take longer to learn this basic exercise, and others, even after learning the game, will relapse and have to be retrained at a later date. Some pups must be reminded with a correction or two each time they are walked on lead. Pups with short attention spans cannot focus on one activity at a time. When they run off lead, there doesn't seem to be any purpose for their activity; they spend their free time running helter-skelter. When there is another dog present, they spend most of their time following the other dog. Scatterbrains can become good family pets, but they require more supervision and guidance as they mature.

A high evaluation score will be given to the pup that has confidence in himself and allegiance to his leaders. He will take notice of me the moment we come in contact. He will appear confident and curious, but standoffish for a few seconds. In short order, he will perceive that I am not a threat and will approach me with only a slight amount of cautiousness. Once he sniffs me and determines that I am a friend, his demeanor will become confident and relaxed.

When I perform a fixed stare, the pup will lower his head and look up at me, as he protrudes his tongue in a submissive manner. Then he will approach me in the same active-submissive manner, wanting to lick my face or hands. When I demonstrate the gripping technique, the pup will allow me to scruff him without resistance, even if I lift him from the ground. When he is rolled onto his side, he will resist minimally and then completely submit by lying still with his head on the ground. When I release my hold, he will not leap up in an excited manner or posture in a dominant manner. Instead of taking exception to my authority, he will be content to remain on the ground as I praise him and scratch his belly.

When the alpha roll is completed, the pup will remain composed. It will appear as if nothing bad has happened—because nothing bad has happened! Young pups are expected to submit in this fashion when they are with their mothers. Pups will not be traumatized when they are disciplined in their customary manner, and they will acknowledge the alpha status of their disciplinarian. As a result, by the time I begin the pup's leash training, he will be attentive and eager to follow my lead.

Quality pups are confident, focused, respectful, and happy. They are eager to have a leader, and they will accept discipline without anxiety or resistance. They also have the cunning to solve problems and learn from their life experience. Finding a pup with these positive traits should be the goal of every prospective dog owner. Stable-tempered pups with great dispositions and high intelligence may be less common than in years past, but they are still out there. People who are passionate about dogs are often those who have owned one of these special dogs. Dogs can absolutely be our best friends when they perceive our alpha status and their membership in our pack-families. When these two factors come together, the resulting relationship is special.

In every litter of pups you will find a microcosm of a wolf pack. At eight weeks of age, each pup will have attained a distinct level of dominance. The most dominant pup is the alpha pup, and the pup with the least dominance is the omega pup. Neither of these pups will be the best choice for an active family with small children, although for different reasons. The alpha pup has six weeks of leadership experience to his credit, and he will be driven to rise to the top pack position in his new home. On the other hand, the omega pups may be too shy to handle an active lifestyle or families with small kids. An omega pup would prefer a quiet, sedentary lifestyle, but an alpha pup should be placed with an experienced handler who can recognize and respond to testing behavior. Dominant-aggressive pups can become good canine citizens, but they will require strong leadership from the start.

After culling the alpha and omega pups, we can then test the remaining pups in the litter for intelligence, independence, adaptability, and aptitude.

Intelligence refers to the dog's ability to solve problems. You can test a pup's intelligence by standing two twelve-inch boards on end, making a giant letter "V" on the ground. The boards will need to be supported with bricks in order to stand on their sides. With the boards in place, you can place the pup head first in the V-corner. The pups that quickly reason out that they must back up a step or two, in order to escape, will get a high IQ score. Some pups will try to climb over the boards time and time again before they solve the problem. A pup's ability to solve problems quickly will be an asset throughout his life.

Independence refers to a pup's unwillingness to follow a leader. These independent rebels are more likely to wander off leaving their owners far behind. You can test for this trait by taking a pup to an unknown location and placing him on the ground before you walk away. If you are able to coax the pup to follow you, he will pass the test. Independent pups will likely go off on their own adventure, instead of following your lead. This independent attitude will not be conducive to your leadership. The pups that follow you are showing the positive trait of wanting to join up with a leader.

Adaptability is the positive trait of handling new experiences without becoming stressed or anxious. A simple test for adaptability can be given by providing an unknown surface for a pup to walk on. If a carpeted floor is a new surface, you can try to coax a pup with a treat to walk on its surface. The pups that are too nervous to walk on a new surface will get a low grade for adaptability, while the pups that overcome their cautiousness will get the higher grade.

Aptitude is the ability to learn from experience. We can test for this trait by placing a pup on a six-inch raised platform, such as a crate, and noting where he jumps from its surface. Do this several times to see if he routinely jumps down from the crate at the same spot. If he jumps from the same spot, it will not be a coincidence. He is remembering a positive experience and demonstrating the ability to learn from his life experience. This trait will make a big difference when it comes time for a pup's training.

By making these preliminary evaluations, you can determine the traits of the puppies you adopt. These tests can be given as early as four weeks and as late as eight weeks of age. Then, after comparing your data with the breeder's test results or observations, you can confidently determine who's who in a litter of puppies.

Positive and negative traits are genetically influenced, so you should also evaluate a pup's parents. Stable-tempered dogs with good dispositions produce more pups with these desirable traits, and they also make better parents. Ideally, you should choose a pup from well-mannered and stable dogs. If you are not allowed to meet the pup's sire, this usually means the dog has a dominant-aggressive temperament or an antisocial disposition.

Making these preliminary evaluations can improve our chances of picking the best pups for our families. If the pup and the parents are sound and stable, and the breeder has participated in the pup's early socialization, you can confidently make the adoption.

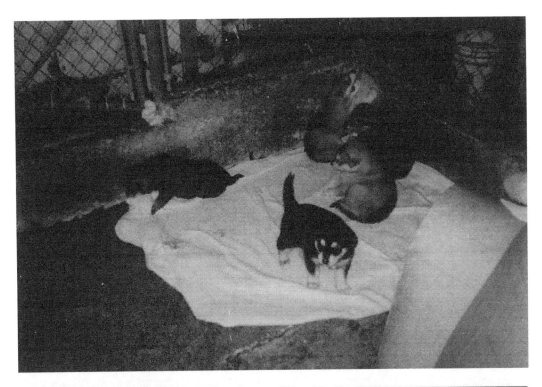

These are Cheyenne's baby pictures. Cheyenne is the black and white pup.
She is posturing her dominant status to her littermates.

Six-week-old Cheyenne, on the left, greets her sire in the top photo.
As a six-year-old dog, she is greeting Lucky, a six-month-old poodle (bottom photo).
Notice how both pups are expressing the same body language.
Cheyenne and Lucky both have dominant-aggressive temperaments.

6

Establishing Social Order with Timid Dogs

What makes a dog timid? Timidity is defined as a tendency to shrink from stressful and difficult situations, or a hesitant or fearful demeanor. While shyness is a normal disposition and submissiveness is a natural temperament, timidity is often the psychological consequence of traumatic events in a pup's life.

A young pup's vulnerable psyche makes him susceptible to trauma. Being roughly handled or repeatedly dropped by a caretaker can permanently damage a pup's vitality. A pup's ill-tempered mother or an unruly child can also stymie a pup's development. You can check for this possibility with an eight-week-old prospect by lifting the pup and holding him on his back. If he seems overly anxious about being upside down, he may well have been dropped or roughly handled. Even if he hadn't been mishandled, and responds with anxiety during this test, he may be expressing his distrust of humans.

Other factors can cause a pup to become timid. A traumatic event experienced at a pup's new home and improper socialization can both cause a pup to appear extremely shy and timid. While a submissive or passive pup will appear shy or standoffish with strangers and unknown dogs, this is not abnormal behavior. On the other hand, a pup that has been socially neglected or physically abused will appear more timid than an omega pup. These pups have a suspicious nature and often respond fearfully when a stranger tries to pet them.

Rolled-up newspapers have damaged many impressionable pups, not from the physical pain of being swatted but from the stress of such an abnormal and sudden event. After all, a pup's mother never disciplined him with a newspaper; therefore, he will not understand what it means when someone uses this abusive technique. The popping sound of a newspaper can be genuinely terrifying to a young pup.

A "kennel-dog" is a good example of a dog that became timid as a result of his upbringing. His timid nature is the consequence of not being socialized to the outside world. Failing to socialize a young pup to civilization increases the likelihood of him becoming a timid kennel-dog. When a kennel-dog is taken away from home, he will appear nervous and distrustful of his surroundings. As a result of the neglect, he will feel safe only when he is in familiar territory.

Wild dogs and wolves will be anxious and terrified when they are caged, because they were not socialized to humans and cages when they were pups. In order to tame a wild wolf, you must gain his trust—and that is easier said than done. In order to gain the trust of a wild wolf, a trainer will sit quietly inside the wolf's enclosure, but he will make no attempt to approach or coax the animal. After thirty minutes or so, he will exit the enclosure after tossing some meat scraps on the ground. In the weeks to come, should the wolf show more interest than fear, the trainer will offer additional meat scraps, tossing them near enough for the wolf to be tempted to approach him.

A timid pup can learn to trust the world, but his therapy will mirror the trainer's effort to gain the trust of a wild wolf. You should not force your will on a shy or timid pup until he has gained confidence in your leadership. When I meet an extremely shy or timid pup, I will sit on the ground and allow him to make the first social move. If I need to stimulate his interest, I can toss him a treat or two. Once the pup has approached me, I will be able to make physical contact without causing any anxiety.

Extremely shy and timid pups need a soothing touch with both hand and voice. No harsh discipline is warranted if we wish to replace their distrust with trust. We must have awareness and understanding that their inhibitions will restrict their social activities until they grow in confidence. We must also have patience with their progress. Timid and shy pups need minimal discipline. Fixed stares will usually be sufficient discipline, and at most, a light snap correction or a light gripping will produce a submissive response from a timid or extremely shy pup. Occasional games of tug-of-war or a little roughhousing will help grow a timid pup's anemic confidence. While these activities can produce dominant-aggressive behavior in dominant pups, a little roughhousing can stimulate a shy pup's confidence without giving the wrong impression.

Hiking on nature trails is an excellent way to boost a timid pup's confidence. Socialization should also be a high priority. Praise and encouragement should be plentiful, while discipline should always follow the rule: Only as much discipline needed to produce a submissive response.

The game of cat-and-mouse, using one of a pup's toys, is a therapeutic game for timid and extremely shy pups. To play the game, sit on the floor and play keep-away by moving the toy around your body and through your legs. When the pup captures the toy, you should allow him to retain possession, while you praise him for a job well done. Unless he drops the toy within your reach or you have a backup toy, the game should end at that time. Most pups will want to encourage another game by dropping the toy within their owners' reach.

Timid pups and dogs are under a lot of stress. Whereas shyness and submissiveness are examples of normal dispositions and temperaments for low-ranking pack members, timidity is an extremely submissive and fearful disposition. The handling of a timid pup will be analogous to the therapy for a traumatized child: stimulation without intimidation.

Pack training is a universal mold for pups. Dominant and stubborn pups will be taken down a peg or two in the social order, and submissive and timid pups will move up the social ladder, appearing more confident in their social behavior. The pack-training strategy is the same for all pups, but the dominant pups will need firmer discipline than the shy and passive pups. Following a pack-training regimen, dominant and submissive pups will appear more alike than complete opposites. They will both be pack members in good standing.

Cheyenne gives a subtle, dominant expression to Jojo, a year-old Chihuahua.
Notice how Jojo lowers his head and averts his eyes
when Cheyenne glances his way and monitors him with her right ear.

Pack members have a great life—no cares, no worries.

7

Establishing Social Order With Dominant Dogs

If your dog is not presenting you with a long list of behavioral problems, he (or she) is a submissive pack member. If you own a problem dog, he is a dominant, stubborn, or dominant-aggressive dog that is testing or challenging your authority.

If your dog is only posturing his dominance and testing the authority of family members, you have a dominant dog in need of discipline and pack training. If your dog bites a neighborhood child, a family member, a friend, or a visitor to your home, you have an alpha dog that is disciplining with his bite. Pack leaders lead with their dominant attitude, and they discipline subordinates and strangers when their authority is tested or disrespected. All dominant dogs test their owners, and some will even challenge their owners' authority.

Alpha dictators are the dogs that are mauling and killing children. While they are rare, there seems to be more of these unstable dogs than ever before. Alpha dictators could be called the "terrorists of the dog world." They are found in nature and occasionally in our neighborhoods. Alpha dictators are extremely dangerous animals because of their desire to punish subordinates and strangers with equal intensity.

Pups attain dominance by winning their tests of authority with family members. Testing behavior includes the following: not coming on command, not submitting readily to authority, demanding owner pet him, demanding owner not pet or groom him, walking out the door first, playing tug-of-war, pulling on lead, soiling the house after house-training, begging for food, biting (hands, feet, clothing), and jumping onto people. Pack leaders demonstrate their dominance by marking the house, destroying their owners' property, growling, snapping, and disciplining family members or visitors with their bites. A typical dog bite is a single bite to the face. The typical dog-bite victim is a child.

What should you do when your alpha dog bites someone? Should you tell him "No?" Should you scruff him by the neck or administer an alpha roll? —Absolutely not! If you try to discipline an alpha dog for biting, you will likely be his next victim. When a dog offensively bites (grips) someone, he is functioning as a pack leader. He is disciplining someone for stepping out of line or challenging his authority. And he will remain the alpha leader until he is defeated in battle. Simple discipline is ineffective for these dogs.

Before explaining more about the motivation and drive of alpha leaders, let me impress upon you that there is no reason anyone should have to experience an event such as this. Pack members do not suddenly become threatening pack leaders.

Anyone who establishes and maintains social order will never have his dog turn on him or anyone else.

In order for an alpha dog to stop biting, he must be demoted from his leadership position. For him to be demoted, he must be defeated in battle. You are not able, however, to battle with a pack leader on his level; and if you choose to beat your dog, you may feel better, but you will still have a problem dog. Your dog will think you "went psycho," but he won't interpret his beating as discipline or a demotion of rank. In all likelihood, he will opt to discipline his subordinates when you are away from home.

Alpha dogs bite as a means of disciplining misbehaving subordinates and disrespectful outsiders. While some are more aggressive than others, alpha dogs are typically not angry with their victims. Regardless of their attitude, alpha dogs are distinct liabilities in their homes. However, if we demote them from their alpha position, they would no longer be a threat to their families or strangers. Because pack members do not have the stressful responsibility of maintaining order, a demoted pack leader's disposition will become relaxed and tolerant. If we do not demote an alpha dog, our remaining options are drugs, confinement, or destroying the animal.

The typical dog that makes its first bite is an adult male dog between one and three years of age. As a pup, he had tested the authority of family members with impunity, and he had growled at family members and outsiders well prior to his initial bite. The dog lives in a home with children, and his first victim is one of the children in the home or a visiting child.

When a child is bitten on the face or head, the dog's owners will be advised or forced to put the dog down. If there are small children in the dog's family, that would be my concern as well. Not that there isn't any hope of rehabilitating a biting dog, but any chance of a child being bitten would not be a gamble I would take. But if there are no children in the home, or the dog can be kenneled until the demotion is accomplished, I will accept the job.

My strategy for demoting a pack leader uses the wolf for a working model. When a wolf challenges a pack leader, there will be a fight for dominance. One of three scenarios will play out when a pack leader is challenged: the leader will be demoted; the challenger will make a hasty retreat; or the challenger will submit to the alpha leader. What causes a wolf to submit? The fear of death is what triggers one wolf to suddenly stop fighting and go "belly-up." At the moment of submission, the alpha wolf will end the fight and decide whether or not to allow the challenger to remain in the pack. The vanquished foe will usually retain his pack membership, but only with a distinct demotion of social rank.

While fighting an alpha dog on his level is not a viable option, if I could lead the dog to believe his life were in jeopardy, he would likely submit to my authority. By submitting to another's authority, an alpha leader will experience a demotion of rank. Dogs are intelligent and cunning creatures that reason through the problems they face. And they usually take the path of least resistance. They certainly know when they are in danger of losing their lives, so we must produce this thought in dominant-aggressive biting dogs.

When I evaluate a biting dog, I must determine if the dog is a pack leader or a fear-biter. Fear-biters represent only ten percent of the biting dogs, but the behavior of the dog will tell me which type of dog I am meeting. Fear-biters will try to avoid my contact. Alpha leaders will try to repel my advance by glaring and growling. Should I approach a growling dog and try to make physical contact, he will likely try to discipline me for ignoring his warning. You may be thinking, "Maybe the dog was only being protective" or "Perhaps he felt threatened." Stable dogs do not think friendly encounters may suddenly turn violent. If "the growling dog" had felt threatened by my advance, he would have moved away or closer to his owner. Because he defiantly warned me with his body language and growls, I would consider him to be a pack leader. So how do we demote a pack leader?

Many authors recommend that their readers consult a professional dog trainer if they have a biting dog. I used to wonder why they didn't address the subject—after all, aren't they the professionals? Now I understand that authors cannot guarantee their readers will comprehend and implement their advice and techniques. If you have an aggressive dog, you should consult with a trainer who has an understanding of pack animal behavior. Your local veterinarians may know a trainer in your area that can help you.

One of the most ruthless pack dictators I ever met was a three-year-old cocker spaniel named Montana. He had bitten each family member on numerous occasions and many of their friends and relatives. And his evaluation was short. The moment I walked into his house, Montana began staring and growling at me. After being shown the collection of scars on the family's hands and legs, I asked them how they usually responded when Montana was growling at their company. They informed me that it usually helped to give the dog a slice of lunchmeat. (Houston, we have a problem!)

Montana's demeanor was as surly as it could be. When we took him for a walk on lead, he pulled hard; and when we walked past a pedestrian or cyclist, not to mention the cars and other dogs, he would shift into the attack mode. Following his demotion, Montana's attitude and outlook immediately changed. As a pack leader, Montana had been on active duty, and he lived in a very active household and neighborhood. The stress of being in charge had adversely affected the dog. However, after his demotion to pack member, Montana was no longer on the clock. It was no longer his responsibility to screen visitors and discipline his family, and his attitude now reflected this peaceful realization. A year later, I contacted the family to check on Montana. I was told me that he had not reverted to his old ways. In fact, he was living happily as a couch potato with their daughter and her new husband.

Being a pack member is the best possible life for a dog—no worries, no cares. Being a pack leader is a thankless and stressful job. An alpha dog's attitude often reflects the stress of responsibility. A pack member does not have the burden of being in charge, so we should relieve an alpha dog of his stressful obligation by giving him a good demotion.

Artist: Cathy Peek—Peek Productions—www.westportwa.com/cathypeek
Fax: 360-258-9559

8

A Good Start

People often ask, "When is the best time to begin a pup's training?" The answer is always consistent: Training begins the day your pup comes home with you. Whereas the training I am addressing is not formal obedience training, it is far more important. The quality of a relationship with a dog depends on this early effort.

The creation of a pack environment begins the day you take possession of an eight-week-old pup, but the process actually began six weeks earlier for your pup. At two weeks of age, a pup begins gathering information and learning from his (or her) life experience. He also begins establishing his social status with his littermates. A pup's parents will teach him a lot, but when he comes home with you, he will learn much more. Waiting until a pup is six months old to begin his training will therefore be a late start. By six months of age, a pup already knows whether or not you are the alpha leader. If he thinks you are a weak, inconsistent leader, his instincts will dictate testing behavior to a greater extent. Should these tests not be consistently disciplined, the pup may well challenge your leadership when he reaches maturity.

A dominant pup will test the authority of each family member. Without a clear understanding of how pups test the authority of their owners, we cannot hope to respond in an appropriate manner to testing behavior. How should we respond to testing behavior? We should always respond like a dog.

To one degree or another, all pups test the authority of their companions. Recognition of testing behavior is therefore crucial to the relationships we are cultivating with our pups. By studying wolf behavior, we will learn how wolves test one another and respond to testing behavior. Instead of traumatizing their testing pups or bribing them with food, wolves and dogs discipline their subordinates in a clear and consistent manner. By disciplining in the same fashion as wolves and dogs, you will be speaking your dog's language. And you won't frighten your pup by behaving in a way that is not instinctively understood. All pups test their owners in the same manner. Testing behavior begins early in their development, usually around three months of age: They bite our hands and feet; they jump onto our legs; they don't submit to authority; they initiate games of tug-of-war; they growl at family members; they don't come when called; they chew up furniture, shoes, and carpet; and they soil the house with their wastes.

Every pup has tested his owners by refusing to come when called. The behavior is saying, "I'll come when I'm ready" or "If you want me, come get me." And when the owner approaches, the pup runs away. Catch-me-if you-can is played by all wild and domesticated pups. When a wolf pup plays this game, a pack leader will warn his subordinate to submit by staring at him and growling. If the pup decides to submit, he will return submissively to the leader, but should the pup ignore the warning, the discipline will escalate.

Progressive discipline creates an orderly sequence of events. When a wolf or dog learns that what comes after the initial warning is more consequential than the warning itself, he will take the path of least resistance. When you discipline in a consistent and escalating manner, your pup will learn the sequence; when your corrections mimic the discipline of an alpha wolf, you will spotlight your alpha status. On the other hand, inconsistent or weak discipline will encourage your pup to take his chances following your warnings.

When a wolf pup ignores the leader's warning, the alpha wolf will take charge by gripping the subordinate with his teeth. While the gripping isn't intended to injure the subordinate, it is meant to restore order by eliciting a submissive response. A submissive response could be lowering the head and body, crying out, or rolling over onto his back. When submission is offered, the leader will release his grip and all will be forgiven. If the pup resists the gripping, the leader will restrain the pup on the ground until he submits.

Maintaining social order is not an option but a necessity. Without order, a pack of wolves could not coexist. Anarchy would rule and cooperation would end. In order to establish and maintain social order, you will need to consistently discipline your pup in his language. When you speak the language, you will be understood and respected. When your pup loves and respects you, he will instinctively be motivated to please you; he will want to come when you call; and he will willingly submit to your authority.

Canine Discipline

Experience is the best teacher when it comes to dogs. When your pup's life experience is consistent, he will quickly learn his daily routine. When you discipline in a consistent manner, he will learn that routine as well. When his corrections prove to be consequential, your pup will change his behavior and gain respect for your leadership.

Dogs thrive on a consistent daily routine. They love knowing the timing of their meals, walks, and training classes. When these activities are consistent in their timing, your dog will be expecting each activity at the appropriate time. This applies to discipline as well. When you discipline in a consistent, coherent manner, your pup will learn the timing and sequence of his corrections. When the consequences are progressive, he will want to avoid the stronger corrections. He must decide this on his own, and he will, when you become a consistent disciplinarian.

An example of giving discipline in your dog's language is as follows:

Your pup is misbehaving. Whether it's biting your hands, feet, or clothing; growling at family members or guests; chewing furniture; or not coming when you call, you should give your pup a warning (fixed stare). When you posture your disapproval, you will be leaning toward your pup and staring at him. He will interpret your body language as a warning to submit. When you combine this body language with a verbal correction and a growl, your pup will stop and take a long, hard look at you. You should continue staring at your pup until he decides whether or not to submit to your authority. If he submits to your warning, he will ask for your forgiveness by submissively approaching you: His head will be lowered; his tail will be lowered and wagging; and he will be licking his lips and your hands. This behavior will not be expressing fear. In fact, it is behavior deserving of praise. This is how wolves and dogs submit to authority. It is a show of respect.

However, if the pup ignores your warning and continues the bad behavior, you must escalate the discipline by lifting the pup by the loose skin (scruff) on the back of the neck. During the gripping correction, you should express your feelings about his behavior before returning him to the ground. Most pups will readily submit when they are gripped, and the rest will resist. Pups that resist authority can also be given a quick shake. This will not be a traumatizing experience. After all, their mothers likely disciplined them in the same manner. If your pup cries out when you lift him by the scruff, he is not expressing pain or fear; he is expressing submission to your authority. A pup that yelps during a gripping will not need the quick shake, because the yelp is his way of expressing submission.

Your pup's reaction to discipline should be noted. Is he submitting to your authority, or is he continuing to test your authority or initiating another bad behavior, such as barking, biting, or jumping onto you? If the pup doesn't submit following a correction, you should escalate the discipline with an alpha roll. By gripping the scruff and the loose skin on the lower back of a pup, you can use leverage to pull a large pup down. Some force is needed. Instead of coaxing the pup to lie down, you should forcibly place him on his side. Because dominant-aggressive pups are usually extremely willful, daily alpha rolls are recommended as a therapy for their obstinate and stubborn attitudes. An alpha roll is not only the third level of canine discipline but also a valid way of demonstrating authority to a dog. As the alpha leader, you have the right to restrain your pack member at your discretion; you also have the responsibility to establish social order with an alpha pup.

Some dog trainers perform the alpha roll by straddling a pup on his back. I do not recommend this technique for large or dominant-aggressive pups. Straddling a large, dominant pup on his back with his head in your hands will put you at risk of being clawed to shreds or bitten. However, by placing a pup on his side and yourself behind the pup, you will not be at risk of being harmed. Once placed on his side, place one hand on the pup's neck, so he can't bite his way free, and the other hand on his hindquarters—and hold on! If the pup struggles to free himself, you should express your disapproval with verbal corrections and growls until he submits. You'll know when he has truly submitted, for he will be lying perfectly still with his head on the ground. And when you slowly release your hold, he will continue to lie still. For this expression of respect, you should praise him and give him an affectionate belly scratch. If the pup jumps up in an excited, dominant, or aggressive manner, he will be expressing his dominance; so you should repeat the alpha roll until he truly submits.

This same pattern of discipline should be used for all infractions around the home. If you have a hardheaded pup that continues to test you following a fixed stare, gripping, and alpha roll, you can administer the fourth level of discipline by banishing the pup for thirty minutes either in the yard or his crate. Banishing a stubborn pup to his crate will not affect his crate training. He will continue to think of his crate in a positive light, but during his banishment, he will use the time to think about the consequences of his rebellious nature.

Banishment from the pack is a profound consequence for a dog. Wolves will also banish an antisocial wolf to the periphery following a serious transgression. From a safe distance, his demeanor will be expressing his desire to reunite with his family. Banished wolves often remain outcasts or become lone wolves. When you banish your pup, he will have time to think about the events that led to the separation. For most pups, this time will be well spent, especially when they realize the cause and effect.

Your pup will make better decisions concerning his behavior when you discipline in a consistent and orderly manner. When you are perceived as a consistent disciplinarian, your pup will readily submit to your verbal corrections. He will also be less prone to test you in the future.

Pack Socialization and Activities

Giving love and discipline will satisfy two of your pup's needs. However, if all you do is give love and discipline, it won't be enough to produce a confident, stable dog. Socializing pups to the outside world may not seem to be important. If this is your thinking, you are not thinking like a pack animal.

Wolves nurture their pups' self-reliance and confidence by allowing them time to explore their environment on their own and taking them for hikes in new territory. Socialization teaches pups to be confident in new environments, and its window for pups is from four to sixteen weeks of age. If wolf pups were not exposed to their surroundings, they would not be motivated to leave the security of their den site. I wonder how wolves know that their pups need to adapt to their world.

Socialization should be given to our pups at a very young age. The rule suggests that pups must be socialized to the world early on in their life. But there are exceptions to this rule. There once was a year-old toy poodle that lived with an elderly, disabled woman. Until the day he came to board with me, his only trips away from home were veterinarian and grooming appointments. So, as expected, the toy poodle cringed and trembled at the back of his kennel run, refusing to move from his spot. We tried all the tricks to gain his trust, but he would have nothing to do with toys, food, or us.

The following day, when placed in an outside run for exercise, he escaped through the opening in the gate. For three days I drove around the neighborhood, placing wanted posters and telling everyone I saw to be on the lookout for one scared toy poodle. I had lost hope by the fourth day when someone responded to a lost-dog flyer. The phone caller, who lived in a distant neighborhood, told me that a black toy poodle had found his way to her home. When I arrived at the home, the owners were standing in the front yard with a black toy poodle, but it was obvious that he wasn't the poodle I was looking for. This dog was standing tall; his tail was sticking straight up; and he had the biggest smile he could stretch.

I nearly keeled over when he answered to his name. Only now, after three days of running wild on Panama City Beach, Pierre was a new dog. He not only survived, he was transformed! So even if the odds are against what you are trying to accomplish with your dog, that doesn't mean it can't be done.

During their first four months of life, wolf pups learn to trust their world. If their environments were restricted to their den sites during that time, they would feel secure only when they were on their home turf. Should they be exposed to unknown territory, without proper socialization, they would be extremely anxious and nervous. Wolves take their pups away from the den when they are old enough to keep up. You should do the same with your pup. By exposing your pup to traffic, strangers, loud noises, strange dogs, strange environments, and kids, you will instill confidence and an outgoing personality in your pup.

The breeder's home or kennel is where a pup learns to trust human contact. If human nurturing is not given by the age of eight weeks, a pup will likely never feel comfortable around strangers, and he may feel insecure with his family as well. He will appear shy and timid at home and fearful around strangers. Insecure pups are under a lot of stress, and their demeanor is comparable to a captured wild wolf. If a newborn pup is hooked up to life support and not touched, he will die—as will a human baby. Both require a loving touch.

Your pup should have had positive human contact before you take possession. I also recommend that you spend some time with your pup at the breeder's home before you bring him home. You can leave an article of your clothing with your pup so he can become imprinted with your scent at the breeder's home. Instead of transporting the pup to your home in a pet carrier, you will lessen the stressful effect of being separated from his natal family by allowing the pup to ride home in your lap. Transporting a young pup in the cargo hold of an airplane is not recommended.

When you arrive home with a new pup, you shouldn't take him inside the house right away. An excited pup will need to relieve himself. He will also need some time to acclimate to his new environment by exploring your property. Large homes can be intimidating to young pups, so it is usually best to expose them to their new homes a little at a time. Restricting a pup's access to your home for a few days will also help keep "accidents" to a minimum. After giving your pup a few days to acclimate to your home, you can begin his socialization. Teaching your pup to trust his world will be the most rewarding time you spend with him. Road trips and stressful environments (e.g., shopping centers, airports, and sporting events) will be advanced socialization, so judge for yourself when your pup's confidence is sufficient to handle these stressful activities.

Taking a young pup for hikes off lead is perhaps the most beneficial pack activity. As well as being socialized to the outdoors, he will be learning to follow your lead and to come when you call. He will also be getting physical and mental exercise as he explores his world. Should your pup excel at the game of hide-and-seek, you can stimulate his aptitude for tracking by recruiting a friend to accompany you on your hikes. While you walk ahead looking for a place to hide, your friend will stay behind with the pup. After you have hidden, your friend can call out, "Go find," as he unsnaps the pup's lead. If the pup runs past your hiding spot, you should call him. Go-find is a beneficial game to play with pups. It is considered a fun activity by most pups; they will be learning to use their senses to solve a problem; and most of all, it is another way we can communicate with our pups from a leadership position. For pups that can't get enough of a good game, go-find and hide-and-seek can be played at home as well.

Teaching a pup the names of his toys is another useful communication exercise. You can teach your pup the identity of his toys by communicating the name of the toy when you engage him in play. Instead of teaching a pup to fetch, teach him to "fetch-ball." When you play cat-and-mouse with your pup, you can use the name of the toy as you play the game. One of Cheyenne's favorite games is go-find-cheese. When she is unaware, I will hide two or three pieces of cheese on doorknobs and bookshelves. Then I will tell her to "go find cheese." Initially, I had to lead her to the locations and point to the hidden treats, but she caught on after one game—after all, it was cheese!

Pack training creates bonds of love and friendship between pups and their owners. Socialization teaches them to be confident in new environments and to follow their owners' lead. Whereas pack training produces a well-mannered dog, socialization instills confidence.

A pack member's agenda is to eat, sleep, play, and follow someone's lead. Pack leaders, on the other hand, have the responsibilities of defending territory, maintaining order, and giving discipline. They are always the problem dogs that you hear or read about. Thankfully, most pack leaders are not trying to harm children when they discipline them. Medium to large dogs have the capability and know-how to kill children with their bites, if that were their intent. However, out of nearly five million annual dog bites, fewer than twenty fatal attacks occur in a given year.

The dog-bite epidemic in this country is alarming, not only for the pain and suffering caused by family dogs but also for the lack of understanding of the problem. Most people do not understand their dogs' aggressive behavior, and the dominance order is not usually a topic of dog-bite investigations. Animal behaviorists tell us not to hit our dogs, but they offer no alternatives for correcting aggressive behavior or solving the dog-aggression problem, other than the following: don't allow the dog to exit the house ahead of you; feed the dog after you eat; make the dog move out of your way, instead of walking around or stepping over him; banish the dog from your bed. These suggestions are like placing a Band-Aid on a gaping wound. They do not address the essence of aggressive behavior, and they will not demote an alpha leader from its position of authority. In fact, these suggestions may place the owner of one of these dogs in harm's way. Forcing a pack leader off your bed or making him move out of the way will often trigger a dog bite.

Pack training is a preventive means of addressing the dog-bite problem. By establishing and maintaining social order, you will ensure the likelihood that your pup will not become a biting dog. If you already have a problem dog, the establishment of social order is critically important. When communicating authority to a dominant dog that has been growling or snapping at family members, it would be advisable to muzzle the dog before offering a behavior-modification lesson. By administering daily alpha rolls to your muzzled dog and restraining him until he totally submits, you will be expressing your authority in the dog's language. Total submission will be expressed when your dog remains on the ground after you release your hold on him. This may initially take several minutes for a stubborn dog, but each time you perform an alpha roll, your dog will submit sooner than the time before. Daily alpha rolls and consistent discipline will be needed until you see a change in your dog's attitude toward family members. When children live in the home, supervision will also be necessary until the dog's demotion has been validated. In addition to discipline, obedience training will also project your alpha status to a dominant-aggressive dog.

Because all dogs speak the same language, pack training is the most effective way of solving and preventing dominant-aggressive behavior. When you speak the language, you will know how to discipline without having to strike your dog. When you discipline your dog appropriately, he will acknowledge your leadership; and when he accepts you as his alpha, his instincts will shape his behavior and attitude in a positive fashion.

If dominant pups are not disciplined, they assume their owners have limited authority. This thought will drive them to attain as much dominance as they can. They become unruly and undisciplined, beginning at an early age. By the time they are six months old, no one will be able to walk them on lead without being dragged or walk through the yard without being shanghaied. At maturity, these undisciplined dogs will be functioning as pack leaders, and one of their responsibilities will be maintaining order with fixed stares, growls, and bites.

By understanding the purpose of your dog's behavior and responding appropriately to testing and submissive behavior, you will shape your dog into being your pack member. Being a pack member is a great life. Being a pack leader is a highly stressful job for a dog, especially in the average American family. An alpha dog must screen everyone that enters his territory. Perhaps this is why older pack leaders are often short-tempered—they're burnt-out from a lifetime of stress. On the other hand, I have seen many menacing adult dogs dramatically change their attitude and behavior following their demotion from alpha to pack member. Their tense and short-tempered dispositions become relaxed and tolerant. They may not necessarily become social butterflies, but they will no longer be in charge.

Leash Training

Teaching a pup to walk on a leash can be difficult if you do not understand what it means when a dog pulls its owner down the street. Once you understand that this behavior is testing your authority to lead the pack, you can proceed with confidence. The only equipment you will need to teach your pup to walk mannerly on lead is a choke collar and a six- to ten-foot leash. Six-foot leashes are recommended for small pups, eight-foot leashes for medium to large pups, and ten-foot leashes for large, athletic pups. If your pet store doesn't stock ten-foot leashes, you can make your own by attaching a four-foot leash to a six-foot leash.

Leash training can be taught when a pup is three to four months old. If this will be the pup's first experience walking on lead, you should give him a few days to get accustomed to the feel of the collar by allowing him to wear the choke collar during your hikes or around the home. Then you can attach the leash to his collar and allow him to drag it behind him for a few minutes. When your pup is accustomed to his leash and collar, you can use the leash to coax him to walk to you. When he is confidently responding to you on lead, you can begin his leash training.

Leash training is a means of demonstrating leadership to a pup. You can project your authority by offering a consequence when your pup tries to dictate the speed and direction of your walks. The leash should be attached to the "free ring" of the choke collar. The free ring is the one that doesn't have the chain passing through it. You can grip the leash by the handle with either hand. Then you can reach down with the same hand and grip the leash at its midpoint between your thumb and index finger. This will create some slack in the leash. Because you will need to release it quickly when the pup begins to pull, you shouldn't coil the leash around your hand.

You can begin your pup's leash training by calling out, "Let's go," as you walk away. When the pup begins to pull against the leash, extend your right arm in front of you and release the slack. After dropping the slack, you should turn and walk rapidly away in the opposite direction. If the pup continues his forward march, and you begin walking away from the pup with a loose leash, he will receive both a correction and a surprise when the leash suddenly snaps tight. This is why you must hold a significant amount of slack leash in your hand; you want to be moving away from the pup when the leash snaps tight.

If you reverse your direction with a taut leash, your pup will not receive a correction; he will only be pulled. By dropping the slack as you walk away from a pulling pup, you will have time to create a little momentum before the correction is made. This momentum will empower you to correct a pup by producing a significant consequence for his inattentive and dominant behavior.

As soon as the correction is made, you should call out in a friendly tone of voice, "Let's go," and continue walking in the new direction. As the pup catches up to you, you can take up the slack and praise the pup for coming along. Each time the pup begins to pull against the leash, you should drop the slack and walk away in the opposite direction. If the pup is pulling to the North, you can drop the slack and head South.

During your pup's first lesson, he will begin taking stock of you. You will be receiving his attention because he wants to know when you are walking away from him. In two or three hikes on lead, your pup will decide that watching you is more desirable that pulling you down the street.

During leash training, instead of making a pup walk by your side, you should allow him to walk in front of you—after all, this is his free time. You only want him to keep an eye on you. When he's walking ahead of you, he'll have to glance back in order to keep track of you. However, if you keep your pup by your side, you will not promote this positive behavior.

Pups that expect their owners to stop while they sniff the ground are also dictating the pack activity. They are determining when it's time to explore new territory. In a wolf pack, the pack leaders make these decisions. Because leash training is leadership training, we should demonstrate our authority by correcting all testing behavior; therefore, you should offer a consequence when the pup decides to stop for a sniff during his walks on lead.

Here's the play-by-play: You're walking with your pup on lead. When he stops to sniff, call out, "Let's go," and drop the slack as you continue walking forward. Should he not respond to the command to go with you, and you continue walking forward, he will receive a light correction when his collar suddenly tightens. Your momentum will likely produce a positive consequence. For large, dominant pups, you may need to amplify the correction by adding a little "snap" to the correction. (Read Chapter 12: Obedience Training for a description of a snap correction)

In order to time a snap correction, you must be looking back at your pup as you walk away. A snap correction should be given when there is a little slack in the leash. Following the correction, call out, "Let's go," and praise him when he comes along. In a few days, your pup will learn what happens when he ignores the Let's-go command. It is not strong leadership to allow a pup to make the decisions concerning pack activities. An alpha wolf would not be coerced, and neither should you. You will be demonstrating your leadership when you correct this behavior.

The only exception to the rule is when a pup stops to relieve himself. When this happens, a pup will suddenly stop, squat, and eliminate, but he will not sniff around for a good place "to go." When a pup stops and begins sniffing unfamiliar ground, he is not looking for a place to go—he is exploring on his own.

By the end of the first week of leash training, your pup will be walking mannerly on lead. When he hears the Let's-go command, his thought will be, "I need to go with my leader." As a result, he will be training himself to follow your lead.

By the time your pup is five months old, you will have logged many miles with his socialization and leadership training. He will be confident when he's exploring trails and walking on lead in strange neighborhoods. He will be socialized to strangers and friends, both in your home and in public. He will also be disciplined and enthusiastic in his temperament and disposition. But most of all, he will see you as his alpha and himself as your pack member.

Top photo: One Norwich terrier is posturing his dominance,
while his sister postures submission by lowering herself onto her owner's arm.
In the bottom photo, Cheyenne, a four-month-old Great Dane,
owned by Jason and Tamara Huff, is expressing her excitement.

From a dog's point of view, dominance and submission are not negative words. Dominance does not suggest aggression, and submission does not express fear. Max, the boxer, is performing a partial alpha roll on a much larger German shepherd.

Kodi, owned by Michael and Sherry Higgins,
Expresses growing excitement with his tail and ear posturing.

9

Advanced Canine Communication

"If you talk to the animals they will talk with you and you will know each other. If you do not talk to them, you will not know them, and what you do not know you will fear. What one fears, one destroys."
-- Chief Dan George

Whether you know it or not, you are already communicating with your dogs; but if you knew what you were revealing about yourself, you might be surprised or shocked. Hopefully, you are communicating that you are the pack leader and your dogs are your pack members. Some dog owners project strong leadership; others express weak leadership; and the rest are communicating an absence of authority.

Communication among higher animals includes vision, hearing, and smell. You communicate to your dog with your voice, body language, disposition, temperament, and as well, your activities and emotions. Your dog always knows your emotional state. He knows whether you are happy, sad, calm, or angry. He can detect your emotional state by reading your body language and body scent. Our body chemistry changes with each of our emotional states, and with chemical reactions there is usually odor. As it turns out, the "smell of fear" is a real smell. This is why dogs are so obsessed with sniffing everything, including us; they are information junkies.

Michael Bright, in his book, *Intelligence of Animals*, suggests that dogs may be detecting "radiations, ranging from heat to the electrical activity of our muscles." He postulates the changes in our emissions may communicate each of our emotional states.

When a dog sniffs another dog's urine or feces, he is profiling the depositor. He is determining the maturity and sex of the dog, the timing of a female's estrous cycle, and even the emotional state of the dog at the time of the elimination.

Your temperament and body language communicate your social status to your dog. Certain activities communicate our low ranking in the pack order (e.g., roughhousing, allowing a dog to pull on lead, and games of tug-of-war). Other activities promote and project your leadership (e.g., hiking, training, grooming, petting, and socialization).

When you expose an eight- to sixteen-week-old pup to unfamiliar territory, such as parks, shopping centers, hiking trails, and friends' homes, he will be inundated with a variety of stressful stimuli. As a result, he will seek security and leadership from someone he knows, and that person will be you.

When you groom or pet your dog, you are initiating an activity and expecting his submission to your intent. In effect, you are communicating your authority when you pet or groom your dog. When you understand that you are expressing not only affection but also leadership and authority when you pet your dog, you will see why children are at great risk when they pet an alpha dog. We should teach our children that some dogs feel the same way about being touched by a stranger as they do.

A positive relationship with a dog occurs when social order is established and maintained. By giving your pup love, discipline, and pack activities, you can establish your alpha position. If you participate only in one pack activity, taking your pup for frequent hikes on nature trails is my recommendation. Because of the strange environment, your pup will often be having the thought, "I need to stay close to my leader" or "Where is my pack leader?" You will know when he is thinking this, for he will be looking back at you at the time of the thought. The mental stress of keeping track of you and dealing with a new environment will be exercising his mind, and the physical exercise will be exercising his body. Both workouts will be beneficial for your pup. When a rambunctious pup returns home following a thirty to forty-five minute run, he will want to take a long nap. He will also be more relaxed during the remainder of the day.

Communicating with dogs involves every aspect of our being. Dogs communicate with us in the same manner. Empathy is one of the special virtues of dogs. When we are sick or melancholy, our dogs will grieve for us and stay by our side for as long as it takes. We also see this loyalty and compassion in the wolf.

Because dogs can sense our emotions, frustrated actors often make good dog trainers. Thankfully, our canine audience is quite gullible so the acting doesn't have to be flawless, only consistent. In other words, we need to impress upon our dogs that we believe what we are expressing when we give them discipline and praise. A monotone voice is not the voice of a dog trainer—and neither is the voice of a drill instructor. Instead of barking your commands, you should express your friendship and leadership with your voice and body language. By monitoring the tone of your voice and the posturing of your body language, you can add emphasis to your commands, discipline, and praise. For example, when you call your dog, the tone of your voice should sound neither like a plea nor a threat. The Recall command should be a confident request, and it should also project some excitement. But when you are tested with non-compliance, your attitude should switch from confident to dominant. While there is no need for heavy-handed corrections to gain a dog's respect, you must be able to give appropriate discipline at the appropriate times. And while there is no need to bribe a dog for good behavior, you must be willing to give sincere praise when he is doing what you want and making good decisions.

When you call your dog, you should be standing upright. When you lean toward a dog, he may interpret your body language as confrontational. When I initially work with extremely shy or timid pups, I will kneel down when I call them. This active-submissive body language will encourage a shy pup to come.

Dogs communicate mainly with their body language, but they also express their will and emotions with their behavioral patterns and vocalizations. Dog vocalizations include yelps (yips), whimpers (yodels), whines, growls, howls, and barks. Yelps, whines, and growls are clear-cut emotional expression; whimpers are comparable to talking (some breeds, especially the Arctic breeds, whimper more than others); and barks can be expressing different emotions at different times. When a dog's tail is wagging in a lowered position, his barking is expressing friendship. When his body is rigid and the tail is held in a high position, his barking is a dominant expression. Threatening barks will be accompanied by threatening body language. As a rule, dogs never mask their emotions—what you see is what you get. You can usually determine the motive of a neighborhood barking dog by your dog's body language as you and he walk past. A threatening bark will be reciprocated with a dominant or submissive response. While dogs bark more frequently than wolves, wolves howl more often than dogs, but both vocalizations are similarly purposeful for both species. Arctic breeds and the African basenji commonly yodel as an expression of joy and excitement.

Knowing how dogs communicate makes it possible to respond to a dog's behavior in a positive and effective manner. When you can read your dog's body language, you will also know his motivation. Knowing when a dog is motivated to misbehave makes it possible to correct him before he acts out in a negative manner. For example, teaching a dog not to chase the neighbor's pet is easier said than done. And should the behavior become an established habit, it will take some effort to break the habit. Preventing bad behavior is always easier than breaking a bad habit. When your dog is staring at the neighbor's pet with his tail, head, and ears held high, he is aroused and thinking of leaving the yard. When his tail moves to a position parallel to the ground, and his body leans forward with his ears pointing forward, the dog is preparing to bolt. Correcting a dog after he has run down the street will usually be too little, too late. The pleasure he had will outweigh any mild correction you might offer. And he will likely want to continue participating in the activity.

When you see your dog posturing his dominance to a neighbor's pet, you should verbally correct him and note his reaction to the correction. If your dog submits to your correction by returning to your side or turning away from the temptation, he is deserving of your praise. But then again, he may decide to ignore your warning. A dog's temperament and disposition will affect his decision-making process. Some dogs are more tractable than others.

If your dog does not submit to your warning, you should go to him and give a gripping correction. If the gripping doesn't elicit a submissive response, you should escalate his discipline to an alpha roll. In order for a dominant dog to submit to authority, he must acknowledge your alpha status. For him to want to change his behavior, he will need to decide that the consequence outweighs the reward. By disciplining a pup in his own language, you will be communicating your leadership and gaining his respect.

You will occasionally meet a dog that cannot be trusted to make good decisions. Rebel, a two-year-old border collie that I rescued from the Humane Society, demonstrated this personality flaw. He also had a problem with dominance. Rebel was extremely bright, but he could not be trusted. You could only trust that he would try to get away with his schemes.

Rebel was gifted in the obedience ring and became an excellent demo dog, but he also had a dark side. Rebel was a dominant-aggressive dog with a cowardly disposition, and his passion was dominating those who feared him. I called him my cowardly serial mugger. It wasn't that he was trying to discipline with his bite, for he never broke the skin during an assault. Instead, he would grip a child's hand in his mouth and glare at his victim. While he never tried to dominate adults, or kids who weren't afraid of him, whenever the right kid came along, Rebel knew it the moment the child entered his yard. Being a cunning dog, Rebel knew how I would respond to one of these episodes, so I never witnessed one of these "muggings"— that is, until I set a trap.

A friend of my youngest son had a fear of dogs. He had never lived with a dog and had been bitten by a dog when he was younger; so when he met my Doberman and Rebel, he was obviously nervous and concerned for his safety. And Rebel knew it before anyone else. When I knew this particular kid was coming over, I drove to a neighbor's house and walked home. While spying from my garage, it didn't take long for Rebel to spring into action. Rebel was posturing and staring at my son's friend as they walked across the yard. When the boy walked past, Rebel quickly approached and gripped the boy's hand in his mouth.

That's when I came storming from the garage yelling, "No...what are you doing!" Rebel's expression changed in an instant, from dominance to passive-submission. He immediately released his grip and rolled onto his back, urinating into the air and crying like a whipped pup—and I hadn't even reached him yet! I finished the correction by giving him a hard gripping and banishing him to the spare bedroom for a long time-out. That was the last time Rebel played the bully in this fashion. He likely decided that I might be lurking nearby, even when he saw me driving away.

For dogs with a habit of chasing neighborhood pets, I will give them many opportunities to experience the consequence of their behavior. By placing a dog on a twenty-foot leash, I can stand away from him and still maintain control. A dog will also be tempted to act out when I am standing eight to ten feet away. Should he begin posturing his dominance or move toward the neighbor's pet, I will quickly offer a consequence. There can be a consequence for this behavior because I know he is thinking about making a mad dash from the yard.

The consequence will utilize the element of surprise. From my position behind the dog, with half of the leash coiled in my hand, I will turn and run away from the dog. As I turn to go, I'll drop the slack leash. If he remains focused on the neighbor's pet when I run away from him, there will be a significant consequence when the leash suddenly snaps tight. My momentum will produce the consequence—the bigger the dog, the faster I run. Let me assure you that there is no chance of injuring a dog in this manner. The sudden pressure of a choke-collar correction is distributed around the dog's thick neck muscles. It would, however, be dangerous to give this correction with a buckled collar. With a buckled collar, the force of the correction is concentrated on the throat of the dog—his most vulnerable spot.

In order to give an effective correction with a choke collar, there must be a little slack in the leash prior to the correction. If the leash were taut when I ran away, I would have only dragged the pup with me. The object is not to pull the pup but to correct him for his inattentive and dominant behavior. No matter what breed of dog you have, his reaction to the correction will verify its efficacy: If the pup is still focusing on the temptation following the correction, the correction wasn't a significant consequence; if he responds in an active-submissive manner, the correction was effective; if he expresses passive-submission or fear, the correction was too forceful.

If the correction was not consequential, you will need to include a little snap with future corrections. A snap correction is a meaningful consequence because it simulates the effect of a gripping correction. When a dog associates discipline with a particular behavior, he will usually stop behaving in that fashion. When your dominant dog is demonstrating self-discipline on lead, you can drop the leash and give him the opportunity to make the right decision when the leash is not in your hands. Leaving the leash attached to his collar works to your advantage. Dogs know their owners are in control when they are on lead. They also know they are more in control when they are off lead. Your dog will be less likely to take his chances, when you are standing away from him, if the leash is still attached to his collar.

In a few weeks, if the dog continues to show restraint, you can unsnap the leash and supervise him off lead in the yard. Having a cookout with the dog in attendance would be a good test for a dog that had been showing improved self-control off lead. However, until you have confidence in your dog's self-discipline, you must prevent any backsliding by not allowing him to chase the neighbor's pet with impunity. If you allow him to be on his own when you are away from home, he will learn that he can get away with his misbehavior at that time. The time needed to change a dog's bad behavior will depend on his stubbornness and how consistently he is disciplined for the behavior. By offering daily behavior modification lessons and giving a dog many opportunities to learn from his mistakes, one can usually change a dog's attitude and behavior. You want your dog to decide that the consequence of chasing the neighborhood pets outweighs the reward. Even when he is thinking about chasing the neighbor's pet, you want him to think there will be a consequence for that as well. Until the habit is broken, your dog will need to be supervised in the yard. My grandfather used to say that one missed correction would cancel out three good days of training. In other words, a dog will remember getting away with misbehavior for a lengthy time.

How should you respond to a pup that ignores your warning and runs out of the yard? As he bolts from the yard, you should communicate that he is making a mistake by posturing and barking, "No!" Should he stop and look back, you should kneel down and call him. If he ignores you by walking or running away, or if he just stands there staring at you, call out, "No!" and start walking toward the pup with the most dominant attitude you can muster. Projecting your emotions is a critical element of dog training. If you don't appear serious, he will not believe you are. Your pup will respond to your dominant behavior in one of three ways—he will correct his mistake, he will submit, or he will resist. Should he correct his mistake by returning to his yard, you can heartily praise his good decision. If he postures submissively as you approach him, give him a light gripping and return him to his yard. Both of these pups, however, will be exceptions to the rule. Most pups will respond in a more dominant and evasive manner.

As you calmly but forcefully walk toward your rebellious pup, your body language will be communicating your disapproval and authority. It is important not to call him again or tell him to stay or offer a treat in order to reach him. You want to be able to correct him when you reach him; therefore, if you call him or tell him to stay, you wouldn't be justified in correcting his bad behavior. Your pup's response to your display of dominance will likely be bolting away when you approach. This evasive behavior is communicating, "You can't catch me" or "Catch me if you can," or the pup will submissively bolt in order to avoid his correction. You'll be able to tell which game is being played—one attitude will be aloof, one will be playful, and the other will be somewhat fearful. It will be evident by the dog's facial and body posturing whether it is arrogance, playful dominance, or a submissive retreat. Usually the pup's agenda will be to make a game out of this bad situation. Regardless of his motive, your response should be the same each time the pup bolts from you.

Because avoidance of your discipline is a test of your authority, you should verbally correct him and continue your pursuit each time he runs away from you. After he has bolted several times from your advance, and you have verbally corrected him each time he took evasive action, he will look for a way out of this stressful confrontation. With each verbal correction, it will register more and more that you are intent on his capture. Following four or five verbal corrections, you will see a change in his attitude and behavior. He will begin thinking that a correction is imminent, and the effect of that thought will cause him to stop and submit. This will usually be a demonstration of passive submission, with your pup crouching low or rolling onto its back or approaching you submissively with his tail tucked between the legs. Your response when you get your hands on him (because you haven't called him) will be to lift him by the scruff as high as you can—preferably eye to eye—and give him a quick shake as you express your discontent. Following the gripping, as you lead him back to the yard by his collar, you can continue to express your dissatisfaction with his behavior. Following any serious transgression, it is helpful to isolate a pup for thirty minutes, either in the back yard or his crate or a spare room. During his banishment, he will recall the events that led to his discipline. When the association is made between his behavior and his discipline, he will likely decide that running down the street is no longer a worthwhile enterprise. He will be thinking of you as his pack leader because you disciplined him in his language, and he will also be grieving because of his banishment from his pack. These are the positive effects of discipline and communication.

It is recommended that you wait until your dog is physically mature
before teaching him to jump over hurdles.
Hip joints can be damaged when young pups are encouraged
to jump during their rapid skeletal development.

Top photo: Baron, owned by Malinda and Victor Wilkes,
expresses his joy with his tail posturing.
Kodi is expressing his relaxed state of mind in the bottom photo.

Cheyenne and my granddaughter, Kodi Peek, on the day they met.
Cheyenne is expressing her joy while Kodi expresses her reticence.

The fixed stare

Active submission expresses respect, not fear.
Jaeger, owned by Stan and Cecilia DeSonia,
happily accepts his pup's wolf greeting in the top photo.

10

Tricks of the Trade

"Dogs respond only to fear, food, and their sex drive" is a common misconception held by many dog trainers and dog owners. Force training, positive-reinforcement training, and clicker training are based on the belief that dogs are simple creatures, incapable of making responsible decisions or responding in a predictable manner to leadership.

Force trainers believe that we must forcibly dominate a dog to produce consistent, obedient behavior, and their techniques reflect this belief. Prior to 1970 the vast majority of dog trainers were using force-training techniques. This was in spite of the fact that many dogs were traumatized by heavy-handed discipline and forceful training techniques.

A commonly used force-training technique for teaching the Down command will give you a better perspective of force training:

A force trainer will attach a leash to a dog's choke collar. Then, with his foot standing on the leash and holding the leash's handle in both hands, he will give the Down command and pull on the leash in an upward direction. Some force trainers pull harder than others. The end result of the hard, upward pull will be a dog suddenly being snatched to the ground, often striking its head. In a few days, this dog will likely be "dropping like a rock" on command. To many observers this would be interpreted as quality obedience training, but it is no different than the chickens that dance on the hotplates at amusement parks and carnivals. They aren't dancing for food—they are dancing to avoid the heat. It is neither training nor entertainment—it is animal abuse.

While dominant and stubborn dogs are more likely to emotionally survive force-training techniques, shy and timid dogs are often permanently scarred by excessive force. The derogatory "that dog won't hunt" remark was likely coined by one of these force trainers. By 1970 many trainers were acknowledging the negative effects of force training, and some were offering an alternative approach to dog training. We know it today as positive-reinforcement training. But they only went from one extreme to another. Superficially, positive-reinforcement training appears to be the antithesis of force training. Whereas force training uses fear as a motivator, positive-reinforcement training motivates a dog with food rewards.

Even though positive-reinforcement training is more humane than force training, I still challenge its merit. Are treat-trained dogs obeying their commands to please their trainers, or do they have their own agenda? Do canine pack leaders offer bribes to their pack members to gain their allegiance? If you treat-train your dog, will he obey when you have no food? Is he motivated by treats when distractions are nearby or when he is running off lead?

Treat training is a temporary fix. Young pups do initially respond to food rewards, but they are less responsive later in life. Many dogs trained in this manner will obey only when a treat is visible to them. And there is no evidence of an alpha wolf offering food to his pack members as an incentive for good behavior. Bribes are bribes. They work only for the short term and are not an effective means of establishing social order with a dog. While positive-reinforcement training and force training appear to be opposite points of view, they are both unnatural means of training dogs.

People often use the same psychology with their dogs and children. Some people believe that they must physically dominate children and pups with heavy-handed discipline. Others believe that rewarding for good behavior is a more effective training technique. One camp thinks harsh discipline is the best way to motivate children and pups; the other believes that positive reinforcement is a better motivator. And they are equally wrong. Kids and pups need love and appropriate discipline, but an omission of one of these basic needs will usually produce insecurity or aggression in children and pups.

For any group of animals to coexist, there must be social order (discipline) and communication (a common language) among its members. This does not suggest the need for traumatic force or treats. You cannot establish social order by rewarding your dog with food rewards. Bribery is unnatural canine behavior, and it restricts our ability to lead our dogs when we behave in such a weak, submissive manner. Many dogs trained exclusively with food rewards see themselves as being the pack leader. In effect, they are training their owners to feed them by sitting, downing, or coming on command.

Some people believe that disciplining a dog involves striking with their hands, but that doesn't mean their dogs understand what they are doing. They surely know their owners are mad at them, but they won't interpret their corporal punishment as discipline. There will also be a lot of confusion about your leadership if you discipline in this manner. Dogs do not discipline by striking with their legs, and therefore do not understand the meaning of a beating. From the resulting confusion comes the trauma. Shy dogs will be affected to a higher degree, but all dogs will be adversely affected by this traumatic and alien behavior. I have seen too many dogs cowering from their owner's hand to believe that force training has any merit. I am not referring to an active-submissive greeting when a dog lowers his head as he greets his owner. I am describing a dog that cowers on the ground or shies away from his owner's hand. These are the broken dogs of force trainers.

Some dog trainers profess an understanding of pack animal behavior, but they either use excessive force to discipline their dogs or a force-training technique to teach a dog a particular command. My response to them would be, "Why use excessive force at all, if you don't have to?"

Pack training is an alternative form of dog training that substitutes food and fear with a psychological connection between a dog and its owner. You can establish order when you understand your dog's language and the dynamics of the dominance order. With this understanding, you can project your alpha status to your dog. Learning how to be a pack trainer is not difficult, but it doesn't happen without effort—and the effort begins the day the pup comes home with you.

Coordinating the arrival of a new pup with some vacation time is recommended. Taking time off from your daily routine will enable you to make a good start with your pup's socialization to his new family and environment. House-training and crate training will also get off on the right foot, if you allow the extra time upon your pup's arrival. Pet carriers with opaque sides are preferable to wire cages, because pups feel more secure in an enclosed space.

Anything your pup does for a few days in a row will become a habit, so by avoiding most of his "accidents" during his first few days at your home, you will have no problem house-training your pup. Until the pup is house-trained, he should be crated or left in the yard when you can't keep an eye on him. Pups will not want to soil their sleeping quarters. By holding his water, a pup's bladder will increase in size, making house-training an easier experience. (Read Chapter 23: Q & A for a house-training strategy)

Gunther Gable-Williams was a world-renowned animal trainer with the Ringling Brothers Circus. As a child, I listened to him speak about his big cats and his approach to training animals. He did not need whips and chairs to get his lions and tigers to perform astounding feats in the ring. He explained that he lived with his cats, and they all belonged to the same pride. By bonding with his tigers and lions, by socializing the animals to the three-ring circus, and by communicating to them in their own language, he was able to train his pride members without having to intimidate them. Their respect for William's authority produced obedient behavior.

Tom Dorrance and Ray Hunt were horse trainers who embraced the belief that communication and understanding were the keys to training intelligent animals. In order for us to communicate our leadership, whether we are training a dog or a horse or any intelligent animal, we must be perceived as a trustworthy and consistent leader.

Tom Dorrance, like many other successful animal trainers, was self-taught by his life experience and his natural ability to read a horse. Mr. Dorrance helped countless riders establish "true unity" with their horses. While many horse enthusiasts consider Tom Dorrance as the consummate horse trainer, his response to their accolades spoke of his character: "Everything I learned, I learned from the horse."

Ray Hunt summed up the psychology of training animals when he wrote: "Practice doesn't make perfect. Perfect practice makes perfect. We need to be more disciplined within ourselves so that we can present our objective to the horse in a way that he can understand. Allow them to learn; allow them to work at things; allow them to figure things out. Make the wrong things difficult, the right things easy."

Rehearsal

Dogs thrive on a routine, and they hate surprises. When a pup's daily routine is consistent, he will confidently learn the timing of his daily schedule. When his daily routine is in disorder, he will not know what to expect. The resulting confusion will often produce an anxious demeanor in a pup. For this reason, consistent handling produces confidence in pups. When your pup detects a consistent pattern during his training, he will quickly learn his lessons. When you are perceived as a consistent leader, your pup will gain respect for your leadership. An inconsistent training regimen will both impede the learning process and produce anxiety or disrespect in a pup.

A good example of inconsistent handling is the trainer who can't stick to the script: The trainer asks his dog to sit, and the dog ignores him; yesterday he responded with a correction, but today he repeats the command over and over. Adding to the confusion, the trainer's voice starts at a normal tone and becomes increasingly louder with each successive command. When trained in this manner, a pup will likely make his trainer repeat the command several times before deciding whether or not to obey. However, when the command and correction sequence is perceived to be consistent, a pup will confidently and respectfully sit on command.

In order to be a consistent obedience trainer, it is helpful to rehearse the sequence of commands and corrections before you begin training your pup. By memorizing your part and knowing how to respond to your pup's behavior, you will not be as likely to alter your training regimen when you're being tested. Many people will emotionally throw consistency out the window when their dogs are testing their authority. By rehearsing your part, you will project the image of a confident and worthy leader by being a consistent handler.

Keeping emotions in check is easier said than done when it comes to training dogs. It may help to remember that testing behavior is both instinctive and natural. It is not a personal affront when your pup tests your authority—it's how he validates your leadership.

Rehearsing is especially helpful when we teach our pups to heel. Your footwork is the key element in teaching a pup that "heel" means to walk by your left side. You can teach a pup to heel by bumping his head with your right leg when he begins to forge ahead. This quick left turn is tricky until you learn the knack of turning your body to the left as you make the turn. When you can square your corner, your right leg will bump the pup's head if he doesn't turn with you. By practicing without the dog until you have the muscle memory to make crisp ninety-degree left turns, you can then confidently and consistently teach a pup to heel.

Breaking Bad Habits

Chasing Cars

When a dog enjoys behaving badly, his behavior will become habitual. Because dogs believe they are defending their territory from outside threats, chasing cars is not only great sport but also a great ego boost. Each time a car speeds away, a dog will be gratified and encouraged by his success. Because car-chasing dogs are typically dominant dogs, creating a consequence to override the joy of chasing a car is not a simple matter. One tried and true method is to allow the dog to experience road rage. If a dog could be led to believe that cars can become a serious threat, he will likely give up his border-guard career. You'll need to recruit some friends to help. In order to produce the desired scary effect, your friends should wear Halloween masks or football helmets. In order to produce a threatening encounter, they should be armed with noisemakers and water balloons. Should the dog begin chasing their car as they drive past your house, the driver should stop the car so his passengers can jump out with their noisemakers "blasting away" at the dog. Banging a metal garbage can lid with a metal object is an effective means of creating noise. Air horns are also effective noisemakers.

Dogs hate surprises. By combining the element of surprise with a dousing of water and a threatening encounter with alien creatures, you will likely produce the needed consequence to break this dangerous habit. This behavior-modification exercise should be offered once a week, until you see a change for the better. The same principle applies for dogs chasing bicycles and joggers. As for any behavior modification, you must break the dog's bad habit. Therefore, you shouldn't leave your dog unsupervised in the yard until he is demonstrating his self-discipline. Depending on the stubbornness of the dog and your management skills, it could take weeks or months to modify this dominant and dangerous behavior.

AWOL

Escaping the confines of their yards and exploring the neighborhood is also a lot of fun for dogs, so you won't be able to bribe or coerce your dog to stay home. He will not be that easily manipulated. If you choose to beat your dog for his wanderlust, he will likely wait until you're away from home before becoming a repeat offender.

For a dog to stop any pleasurable activity, he must first want to stop. When there is a significant consequence for a particular behavior each time the dog indulges himself, he will take the necessary steps to avoid its repetition. But he will stop only when he decides it's in his best interest to do so. For this reason, an "electric fence, or hot wire," is the best way of confining a dog suffering from wanderlust. It's not the physical pain of the electric wire but the surprise that creates the consequence. The wire's current is comparable to the effect of a bee sting. The consequence of the surprise, combined with the "buzz" he feels when he touches the wire, will usually break the habit of going AWOL.

Underground pet containment systems can also be an effective means of confining a dog to his yard, providing you teach the dog that there will be a consequence when he crosses the property line. After installing an electronic underground fence, and with your dog on lead, you should allow him to experience the consequence for a few days before you turn him loose in the yard. By doing so, you can control his behavior and learning experience. Some unsupervised dogs will learn that they can reduce the effect of the shock by running across the boundary line. Others will be traumatized with multiple shocks when they crisscross the property line.

You can condition your dog to respect the boundary of your property by allowing him to experience the warning sound and the consequential shock when he crosses the property line. When your dog is taking the initiative to avoid the consequence, you can give him the opportunity to make the same decision when he is off lead. After a week or two of walking the dog around the perimeter of your yard, you can unsnap the leash and observe his behavior. If he continues to respect the boundaries, you can begin trusting him to be on his own in the yard.

Garbage Can Raiding

A dog will decide the garbage can is not his fast food take-out restaurant if there is a consequence than outweighs the reward. An unexpected occurrence is always a worthy consequence for a dog. You can use a mousetrap for this purpose. Instead of baiting the trap, place a set trap near the top of an open garbage can. When the dog sniffs inside the can and springs the trap, he will not forget the experience. There is no need to worry about his nose being caught in the trap—dogs are much too quick for that. If this seems too risky, you can place a single sheet of newspaper over the trap to increase the noise level and reduce any chance of the trap striking the dog. You should repeat this exercise each day until you see him making a conscious effort to avoid the garbage. Until the habit is broken, the pup should not be given an opportunity to raid the garbage with impunity. We want him to think the garbage can is always booby-trapped. If he decides this is not the case, he will use his cunning to decide when it's safe to dine out.

Sprinkling cayenne pepper on top of the garbage is also an effective means of repelling a dog.

There are commercial products that will train a dog to stay off the furniture. A "scat mat" works on the principle of giving an irritating buzzing sensation when a dog touches its surface.

Jumping (Riding up)

Dogs jump onto people for different reasons: to express dominance, to initiate an activity, and as part of a greeting ritual. When dogs are reunited with canine friends, whether they have been apart for minutes or days, they will want to lick one another on the face. This behavior is not indicative of a short memory—it is a greeting ritual we are witnessing. When we arrive home, our dogs want to greet us in the same manner. They jump onto us to get closer to our mouths.

Riding-up can communicate a different message at different times. When we arrive home, our dogs jump up to greet us. Later they jump onto us as a show of dominance or to initiate an activity, such as "feed me" or "play with me." When dogs jump onto small children, it is usually an expression of dominance.

If you know your dog's social status and temperament, you can usually determine what his behavior is saying at a particular time. If your dog is a stable pack member and not considered to be the testing type, his riding-up behavior is likely just an attempted wolf greeting. Even though the wolf greeting is not a testing behavior, you still have the right to correct the behavior. By offering a mild consequence when he jumps onto your legs, your pup will want to modify his greeting.

A quick knee in the dog's chest is preferable to pinching his toes or stepping on his feet or commanding him to sit when he jumps up. The effect of a knee in the chest will both be a physical consequence and a surprise. You can also include a verbal correction and a fixed stare for the dominant jumpers, but there is usually no need for stronger discipline—that is, if your knee correction was taken as a consequence. If your dog continues to jump onto you following a knee correction, the follow-up knee correction should be more forceful. If the second correction doesn't stop the behavior, or you are unable to execute the knee correction, a gripping or an alpha roll will be needed.

For habitual or chronic jumpers that like to get a running start before bouncing off your legs and chest, an even stronger consequence is required. When your dominant dog is running toward you, you may be able to ward off his assault by thrusting your knee up and down like a drum major in a marching band. If this doesn't discourage his behavior, you can drive your knee into his chest when he jumps onto you. His momentum, countered with your opposing knee, will propel him backwards and hopefully flat on his back. Following the knee correction, continue to posture your dominance while you observe the dog's response. If he displays active submission, you can respond with a compliment. If he continues to jump onto you, you should escalate the discipline with a gripping or alpha roll. Should he continue to jump onto you following the alpha roll, you can banish the pup for thirty minutes.

The key to giving effective knee corrections is timing and consequence. The knee correction is not meant to push the dog away, and it isn't intended to take his head off. However, if you can counter his momentum with the momentum of your knee, it will prove to be an effective consequence. If you are physically unable to give an adequate knee correction, there are other ways of producing a consequence for jumping. Squirting a dog in the face with water or using a sonic dog-repelling device should give you the needed leverage. Whatever you use, it will have to be considered a consequence by your dog to have the desired effect.

Cheyenne, my wolf dog, modified her greeting ritual when she reasoned that it was permissible to greet me, as long as she keeps her paws off me; consequently, she stands on her hind legs, pirouetting on point, as she gets her licks in.

If you cannot convince your guests to give a knee correction to your exuberant dog, you can take charge by having the dog on lead when friends enter your home. Should your dog jump onto them, you can correct the behavior by giving him a snap correction in a downward direction.

My approach to discipline is to produce a consistent consequence for bad behavior. When a dog associates a consequence with a particular behavior, he will do what it takes to avoid the unpleasant experience. Dogs are quite capable of making good decisions for themselves when it's in their best interest.

Separation Anxiety

Separation anxiety is a common problem behavior. As it sounds, dogs with this disorder will become extremely anxious or frantic when separated from their families. Their owners often return home to find the furniture chewed or their personal items and clothes strewn throughout the house. The front door and doorjamb will often bear the brunt of the damage. In each of these examples, the dog was grieving for its owners. Some dogs chew to relieve their anxiety; others try to reunite with their families by trying to escape their confinement; and they all use their owners' clothing for security blankets as they grieve for their families.

Because they were not taught to be self-reliant, dogs with separation anxiety are dependent on their owner's presence. Separation anxiety is preventable, but once a dog has this condition, you have entered the mental health ward for neurotic dogs—and help is hard to find. Many veterinarians prescribe tranquilizers for this emotional problem. Trainers offer behavior modification classes that are designed to increase a dog's confidence while reducing his anxiety, but progress is usually painstakingly slow.

It's the anxiety of being left alone that panics these dogs. They panic because they were not conditioned as young pups to feel secure by themselves. By studying wolf behavior, we can learn how to prevent separation anxiety from affecting our pups. Wolves will occasionally allow their young pups to explore on their own. Because this is done, the pups learn to be self-reliant when their parents are not nearby. Wolves will also take their pups for hikes so they will feel secure when they are away from their den site.

This is what you should do with your eight- to sixteen-week-old pup. In addition to giving him time to explore new territory, you should give him a little time each day to be alone in the home, in the back yard, in a spare room in the house with the door closed, in his crate, or at a friend's home. With eight-week-old pups, we can begin their self-reliance training by leaving them home alone for a brief period of time and repeating the exercise throughout the day. Teaching a pup to be independent is a progressive undertaking. You can begin by walking outside the home for one minute before returning inside. There should be no farewells or greetings at the front door—that is, if you don't want to condition your pup to become anxious and excited when you leave and arrive home each day. You should make your departures and arrivals uneventful life experiences. By slowing increasing the time your pup spends alone, he will become increasingly confident during his solitude. If we leave our pups alone for only a minute or two each day, they will be conditioned to expect us to arrive home in a couple of minutes. By slowly increasing a pup's time alone, you will soon be able to walk outside for five minutes, and soon thereafter ten minutes, without creating any anxiety for your pup. Using the same time schedule, a spare room can serve as a playroom for your pup and his toys. Feeding a pup outdoors will also be helpful in producing this sense of security.

You can evaluate your pup's progressing confidence by taking him for a ride to a convenience store. While inside the store, you can observe the pup's behavior in the car. If he is calm and attentive as he looks for you, you are well on your way to having a confident dog.

When your pup is comfortable being home alone for ten minutes, the next step is to leave him in the car while you go inside a grocery store for ten minutes. In time, you can increase his time alone to twenty minutes. Until you have confidence in your pup's stability, having someone observe the pup's behavior while you're inside the store is recommended. Evening grocery-store trips will be necessary in hot climates. With the exception of the hairless breeds, dogs do not have sweat glands.

They must therefore cool themselves by panting, so it takes only a few minutes in a closed car on a hot day to put a dog in dire straits.

Day-boarding your pup at a friend's home or a commercial kennel for a few hours are other means of teaching a pup that he can be safe by himself. Dog parks are also beneficial during a pup's development.

By following these guidelines, separation anxiety will likely never come into play with your pup. But if you already have an anxious pup, a confident companion may give him what he needs to feel secure. A companion doesn't necessarily need to be another pup. A puppy and a kitten can provide companionship for one another throughout their lives.

Leaving the stereo or TV on can be soothing to an anxious pup's nerves, and exercise will be a benefit as well. When an anxious pup is frequently exercised, he will be less likely to react to stress. Frequently offering new chew toys will also provide a positive outlet for his nervous energy when you are away from home. There are herbal supplements, such as Solid Gold's Pet Calmer, that can be used during a pup's self-reliance training. While these products may have a soothing effect on a dog's nervous system, they are not a cure for separation anxiety. Separation anxiety is easier to prevent than cure. There are no quick fixes, and drugs are only a temporary fix. Conditioning anxious pups to feel secure when they are alone is possible, but they all will be affected by the neglect to some degree.

An adult dog may also become anxious or fearful when he experiences a stimulus for the first time. The therapy for an anxious dog is to slowly build his confidence by exposing him to an irritating stimulus a little at a time. If high anxiety is triggered by loud noises, such as gunfire, semis, or motorcycles, you can expose your dog to the noise at a distance where he feels a little anxious. When he becomes composed at that distance, you can move a little closer to his fear factor. It may take weeks for him to feel safe around loud noises; but then again, it may take only a few experiences to make a real difference in how he reacts to noise. His body language will tell you when he is relaxed: His mouth will be open; his facial expression and tail position will be expressing a relaxed state of mind; and his attention will not be focused on the anxiety-producing sound.

The strategy is to give an anxious dog the opportunity to form a positive association with an aggravating stimulus (e.g., "loud noises can't hurt me"). You will be dulling his reaction to loud noises by conditioning the dog to form positive thoughts in association with these experiences.

While it's human nature to console loved ones when they are stressed or frightened, it will not help your dog if you try to calm him during a stressful episode. Consoling an anxious or frightened dog can be interpreted as praise for the fearful behavior. It would be better to ignore your dog's panicky behavior. The adrenalin rush of the fight-or-flight response will last for ten to fifteen minutes, so until the adrenalin rush is spent, you should be calm and composed for your dog. If your dog is severely stressed, you can move farther away from the stimulus.

Digging Holes

Most pups will be diggers during their development. Digging is natural behavior when a young pup hears crickets or other insects in the ground. When this is the case, you will find many small holes in the yard, just big enough for him to sniff underground. It's a natural instinct to hunt bugs when pups are starting out in life.

Dogs will also dig large holes to cool themselves on hot summer days. Others dig just because they can. If your dog is digging to cool himself on a hot day or to relieve the boredom of a long day, you might consider providing a wading pool or landscaping a den or playground with objects to climb and crawl through. If your dog likes to sleep on the porch or veranda, a fan can provide a cooling breeze. If we provide shade, water, and a cool breeze, our dogs can be comfortable even in a tropical climate.

You can usually break the digging habit by burying the pup's feces in his holes. Should he return to "the grime scene" and begins digging again, he will not like the end result when he steps in his own feces. Sprinkling cheap perfume or aftershave lotion in his holes may also produce a negative association with digging. Most young pups will find something else to do when they associate their digging with a consequence.

If you have bugs underground, you have the options of insecticides or just waiting it out. Pups are less likely to be diggers when they are mature and no longer interested in bugs. Two alternatives to pesticides are spraying your yard with the "gray water" from your washing machine and spreading Tide detergent on your lawn and turning on the sprinklers. Both are effective means of controlling the insect population in your lawn. A natural means of controlling insects is diatomaceous earth (Diatomite).

Off lead exercise will provide a positive outlet for a pup's nervous energy and produce a more relaxed pup at home. New bones and toys will also help keep a pup's mind on more positive activities.

Chronic Barking

With the exception of the yodeling African basenji, barking is a natural means of communication for dogs. However, it is considered abnormal behavior when a dog barks incessantly. Chronic barking is one of the most difficult habits to break. Because we are not always home to correct the behavior, dogs will learn when it is safe to bark and when it's not. If they're bull-headed, and decide to sound off, they won't care whether we are home or not.

Because of their consistency, bark-control collars are helpful in solving this problem. Most bark-control collars will shock a barking dog, but I prefer the citronella collars that spray a perfumed mist in a dog's face when he barks. Dogs hate sweet odors. Perhaps this is why dogs try to roll off the residual perfume of their shampoo following their baths. When a chronic barker associates his barking with a disgusting odor, he will usually take the easy way out by remaining quiet.

It is also possible to modify a dog's chronic barking behavior without using a bark-control collar. You can teach your dog to sound the alarm when someone enters your yard, and to stop barking after the announcement. The training includes praising the dog (whenever possible) following the initial set of barks; but following the alarm, you should correct all subsequent barking by calling out, "No...that's enough!" Then, following a short pause, you should tell him to be quiet, and if he remains quiet, praise him, "Good quiet!" Should he ignore the Quiet command, you need to go to him and give a gripping correction. Following the gripping, you can command him again, "Quiet," and praise him should he comply. But should he ignore your command, you can escalate the discipline to an alpha roll or banishment. Until a good habit is established, this procedure will have to be done each time he begins to bark.

It will take considerable time to modify the behavior of a chronic barker. Your management skills and the stubbornness of your dog will determine your level of success. By offering a significant and consistent consequence, we can usually modify a dog's chronic barking behavior, no matter how long he has had the habit. The objective for any behavior modification is to have dogs make the right decision concerning their behavior. When your dog knows there will be a consequence each time he chronically barks, he will decide that silence is golden, but if he learns that he can bark with impunity when you are away, he will likely wait until you leave home to exercise his vocal cords.

There aren't many dumb dogs, but many dogs have trained their owners to believe in their stupidity, and others will use their cunning to "beat the system." If your dog knows he can bark with impunity when you are away from home, he needs to learn why this is not his reality. After recruiting a neighbor's assistance, you can spy on your dog from his yard while the neighbor walks past your house. Should your dog begin barking incessantly, he will experience the consequence of surprise when you come storming back into your yard. After disciplining the dog, you should banish him for thirty minutes in his crate or a spare room. Do this a few times and your dog will likely expect a correction for his barking whether he thinks you are home or not.

Destructive Chewing

Pups chew for a variety of reasons: to relieve teething pain, to relieve boredom and anxiety, and just because its fun. Pups have occasional teething pain until they reach maturity. Some pups chew to relieve their nervous energy, and others like to run off their pent-up energy. Taking these pups for long runs on a regular basis will help satisfy their needs. By offering new cow hooves, knuckle bones, and other natural chews each month, pups will be more likely to look for them when they get the urge to chew. To hold a pup's interest in his toys, you can alternate different sets of toys each month. You can create more interest in his toys by occasionally tossing a treat into his toy box for him to discover. Most pups enjoy their toys, and sometimes a pup's favorite toy is a plastic soda bottle. As long as you discard them before they become shredded, plastic bottles are safe toys for pups.

But if you have tried all this, and your pup still looks for a chair leg to gnaw, you can repel him from chewing the furniture, carpet corners, and woodwork by spraying the furnishings with something that tastes bad. You can purchase such products at pet stores or make your own by mixing 16 oz of isopropyl (rubbing) alcohol with 1 tsp of hot cayenne pepper—the hotter, the better. Pups will often chew where they like to rest. Doorjambs, baseboard corners, and furniture legs are really tempting to young pups, so you will need to spray the repelling mixture on a problem spot and observe the pup's reaction to the taste. I've seen pups lap up Bitter Apple and Tabasco with relish. When you find a suitable repellent, you should spray or apply the foul-tasting mixture daily on the spots where the pup has chewed or may want to chew.

If his chewing habit is well established, you will need to temporarily supervise your pup in the home. When you are away from home, crating an unsupervised pup will be advisable until the pup can be trusted on its own, especially if he's destructive in the yard as well as the house.

I have had mixed results using cheap perfume and aftershave lotion as a repellent for furniture legs. Lavender oil and citronella oil have also been effective repellents for some pups. When you find a substance that tastes or smells bad to your pup, apply the solution each day to the surfaces until you are sure the habit is broken.

Catch-Me-if-You-Can

Pups play catch-me-if-you-can by ignoring their owners' call and taking evasive action when they approach. Most pups have tested their owners' authority with this instinctive game. Each time your pup wins the game, he will gain a little more of your authority for himself.

When you call your pup, and he ignores you by walking away, you should warn him to stop by calling out, "No!" As you posture with your dominant body language, you will be projecting with your voice that you are unhappy with his behavior. Your body will be leaning toward the pup as you give him your out-and-out attention. If he decides to submit to your authority, he will submissively approach you while protruding his tongue and wagging his tail. You should praise his good decision.

But should he ignore the warning by walking farther away, you should escalate the discipline by giving another verbal correction and going after him. Do not call the pup following the second verbal correction, and each time he bolts away from you, you should repeat the verbal correction and continue your pursuit. It may take four or five verbal corrections for the cumulative effect to manifest, but when it does, the pup's attitude will instantly change. Instead of playing catch-me-if-you-can, he will become passive and submissive as he lowers himself to the ground or rolls onto his back. His behavioral attitude will change from "catch me if you can" to "please forgive me and I'll never do it again." This will not be a fearful response but an attempt to avoid your discipline.

Your attitude and response should be showing him that this risky behavior always results in a gripping correction. As you express your disfavor, you should give him a quick shake as you stare into his eyes. Following the gripping correction, you can determine if the correction was adequate by taking a few steps away, kneeling down, and calling him in a friendly manner. If the correction was effective, your pup will eagerly and submissively come when you call.

If you have an extremely stubborn pup that persists in this activity, you can improve your chances of catching the runaway by attaching a twenty-foot lead to his collar before giving him an opportunity to test you in this manner. Should he decide to play the game, you can walk toward the end of the leash without causing the pup to bolt. Then, by stepping on the leash, you can take control of the situation.

The purpose of discipline is to elicit a submissive response. Your pup's response to a correction will confirm its effectiveness. Does he appear apologetic, "freaked-out," or indignant? Indignation or defiance following a correction is saying just what it appears to be saying: "Is that all you got?" or "How dare you do that to me!" A pup that becomes terrified following a correction is being handled too forcefully. Should he express active submission, the correction was just right. If the pup yelps during the gripping, he is not expressing pain, but submission. So don't be fooled!

Stealing

No known cure, but consider it a compliment when your dog steals your personal property. Wolves steal from those they love or as an invitation to play. Some nineteenth-century Native American tribes also played the game of thievery. American Plains Indians loved to steal horses from neighboring tribes. They didn't steal for profit—they did it as a practical joke. If the thieves were caught in the act, the joke would be on them.

A client had tethered her Siberian husky in the front yard while she was cleaning the house. When she heard steps coming up the stairs, she turned to see the neighbor's Doberman entering her home through the open sliding-glass door and sneaking across her living room. Then she watched as the pup picked up one of her pup's toys and trotted back home with her ill-gotten gain. The Doberman pup had never gotten to socialize with her pup, but she apparently had amorous feelings for the husky. Dogs also steal from those they love.

Eating Feces

When I encounter a feces-eating pup, the first thing I check is the pup's diet. If the pup is eating a corn and by-product diet, my advice is to change his diet. In most name-brand dog foods, the main ingredients are corn and by-products. According to the FDA, corn cannot be fully digested by dogs. Therefore, the undigested corn is eliminated. Forty percent of whole corn cannot be digested, so a pup can smell the undigested corn in his feces. If the pup stops eating his feces when his diet is changed from corn and by-products to a chicken and rice or lamb and rice diet, you will have solved the problem. If this doesn't stop the habit, your vet can give you a product, such as Glutanic acid, that will help repel the pup from his wastes. Usually, if all else fails, the behavior will correct itself as the pup matures.

If your pup is eating a quality diet and still eats his feces, you can improve his digestion by adding enzymes to his food.

Submissive Urination

It is not uncommon or unnatural for a young pup to have occasional incontinence, especially in the presence of a dominant dog or human. Adult dogs that submissively urinate in your presence are either extremely submissive dogs or suffering from bladder problems. Correcting dogs for this behavior is not the answer because it is not a test of your authority. Discipline will only escalate the problem behavior. If it has been determined that the dog is healthy, we can approach the problem as we would for any timid behavior, with a lot of patience and understanding.

If submissive urination is a common occurrence for your dog when you greet him at the front door—then don't greet your dog at the front door! Instead, calmly speak to him as you enter the house and take him outside before greeting him formally. Then, if the pup decides to express passive submission by urinating, it will be outdoors.

As for all timid dogs, I recommend boosting his confidence in any way you can. Playtime with other submissive dogs and off lead runs will be therapeutic. With an extremely shy or timid dog, gentle roughhousing or games of tug-of-war will help boost his confidence. While these games can affect a dominant dog in a negative manner, they will not be problem-producing activities for a shy dog.

Begging for Food

Begging for food is a good example of canine memory. Dogs do not forget anything good or bad in their life experience, and when the experience involves food, a dog will assign special importance to the memory. "Dogs will always beg for food if you feed them from the dining room table" is an adage that correctly identifies this trait. For some dog owners, begging is not an undesirable behavior; for others, it is.

If you don't want your dog to beg for food, you should never feed him from the table. If your dog already has the begging habit, you can address the problem by disciplining the dog as you would for any problem behavior. "Go lie down" is a command that is understood by most dogs, so you can include it with your verbal correction. Should the dog ignore your command, "No…go lie down", you should enforce your rule by banishing the dog to the yard or his crate. If your dog knows the Down command, you can take the dog away from the table and have him Down and Stay while you finish your meal.

This young wolf pup (below) is expressing anxiety and submission. His right ear is expressing submission to his owner, while the left ear is monitoring the sounds behind him. The tail is being held close to his body—ready to tuck should the photographer approach any closer—and his body posture is lowered and drawing back.

Sandy was a six-month-old yellow Labrador retriever with a dominant-aggressive temperament when she enrolled in my obedience school. During her first alpha roll, she fought like a wildcat to free herself. In her graduation picture is the new and improved Sandy with her owners, Midge and Zeke Stevens.

Kodi, the German shepherd, is feeling the excitement.
Cheyenne is posturing her relaxed demeanor.

11

Reading a Dog

Determining the attitude and emotion being expressed by a particular behavior or facial expression is what is commonly known as "reading a dog." For example, a dog that snaps at someone's hand is either acting out in a disciplinary fashion or reacting to fear. Determining which emotion is being expressed depends on your ability to read a dog's body language. Does he look really teed off, or does he seem nervous or scared as he projects a defensive posture? Is his body language posturing dominance, or is he pulling back from the encounter? The motives of a fear-biter and a dominant-aggressive dog are distinctly different and easily read, but determining whether a dog's behavior is expressing obstinacy or confusion takes a little more consideration.

Your "reading skills" will be put to good use during your pup's obedience training. With an understanding of canine body language, you will know when your pup is expressing dominance or submission, stubbornness or eagerness, confidence or confusion, calmness or anxiety. However, there will be times when his body language will not clearly express his motive or attitude. For instance, if you think your pup is confused during obedience training, you can offer your assistance by placing him in the position you want and noting his response to your help. If he was only confused before you gave assistance, he will respond with a smile and a wagging tail. If you place him and he doesn't respond with an active-submissive response—deciding instead to look away from you—this is usually indicating testing behavior. In effect, he will be training you to place him when and where you want. Novice trainers often fall into this trap, because they think their pups do not understand a particular command. Instead of correcting their stubborn pups for not executing a command they have been teaching for many days, they will continue to place them in position.

With a basic understanding of pack animal behavior, you can make most of the judgment calls concerning your pup's behavior. Canine body language can be extremely subtle, but we can gain some understanding by learning how wolves and dogs communicate. In general, dominance and stubbornness are expressions of confidence and obstinacy; active submission is characteristic of a happy, congenial demeanor; and passive submission indicates a more fearful or stressful attitude.

Dominance is expressed by a dog's behavior and disposition. Dominant behavior includes rough play, competitiveness, and dominant body language. Aggressiveness and stubbornness are dominant dispositions. Aggression is expressed during play and confrontations with other animals and people. Stubbornness expresses itself as arrogance or a defiant attitude. An aroused, dominant dog will express himself by standing tall. His head and ears will be erect, and his mouth will be closed. The tail will be held high over the back, and it will wag excitedly in short strokes. Should his dominant expression not be met with appropriate submission, the expression may turn into a warning. The dog's body will then lean toward his adversary, and the hackles may also rise on the base of his neck, shoulders, and back.

In comparison, an active-submissive greeting will be more relaxed in appearance. The dog's body will be slightly lowered, as will its tail carriage. The tail will neither be tucked between the legs nor held at its highest position, and it will be wagging in slow, methodical wags. The head will also be slightly lowered much like a bow, and the ears will be pulled close to the head, flattened, or cupped to the side. A passive-submissive greeting will appear more fearful as the dog hunkers down with its tail tucked between the legs.

Dogs also use their facial expressions to express their emotions. An open mouth with a hanging tongue, combined with a wagging tail, is the classic smiling expression. Some smiling dogs will raise their upper lips, exposing their front teeth. A closed mouth may be an expression of dominance, submission, or contemplation, depending on the accompanying dominant, submissive, or relaxed body language.

When reading a dog, consider all the signals the dog is communicating:

If his body is standing tall, and his tail is held high and motionless over its back, he is expressing dominance or social confidence; if the tail begins to wag excitedly, increasing agitation or excitement is being expressed. When a dog stares at a rival and leans forward with his tail held over his back or horizontal to the ground, he is threatening to discipline; when a dog is expressing dominance by barking in an agitated manner, and his body posturing is drawing back and somewhat lowered, he is expressing fear-aggression. When his body and tail posture is slightly lowered, and the tail is wagging slowly, he is expressing active submission. An extremely low body posture with a tucked tail is expressing passive submission. When a dog is concentrating or contemplating something in the distance, his mouth will be closed, his ears and head will be held high, and his tail will hang motionless.

While dominant dogs will not necessarily be dog aggressive, they will likely defend their position in the pack order; and they will usually be the dominant player during activities with other dogs. If you own more than one dog, it is common for a dominant and submissive dog to take turns being the dominant dog during their play.

Tempers will occasionally flare when dominant dogs play together. This is normal behavior and should not necessarily be corrected. If a squabble erupts from dominant play, most dogs can resolve the conflict without any assistance. In fact, we should allow our dogs to settle these social-order disputes unless push comes to shove, or one dog is being harmed or traumatized. You should give them a minute or two to restore order; if you are nearby when tempers flare, walk away from the dispute as you express your disfavor, "Cut it out!" By walking away, you will usually defuse the confrontation before it escalates. Trying to intercede or mediate an altercation may trigger a dogfight.

Breaking up a dogfight can be a dangerous undertaking. During a fight, dogs will often bite anything that touches them; therefore, if you try to pull two dogs apart, they may respond to your touch as a threat. Spraying dogs with a water hose will usually stop most fights. If two people are present, they can safely pull the dogs apart by their hind legs. A sudden noise, such as the blast of an air horn at close range, can also be an effective means of breaking up a dogfight.

Knowing your dog's temperament will also pay off should you decide to add another dog to your family. If you know the temperament of your dog, you can determine which temperament would be compatible with him. If you own a dominant-aggressive dog, it would not be advisable to adopt another dominant dog. Neither would an omega dog be a good companion because of the inherent passiveness. A dominant-submissive dog would be more compatible with a dominant-aggressive dog. A dominant-submissive dog will submit readily to a dog with a higher social status, and he will also be confident enough to handle the attitude of a dominant dog. If you have a shy or timid dog, an omega pup would be the best match, as far as compatibility goes.

As a general rule, a male and female dog are more likely to coexist in harmony, but the temperaments and dispositions of the dogs are more relevant than their gender. Dogs of the same sex can live in peace, if their temperaments and dispositions are compatible. When you find a compatible dog, and it comes time for the two dogs to meet, you should allow them to meet on neutral territory. Allowing dogs to meet away from home makes it easier for them to accept one another. When you introduce dogs at your home, the territorial issue may come into play. Taking them for a run off lead would be a preferred means of introducing dogs.

Another aspect of reading a dog is recognizing when a dog is in the decision-making mode. You will usually witness this when you are teaching your pup his obedience commands. When a pup is considering his options, he will move his head from side to side. This usually occurs following a command or a correction. When you witness this behavior, you should be patient while your pup makes a decision. When he decides on a response and takes action, you can then appropriately counter his response with praise or discipline.

When a dog cocks his head to the side, he is likely trying to determine the significance or meaning of a stimulus, whether it's an unusual sound or a conversation with his owner.

Smile!

Dominant dogs are usually in character.

Lucky, the poodle, grins as Cheyenne decides to take a sniff.
Lucky and Cheyenne are both dominant-aggressive dogs.

Some dogs can't keep a straight face.

Cheyenne's state of alert is telling me she is considering chasing the heron up ahead.

12

Basic Obedience Training

We are what we repeatedly do. Excellence, then, is not an act, but a habit.

-Aristotle

Obedience training could be called advanced leadership training because this is the goal and purpose of the activity. Your role will be a teacher, teaching a student the meanings of certain commands and expecting an obedient response upon his comprehension. Being able to read your pup will serve you well, because you will need to determine when he understands and when he doesn't. Small breeds can begin their obedience training when they are five to six months old; large and giant breeds can begin their training when they are four to five months old. Large breeds usually mature faster than small breeds.

Because of his socialization and pack training, your pup will already be a stable pack member. Without fear or attitude, he will be disciplined and submissive to your authority. He will be walking mannerly on lead, ranging close off lead, and anxiously coming when you call. All in all, he will be a pup that is confident, happy, and eager to follow your lead. Because of your leadership, he will be anxious to learn whatever you want to teach.

I do not recommend beginning a pup's obedience training in a group class. It is better to begin your pup's obedience training in familiar territory with few distractions. In a week or two, when he has learned the meanings of Heel, Sit, and Stay, you can move your training class to a new location, such as a park or a different neighborhood. Once the pup is working confidently in public, a group training class will be beneficial advanced training.

Most group classes are composed of pups that have had little or no training and socialization. This is where most people go wrong. They take unruly pups to a group class, and their pups are more interested in the other pups than they are their lessons. Some will be barking, others will be pulling on their leashes, and the rest will be unsettled by all the commotion. As a result, the owners often become frustrated when they cannot hold their pups' attention. When their pups don't seem to learn much, the owners will either drop out of class or settle for something less than a well-trained dog. Taking an unruly pup to a group training class is like taking a first grader to school at an amusement park. The child wouldn't learn much, and his parents would likely consider pulling him out of school.

Prospective clients often tell me they are looking for a group training class so their pups can be socialized to other dogs. Participating in a group training class is not the best way to socialize pups to other dogs. Socialization should be given long before you begin a pup's obedience training.

The greatest benefit of a group training class is proofing a trained pup under extreme conditions. However, a group class can be a frustrating experience if you haven't already established social order with your pup. Under the extreme conditions of a group class, your pup's self-discipline will be exercised and strengthened each time he makes the decision to follow your lead. The more your pup makes these decisions to obey in stressful situations, the better his and your life will be together. While all pups test their owners, their instinct is to follow their leader when they are experiencing something new and stressful. In effect, a pack-trained pup will defer to his owner's authority when participating in a group training class.

The progressive steps of pack training—bonding and establishing social order, socialization, basic obedience training in private, basic obedience training in public, and advanced training in a group class—will produce a confident and obedient pack member.

Let's Work

You have already taught your pup many words and commands. He knows that the Let's -go command means his pack leader is heading down the trail. He is free to have fun as long as he pays attention and doesn't pull on the leash. Now you can teach him when it's time to go to work. Following a fifteen to twenty minute walk on lead, you can call out in an excited tone, "Let's work!" As you give the command, you should turn away from the pup so he has to return to you on your left side. You may have to guide him there. You should praise the pup when he comes alongside, while steadying him with you left hand. In a few days your pup will be returning to your left side without any assistance.

For obedience training, a six-foot nylon leash is recommended. Metal training collars with small links (choke collars) are preferable to buckled collars, harnesses, or heavy choke collars. Because of their lesser weight, nylon choke collars are recommended for toy breeds and extremely shy pups.

You can make a training collar out of a choke chain by threading the chain through one of the rings and pulling it through. Then you can hold the collar with both hands, in such a way to form the letter "P", before placing the collar over the pup's head. When used properly, a choke collar will quickly release the pressure on the pup's neck following a correction. When the collar is placed on the pup backwards, the collar may keep pressure on the pup's neck following a correction.

A choke collar's function is to discipline a dog, not to choke him. Lightweight choke collars are preferable to heavy choke collars. The chain of a heavyweight choke collar does not slide through the ring as efficiently as the lightweight collars with small links. You can determine the size of your pup's collar by measuring the pup's neck and adding two inches to the measurement for a small pup and four inches for a large pup. If your pup's neck measurement is twelve inches, buy a fourteen-inch collar; if his neck measures twenty inches, he needs a twenty-four-inch choke collar. It is advisable to remove the choke collar following each training class, because a pup may get the chain caught in his mouth.

Sit

You can begin your pup's obedience training by teaching him to sit on command. With your pup standing by your left side, you can give the Sit command in a normal, confident tone. You are his leader, not his dictator, so there is no need to bark your commands. After you ask him to sit, you should pause for two seconds before placing him in the Sit position. Once placed in the sitting position, you can steady him with your hands while you repetitively praise him, "Good sit!" Pups can read our emotions, so your praise should be sincere and heartfelt but not necessarily inciting. By combining the praise (Good) with the command (Sit), you will produce a positive association with the obedience commands.

You will use the same sequence for each of the obedience commands: give the command, pause for two seconds, and then place him in position. A small pup can be placed in the sitting position by pushing down on its rear end. A large pup can be placed by pushing against the back of the pup's hind legs at the knee (stifle) joints. It may also help to push against the pup's chest while you buckle his knees with your other arm.

Your pup's body language will be telling you how he is receiving his instruction. A smiling face is expressing confidence and enjoyment, but a closed mouth and a lowered body posture are communicating some anxiety. More encouragement and praise is needed for anxious and confused pups.

There is a reason why I pause following my commands. Dogs are intelligent animals, but they process information slowly. For this reason you should pause following each command. You want your pup to make good decisions, so you should give him the time he needs when he is learning something new.

Does a slow-processing brain make a dog mentally subnormal? At the age of twenty, I was camping on the Hoopa River in Willow Creek, California with a friend from the Yurok tribe. One day I asked him about his tribe's opinion of the white race. Jim paused before answering, "Our tribal leaders believe the White Man think very fast but make many mistakes. Indians think slow but make fewer mistakes." Ditto for dogs!

By the fifth day of training, most pups will have sat on command without any assistance. Whether it's a pup's fifth day of training or he has previously sat on command, you should stop placing him in position and begin correcting his stubbornness. Dogs are not forgetful. If your pup sat on command yesterday, he will not have forgotten what "sit" means today. He will, however, be testing your authority each time he disobeys a command he understands. Instead of giving in and placing him in position, you should discipline the testing behavior.

I've yet to meet a pup that couldn't learn to sit within four days, so don't mistake your pup's inaction for confusion. His attitude will be expressing his stubborn disposition. Your response should be firm and consistent each time you are tested: with authority, tell him, "No!" and give him a snap correction in an upward direction with the leash.

A snap correction is not a chokehold, and it is not meant to nudge a dog into a sitting position. And it should only be hard enough to produce a positive response. In order to execute a snap correction, there must be a little slack in the leash prior to the correction. If a dog is corrected with a tight leash, the collar will only be increasingly tightened around the dog's neck. A correction made with a tight leash will not correct a pup; it will only choke him or lift him from the ground.

When you properly execute a snap correction, the choke collar will quickly tighten around the dog's neck, and once it tightens, it will quickly loosen again. You can get the feel of a snap correction by placing a choke collar on your arm and giving yourself a few corrections. There should be a little slack in the collar prior to the correction. By holding the collar by the free ring, you can snap your hand up, causing the collar to quickly tighten around your arm. As soon as the collar tightens, your hand should move down to its original position.

Some dogs need firmer snap corrections than others. It's not the size of the dog but his temperament and disposition that determines how strong a correction is needed. A snap correction is neither a pull nor a snatch, but a quick snapping action with your arm moving up and down like a piston in an engine. When you execute a snap correction with a metal choke collar, you'll be able to hear the correction. The chain will make a distinctive "zipping" sound when it is quickly pulled through one of the rings.

You can judge by your pup's reaction whether or not a snap correction was effective. An effective correction will be countered with an active-submissive response, but an ineffective correction will be ignored. By combining a snap correction with a verbal correction, a pup will also learn to associate your verbal correction with the gripping correction of the choke collar. When this association is made, you will see a dramatic change in how your pup responds to verbal corrections.

How do you handle a stubborn, testing pup that refuses to sit on command? You know he understands what to do because he has previously sat on command. You should ask him to sit and pause for two seconds following the command. If he refuses to sit, you should correct him. Now you will pause for two seconds while noting his reaction to the correction. If the pup expresses active submission by looking at you and wagging his tail, or if he corrects his mistake by sitting, the correction was effective. If the pup ignores you by looking away following a correction, the correction wasn't considered to be consequential; therefore, initial corrections will need to be more forceful in the future.

Following the initial correction and pause, you can repeat the Sit command. If he is still standing following the second command and short pause, you should give a firmer correction to the pup. In a few days you will know how forceful a correction is needed to produce the desired effect. On the other hand, if a pup reacts with alarm or fear, the correction was too harsh.

When you discipline a pup for testing your authority during obedience training, he will usually execute the command during the two-second pause. This suggests that the pup was ignoring a command that he heard and understood. When the pup sits on command or following the correction, your praise is warranted. If he is still standing following two commands and two corrections, you can ask him to sit for the third time. Then, following a short pause, you can gently push at the base of his tail as you coax him to sit. If he refuses to sit, you should place him in the Sit position. The pup's response to your assistance will communicate his motive for not sitting on command. If the pup had been demonstrating his stubbornness following the third command, he would have resisted the gentle push on his back end. However, if the pup had only been nervous or confused, he would have readily responded to the push. A stubborn pup will need more forceful corrections in the future. Once you determine the level of discipline needed for him to consider a consequence, you should give all initial corrections with equal force.

The universal key to learning is consistent and repetitive experience. Not only will dogs learn faster when they experience consistent handling, they will learn with confidence when they know what to expect. Dogs love knowing when it's time to go for a walk or eat a meal, and they will take the necessary steps to encourage these activities at the appropriate times. If there is something they would rather avoid, they will take the necessary steps to achieve that as well. When a consequence consistently follows a particular behavior, a dog will change his attitude and behavior. Therefore, if a dog knows that a significant snap correction follows his noncompliance, he will want to obey your commands. Because he can depend on you to praise and correct him appropriately, he will gain more respect for you.

Practice the Sit command three or four times during each training class. While many herding and sporting breeds enjoy repetitive activities, for the average pup, extending a lesson by practicing a particular command over and over will only produce boredom. Praise and discipline should be timely, heartfelt, and consistent. And both should only be strong enough to produce a positive response. While excessive praise can be inciting and disruptive, excessively forceful corrections will only frustrate a pup that is having trouble learning. As a rule, I will give a pup two chances to obey a command he understands, and the second correction will be stronger than the first. If the second correction doesn't produce an active-submissive response, I will make initial and follow-up corrections more forceful in the future. Following the third command, however, I will give the pup some assistance by pushing down on his rear end.

Stay

You can teach the Stay command when your pup is sitting on command. With your pup sitting by your left side, you can tell him to "Stay," as you sweep your left hand in front of the pup's face. Then you can take one step away and face the pup for ten seconds. Following the ten-second Sit-Stay, you can return to your pup and praise him for a job well done. When you step away from the pup, you should take the step with your right leg moving first.

When you train a pup, your attitude and body language should be confident and relaxed. You should not repeat the Stay command over and over or move in a tentative manner, as though you might cause the pup to move from his spot. Your objective is to correct mistakes, not prevent them. So when he stands up, you should respond with a verbal correction and a light snap correction in an upward direction. Following the correction you should pause for two seconds while the pup considers his options. If he sits, you should offer a compliment and remind him to stay; if he expresses active submission but remains standing, you should return to him and ask him to sit and stay; if he approaches you, take him back to the original spot, have him sit, and repeat the exercise.

When you begin teaching the Stay command, your pup will make some mistakes. Mistakes should be corrected in a timely manner, not three seconds later. Therefore, you will need to manage the leash so you can correct him the moment he stands. By extending your right arm in front of you and maintaining a little slack in the lead, you will be able to correct the pup in a timely manner when he stands up.

During obedience training, confusion and anxiety should be avoided at all costs. For this reason, you should take only one step away when he is learning the Stay command. If you walked six feet away during a pup's first Stay, he will likely feel the need to go with you. Up until now his reality has been to follow you; so when your pup sees you walking away during his first Sit-Stay, he will think you want him to follow your lead. This thought will cause him to make one mistake after another, and multiple corrections for submissive behavior would be counter-productive. By staying close to your pup for a few days, until he grows both in understanding and confidence, you can then gradually increase the distance you move away.

By adding five to ten seconds each day to the time of his Stays, you will expand his comfort range in an orderly manner. When the pup is staying for thirty seconds at close range, you can move six feet away during the exercise. When the pup is confidently staying at that distance for thirty seconds, you can begin moving from side to side in front of the pup. In a few days, you will be able to walk around the pup during a Sit-stay. In a week or two, you will be able to drop the leash and work the pup from ten feet away. As the pup's confidence increases, you can gradually increase the distance to fifty feet. When your pup moves from his spot, when the leash is not in your hand, you must verbally correct him before returning and repeating the exercise.

Heel

Heeling is the most difficult exercise to perfect for both you and your pup. This is because the pup will have to be diligent to remain in the heeling position, with his neck aligned with your left hip, and you will have to be nimble on your feet. Dogs that heel with precision love to work for their owners, so we should make our pups' heeling exercise as much fun as it is challenging.

Each obedience-training class should begin with a brisk walk on lead or a short run off lead. Pups experience a ten to fifteen minute adrenalin rush at the beginning of each training class. For this reason, we should give them some time for their excitement to wane. When you are both ready to go to work, you can give the Let's-work command and bring the pup to a sitting position by your left leg. Now you can prepare to heel your pup: coil the leash in your right hand, hold your right arm about waist high and horizontal to the ground, and adjust the amount of slack you're holding so the leash drapes across your left upper leg.

When you heel your pup, instead of holding him by your side on a tight lead, you should maintain a little slack in the leash. Dogs that are held in position by their owners' side do not have to pay attention. When their owners change direction, they can feel the pull of the leash. When pups are heeled on a slack lead, they will learn to pay attention in order to see us changing direction.

You can begin the heeling exercise by calling out, "Heel," and taking the first step with your left leg. Instead of plodding along, it's best to walk at a normal pace. Instead of walking in a straight line, you want to give your pup a reason to watch you. You can begin this process of gaining your pup's close attention by making frequent ninety-degree turns to the left. By making sharp left turns you will bump the pup's head, either with your right leg or knee, when he is in the way of your turn. As a result of the consequence, your pup will soon decide to heel by your side in order to avoid your crossing leg.

This sharp left turn is a little tricky to execute. You will find it helpful to practice this turn without your pup, until you master the mechanics of squaring your corner. To make a ninety-degree left turn, you must turn your upper body to the left before you actually make the turn. This is possible when you plant your left foot pointing to the left (toward the pup at a forty-five-degree angle). By standing on the ball of your left foot, you can pivot the foot to a right angle, making it possible to swing your right leg, as a pendulum, across the path of the pup. When you make a left turn, instead of stepping in front of the pup, plant your foot where it would have normally stepped—only point it to the left.

The key to making a left turn is timing. If the pup has forged ahead of you, you can't make a ninety-degree turn without falling over him. Therefore, you should make your left turns before he walks in front of you. If he forges ahead before you can make the turn, you can pull back on the leash with your left hand. This will enable you to move up to a position where you can make a left turn. If your pup gets a full body length ahead, you can drop the slack leash and give him a snap correction as you walk away in the opposite direction.

By heeling your pup in a counterclockwise square, making left turns every four or five steps, he will soon be watching for the crossing leg and turning on cue. In his mind, he'll be thinking, "My leader can't make up his mind where he wants to go, so I need to keep an eye on him." Once the pup is turning on cue, you can teach him to make a right turn.

The right turn is easier for us but harder for our pups to execute. Because you will be turning away from him, he'll need to increase his pace to avoid the consequence of falling behind. When you make a ninety-degree turn to the right, move your right arm toward the pup and release the slack leash. As you walk slowly to the right, you should observe your pup's response. Is he coming with you, even though he is a step or two behind, or is he looking away and not following your lead? The former response should be met with praise and encouragement. The latter response is a mistake that needs to be corrected with a snap correction. The snap correction must be made when there is a little slack in the leash. This is why you must be looking back at your pup when you walk away—you must be able to time the snap correction. If there is too much slack in the lead, you will not be able to snap the collar tight. If there is no slack in the lead, you will only be pulling or dragging the pup where you want him to go.

Your pup will also try to cross behind you to the right side when he is learning to heel. You can correct this mistake by lifting your left knee when he begins to walk behind you. Leash management will be needed to execute this correction, for the leash must be crossing your left upper leg when you lift your knee. In order to produce the needed leverage, your right hand must also be positioned on your right hip when you lift your left knee. Not only will a pup receive a snap correction, he will also be brought back alongside your left leg following a knee-lift correction. The same knee correction can be used for pups that lag behind when they are heeling. Pups that lag behind are usually shy and submissive pups, so you should encourage your lagging pup to heel by patting your leg and coaxing him. If your persuasion doesn't get results in a few seconds, a light knee correction will be needed. Stubborn pups will need firmer knee-lift corrections than shy pups.

Teaching your pup to heel will condition him to pay closer attention to you. When he is being attentive, he can see you changing direction and avoid the resulting consequence. For this reason, it is important to enthusiastically praise a pup that is making an effort to follow your lead. Even though he is a step or two behind when you make a right turn, you should enthusiastically praise the pup when he turns to go with you. It would be counterproductive to ignore or correct him when he is trying to learn a new task and making good decisions. No verbal reprimand is needed when you correct a pup for not following your lead; you are simply producing a consequence that will encourage him to pay closer attention.

These are the two basic turns. As the pup progresses in understanding and confidence, you can keep his lessons fresh and challenging by heeling in intricate patterns and at different speeds. For your pup's training to be considered a fun activity, your attitude should be enthusiastic and lighthearted. You should be complimenting him whenever he is heeling by your side and following your lead during a sudden turn. Praising obedient and attentive behavior is the mark of strong leadership.

Praise and discipline are equally important. As with discipline, the same rule applies for giving praise: Just enough to produce a positive response. Whereas excessive praise can cause a pup to become overly excited, weak praise will not motivate a pup to work hard. When your pup receives ample praise, he will gain confidence in himself and your leadership. You will know when he's truly complimented, for he will be responding with a smiling face and a wagging tail.

After a week of daily lessons, your pup will be making good progress with his heeling exercise. During a fifteen-minute lesson, practice three or four Sit-stays in addition to his heeling exercise. Ending each lesson with an enjoyable activity is also recommended.

Consistent handling is a key component of dog training. We know that dogs are constantly processing information from their life experience, and that includes us.

As a pack trainer, you have been expressing your leadership. You will also be projecting strong leadership when you train your pup in a consistent manner. Consistent handling also produces a confident attitude in pups. When your pup knows what to expect from you, he will respect your alpha position and desire your good favor. This is why consistent handling is so important—it promotes your leadership.

When you're teaching a pup to heel, you must eventually come to a stop. If you stop by planting your right foot and bringing the left foot alongside, your pup will likely wind up a step or two ahead of you. However, if you stop by first planting your left foot and bringing the right foot alongside, the pup will be more likely to stop on cue. By this time in his obedience training, your pup has learned that you want him to stay when he sees your right leg move first; and he is now learning that you want him to heel when your left leg moves first. Therefore, if you stop on the right foot, and bring the left leg alongside to complete a stop, he will see the left leg movement as his cue to continue heeling. This thought will cause him to walk ahead of you.

You can also help a pup learn to stop on cue by pulling back on the leash with your left hand when you come to a stop. In a few days, you can correct him when he understands that he is supposed to stop on cue and fails to do so. Until then, you can rein him back with the leash when you heel to a stop.

Pups test their boundaries. We see this commonly during leash training and obedience training. Most pups will initially pull against the leash during leash training and forge ahead when they are learning to heel. Others will refuse to walk, and some will bite and tug on the leash. When a dominant pup bites the leash or plays tug-of-war, he is trying to escape the control of his owner. He knows that the leash gives his owner control over his behavior, so he is trying to bite or pull his way free of that control. Because these tactics are tests, there should be a consequence for both behaviors. If your pup refuses to walk with you, you should continue to walk as you coax him to come along. You won't drag him far before he decides to walk with you. If your pup plays tug-of-war or bites the lead, you should follow the four sequential steps of discipline: first offense—verbal correction and fixed stare, second offense—gripping, third offense—alpha roll, fourth offense—banishment.

Down

You can teach the Down command using the same training sequence: show him for a few days what you want him to do, and then correct him when he tests your authority with disobedience. You can teach the Down command after he has learned the Sit and Stay commands: with the pup sitting by your left side, give the Down command as you move your left hand—palm down—past the pup's head and toward the ground. You can encourage him to lie down by tapping the ground or pushing gently on the leash with your left hand or doing both at the same time. Instead of pulling the pup to the ground, your demeanor should be coaxing him to lie down by repeating the command and keeping some pressure on the leash. If you cannot coax him to lie down within ten seconds, you should place him in the Down position. With your left hand on the pup's shoulders (to steady him), you can pull the pup's right front leg forward and toward you with your right hand. This will cause a large pup to lie down. A small pup's legs can be lifted together when you place him down. Once placed in the Down position, you should hold him gently in position while you repeat the praise, "Good down." Once he is steady in the Down position, you can continue to praise him and show your affection for a minute or two; but if your pup stands up, you should correct him, pause for two seconds, and, if needed, repeat the Sit and Down commands.

Your pup may roll onto his side or even go belly-up when he is learning to lie down on command. Some people think pups are testing them when they roll onto their sides during the Down exercise. The reason a pup rolls onto his side, when placed in the Down position, is to express additional submission. After all, we are dominantly positioned over the pup and have placed him in a submissive position, so it would be natural for a submissive pup to roll over and demonstrate more submission to its leader. There is no reason to correct a pup when he rolls over because this is not testing behavior; it's an expression of submission.

By the fifth day of teaching the Down command, many pups will have lain down with a little coaxing; the rest will be expressing their stubbornness. Following four lessons, you should stop coaxing your pup to lie down. Instead of enabling his stubbornness, you should follow the same training sequence of one voice and hand signal, a two-second pause, and a correction when he refuses to obey. If you continue to coax or place the pup in position, he will be training you to place him down.

The correction for not downing on command is a downward snap correction and a simultaneous verbal correction. In order to snap the lead downward, you will need to grip the leash a few inches from his collar and create a little slack by moving your hand toward the pup's neck. Then you can snap the leash downward as you verbally correct the pup. As you did when you taught him to sit, you should follow the same regimen of two commands and two corrections before giving any assistance. When your pup is relaxed in the Down position, you can add the Stay command to the exercise. With a shy or anxious pup, you may need to stay close to him until his confidence grows. In a day or two, you'll be able to walk farther away without causing any anxiety. By following the same schedule as the Stay command, your pup will soon be staying for three minutes at a distance of fifty feet. Your pup's body language and behavior will be communicating his emotional state and attitude. Anxious and stubborn pups will make more mistakes than stable and submissive pups. Anxious pups feel insecure when they are away from their owners, and stubborn pups want to test their owners' authority by standing up and walking away.

Recall and Finish

If you have pack trained your pup, he will already be coming when you call. Now you can refine the command so he comes to a sitting position in front of you, and then finishes the exercise by walking around you and returning to a sitting position at your left side.

The Recall and Finish exercise begins from the Sit-stay position: walk out to the end of the leash, wait a few seconds, and call your pup by name, "Max, Come," as you extend your left arm and sweep it back to your chest. Once he responds, you should back away as you praise him for coming on command. This backward movement will encourage him by making the exercise a game of follow-the-leader. As he comes to you, you can take up the slack leash, without pulling the pup. When the pup is close to you, you can grip the end of the leash with your left hand and come to a stop. You will now have the pup on a short lead directly in front of you. If there is slack in the leash when you stop, the pup may walk past you. Until he learns what you want him to do, you should have him on a short lead when you stop. You can now teach him to sit while he is standing in front of you.

You may be wondering why you need to teach your pup to sit when he is standing in front of you. When you began training your pup, you taught him to sit when he was standing by your left side. For many pups, this is what Sit literally means. When you ask one of these pups to sit when he is standing in front of you, he will not clearly understand the command. In effect, this will be a new command because something is different.

Pups often balk during this part of the Recall exercise. Because it is not a test, we should treat this as a new command: ask him to sit, pause for two seconds, and then place him by pushing down on his rear end. He'll understand your intent and will respond appropriately to the push. When he sits, you can praise him for coming and sitting in front of you. You should allow him a few days to learn this variation of the Sit command before offering a correction for not sitting.

Now you can finish the exercise by teaching him to walk around your right side and return to a sitting position by your left side. Although any word would suffice, as long as it conveys the same excitement, the Finish command is usually the word "heel." Because you are essentially asking your pup to return to the heeling position, I recommend that you use the Heel command when teaching the Finish exercise.

With your pup sitting in front and facing you, you can begin teaching the Finish command: with some slack hanging from the dog's collar, coil the leash in your right hand; give the Heel command; and swing your right arm backward as you take one step back with your right leg. The pup will likely respond to your leg cue or when he feels the gentle pull of the leash. If he doesn't respond, you should coax him while gently pulling him to a standing position. As soon as he stands and begins walking toward you, you can step forward with the right leg to a position ahead of your left leg. So it's one small backward step with the right leg, and as soon as the dog is up and moving, it's one giant step forward. As you step forward, you should pass the leash behind your back to your left hand. As you do this, you will be leading the pup around to your left side. With the leash now in your left hand, you can step forward with the left leg, bringing it alongside the forward right leg. As you steady the pup by your side, ask him to sit before praising his Finish. This three-step technique will be a continuous movement, once you and your pup get the timing down.

This exercise is more complicated than the other obedience commands, so be patient with your pup's progress. Following five to ten lessons of leading him around your backside, your pup will have an understanding of the exercise. If you continue to lead the pup around, he will never learn to do it without your assistance. Therefore, you should increase the amount of slack in the lead so you won't pull the pup when you step back and tell him to heel. You may need to coax him with your voice to get him started, but as soon as he is moving on his own volition, you can reduce the other signals you have been giving. Perhaps by the end of the second week, you will be able to give the Heel command with the right-hand and right-leg signals as before; but instead of stepping forward with the right leg to a position ahead of the left leg, you can step up to its original position by the left leg. By the end of the third week, you can stop giving the right-leg signal altogether. When a pup understands the Finish command, you can give the Heel command, with your right arm sweeping back, and expect him to walk around you on his own.

Lots of encouragement, such as patting your left leg as the pup walks around you, or using a treat to lead him around, will help him put it all together. Treats can be used sparingly once social order has been established.

Automatic Sit

The Automatic Sit teaches the pup to finish and sit as one exercise. When he is finishing on his own, you can stop giving the Sit command. Instead of asking him to sit when he finishes the Recall command, you should pause for two seconds and give him a correction if he hasn't sat by that time. If he doesn't sit during the next two-second pause, you can then ask him to sit. In a day or two, he will understand that you want him to sit without having to be asked.

The Automatic Sit can also be used when you heel to a stop. Instead of asking the pup to sit when you heel to a stop, you can pause for two seconds and correct him if he is still standing.

Stand For Examination

The Stand command is a useful exercise in obedience trials. In obedience trials, a dog is told to stand and stay as the handler moves away from his dog. A judge will then make physical contact by running his or her hand from the dog's head to its tail. The dog must remain in place and accept the touch of the stranger. This demonstrates that the dog has been properly socialized to strangers.

Your pup can learn to stand on command from the sitting position or while he is heeling. Confusion may come into play when a pup is learning to stand; therefore, it is not recommended to teach a pup to stand from the sitting position. After all, he will remember being corrected for standing up when he was learning to sit on command. For this reason, I recommend teaching the Stand while your pup is heeling by your side.

By this time in your pup's training, your pup knows that when you heel to a stop, you expect him to sit. Therefore, if you heel to a stop and ask the pup to stand, he will be a little confused. He will be thinking, "When we stop, I'm supposed to sit." He will know the command was different, but he will not understand what you want him to do. Consequently, your pup may decide to sit.

For the sake of their confidence, pups should not have to experience a lot of confusion during their training. Instead of heeling to a stop and asking your pup to stand, you should give the Stand command and hand signal while he is heeling by your side. Then you should step away and turn to face the pup. The hand signal is a forward sweeping motion with the left hand. Once you are facing the pup, you can give the Stay command and compliment him, "Good stand," if he remains standing. The Stay command should be given in combination with the hand signal, with your left hand directed at the pup like a traffic cop.

Should the pup try to sit, you can give a backward snap correction the moment he begins to sit. The snap correction will correct the pup and prevent him from sitting by snapping him forward a little. Should he sit without being corrected, you should give him a snap correction and a verbal correction. Following a short pause, you can repeat the Stand command and hand signal. Following another short pause, you should gently pull the dog to a standing position by applying increasing pressure with the leash. By steadily increasing the pressure on a pup's neck, he will take the path of least resistance. As soon as he stands, you should release the pressure on the leash and praise him, "Good stand," before repeating the Stay command.

If your pup walks toward you, you should express your disapproval with a verbal correction as you lift the leash with your left hand. This will restrict his ability to approach you. As you apply upward pressure with the leash and remind him to stay, you should maintain your three-foot distance from the pup. If you allow the pup to walk closer to you, he will likely want to sit.

If you are working with a shy pup, he may become anxious about the Stand command. This will cause the pup to repeatedly sit during this exercise. With an awareness of your pup's shy disposition, you will know it's not a testing attitude but his insecurity that is causing the problem. Instead of treating it as a test, you can give the Stand command, return to his side, and support him with your hand on his belly as you praise him. In a few days, he will no longer need your support.

Leave it

"Leave it" is a useful command to teach pups. Pups love to pick up garbage when they are walking on lead with their owners. You can teach your pup to bypass the garbage on the road when you call out "Leave it." You can teach this command by tossing a treat on the ground and leading the pup toward the treat. When you see his attention focusing on the bait, you should give the Leave-it command. If he tries to pick up the food, you can give him a snap correction and a verbal correction. If he doesn't take the bait, you should praise his decision. After a few repetitions, your pup will know the consequence for eating roadside garbage.

Variations of the Obedience Commands

After your pup has learned the basic commands, you can keep the workouts fresh and challenging by not following a set routine. Dogs learn by remembering the sequence of events in their life experience. As a result, they will often be anticipating our commands if we follow a set routine. For example, if you always practice the Down-stay following the Sit-stay, your pup may anticipate that the Down command follows the Sit command. As a result, the pup may lie down when you ask him to sit. In order to keep your pup on his toes, you should mix up the order of the obedience exercises.

Once he has learned the basic commands, you can teach your pup to lie down from the Stand position and to stand from the Down and Sit positions. When you teach your pup to stand from the Sit position, you can substitute the Stand command for the Heel command as you take one forward step with your left leg. In addition to giving the voice and left-hand signal to stand, the movement of your left leg will serve as a cue. If your pup doesn't stand, you can gently pull him to a standing position.

You can also teach your pup to sit and lie down when you are standing in front of him. Because you are changing the dynamics of these commands—you are now standing in front of the pup instead of by his side—many pups will perceive these to be new commands. Therefore, you will need to teach him the meaning of the Sit and Down commands when you are standing in front: move a step away and face the pup; and with your left arm raised over your head, give the Down command and bring your hand down onto the leash, gently pushing downward. By standing close to your pup, he will not feel the need to return to you before lying down. After praising him for lying down, you can teach him to sit from the Down position by giving the Sit command and lifting the leash with your left hand. As soon as he sits, you should release the pressure on the leash and praise him. In a few days your pup will be responding to the voice and hand signals without the physical cues. You can then begin increasing your distance from the pup when you give these commands. The hand signal for Sit is an underhanded, upward motion, and the opposite motion for the Down signal.

You began teaching the obedience commands by giving exaggerated hand signals. When your pup fully understands a particular command, you can begin shortening the hand signal. When you taught the Down command, you began with your hand held high above the dog's head and moving it all the way to the ground. Now, instead of moving your hand all the way to the ground, you can end the signal about waist high. In time you will be able to shorten the hand signal even more.

Up until now you have been using simultaneous voice and hand signals. Now you can use either the voice signal or the hand signal, instead of both at the same time. This will not confuse the pup because he will be associating both the voice signal and the hand signal with a particular command.

By this time your pup will have learned as much about your body language as he has your verbal language. Our dogs are extremely observant and cunning creatures, and the following exercise will prove my point:

From the Sit position, begin heeling your pup without saying a word—did he begin heeling when you stepped away with the left leg? From the Sit position, and without saying a word or giving the hand signal, walk away from your pup, taking the first step with your right leg—did he stay? Most pups, after a few weeks of training, will be reading your body language. They know that when you walk away with the right leg moving first, you want them to stay, and when you step away with the left leg, you want them to heel.

Let's work!

Begin heeling by giving the Heel command
and taking the first step with your left leg.

Lagging and Forging

Becky Taipalus executes the left turn with her year-old Rottweiler, Bruiser

Pack-trained dogs follow their leaders
because of their desire to please.

Heeling a dog on a slack lead produces attentive behavior.

Stay

Down from the side and Down from in front

The Recall

The Recall (part 2)

The Finish

The Finish (part 2)

Stand for Examination

When your dog believes you are the pack leader,
you won't need treats to hold his attention.

13

Voice Control

Where there is a belief in authority, there will be obedience.

Many dogs that are trained by conventional methods will obey their owners only when they are on lead or when treats are in the offing. And should there be any distractions nearby, treats will often have little effect in holding their attention. Off lead training for dogs that are trained with force or treats is usually difficult, because their owners have not established their leadership position. For a dog to have the incentive to work off lead, he must respect the authority of his handler.

Champion working dogs score high in competition because they intently watch their handlers. They don't focus because they are fearful or hungry—they are attentive because they want to please their leaders. Pack training produces this incentive and motivation in a dog. A dog's attitude and demeanor will be subservient when he respects his owner's authority. You earned his respect when you bonded with your pup and established social order.

By giving appropriate socialization, discipline, praise, and love, you have connected with your pup and produced a stable pack member. Whereas socialization and hiking runs on nature trails are enjoyable activities for pups, they are also learning experiences. Socialization not only teaches pups to trust their world but also to follow their owners' lead. Young pups are somewhat anxious when they are exploring new territory, and especially nervous when they discover something new. As a result, pups will depend on their owners for security and leadership when they explore new environments. Everyone has witnessed a pup discovering his first frog, turtle, or crab, as he cautiously approaches the alien creature. This is how a pup functions when he is exploring new territory: curious but cautious. By taking your pup for frequent hikes, you also taught him to range close and to come when you call. Pups will look for someone to follow when the need arises. Your job has been to produce the need.

Obedience training taught your pup to pay closer attention to you. You did this by producing consequences for his inattentiveness. Whereas the game of hide-and-seek taught your pup to occasionally look back to check on you, obedience training taught him to focus on you. Now you can utilize this trait to teach him to work off lead.

Off lead training is a natural transition for most pack-trained pups. However, if you haven't already established social order, you will not find your dog to be very attentive on lead, and especially inattentive when he is off lead. When a pup is learning to heel off lead, you can teach him to watch you like a hawk by producing a consequence for his inattentiveness, and you can encourage him to work hard by making a game out of the activity. This is why I recommend heeling dogs on a slack lead during their basic obedience training. By not being able to feel you change direction through the pull of the leash, your pup learned to pay attention in order to avoid the consequence. Praising pups when they turn on cue, and correcting them when they don't, stimulates them to focus on their trainers. Using the slack-lead technique during obedience training produces attentive behavior.

Pack training produces a pack-member mentality in pups. As pack members, pups will be responsive to leadership. This is commonly known as "voice control." Because of the positive effects of pack training, you will find your pup to be a receptive to the idea of working off lead. Not only is off lead training possible, it's a natural progression for pack members. In fact, off lead training will likely be easier than his basic training because of his desire to follow your lead.

The length of an off leash training class will depend on the work ethic of your pup. For most pups, fifteen- to thirty-minute lessons will suffice. At some point during each lesson, a pup's interest will peak and begin to wane, so it should be your goal to end each class on a high note. Your pup will let you know when he is losing interest in his lesson.

Teaching a pup to heel off lead is a two-step process. The first step is to allow your pup to drag the leash behind him when he's heeling. Allowing your pup to drag his leash will help him make the transition to working off lead. Unsnapping the lead right away may cause some confusion because of the radical change in the exercise, or the pup may think it's time to run free. However, if you drop the leash when he is heeling by your side, your pup will likely continue to heel by your side. It also works to your advantage when the leash is dragging behind your pup. Your pup knows the leash gives you control over his behavior, and when he decides to test the boundaries of off lead heeling, you will be able to correct him without having to pick up the leash.

When your pup begins to forge ahead, you can correct him by stepping on the leash as you continue walking. If you stop and pick up the leash, you will not be able to correct him at the time of the mistake. By continuing to walk after you step on the leash, your forging pup will receive a correction at the proper time, and following the correction he will be back alongside your left leg. After a few corrections, your pup will learn that the same rules apply for off lead heeling.

Your pup will also try to walk away from you. When this happens, you shouldn't walk toward him and step on the leash—that would be following his lead. Instead of going after him, you should stay on course as you posture your disapproval and verbally correct the pup. When you posture your disapproval, you will be glaring at the pup and leaning in his direction. Your pup should submissively return to you, but if he ignores you, you should call out, "Heel-up," as you clap your hands or slap your leg. You shouldn't stop and wait for your pup, but you should give him a chance to correct his mistake. If your pup does not correct himself by returning to your side, you should escalate the discipline by going to him and giving him a snap correction with the leash. Following the correction you should continue the pup's heeling exercise on lead before offering him another opportunity to drag the leash.

As a pack trainer, you have earned your pup's respect. During obedience training you conditioned your pup to associate your verbal corrections with his snap corrections. As a result, he will likely respond to your verbal corrections when you begin his off lead training. When he doesn't respond to your verbal correction and you consistently correct his testing behavior, he will soon make the transition to working off lead—and you will have voice control.

In addition to giving timely corrections, you should also be encouraging and enthusiastic when a pup initially goes off lead. Because you are changing the dynamics of the Heeling exercise when you drop the leash, your pup may stop and look at you, as if to say, "Hey Butterfingers, what's up with this?" If he does this, you should continue to walk along as you encourage him to heel. Pups realize that something is different when the leash is dragging on the ground, and some will be confused by the change in the routine. Because this is closer to confusion than a test, they are in need of encouragement, not discipline.

If you cannot coax your pup to drag the leash, you should give him time to become accustomed to the sound and feel of a dragging leash. By holding the leash at its midpoint in your left hand and allowing the end of the leash to drag on the ground, you can help an anxious pup to heel with the leash dragging behind them. With a little assistance, an anxious pup will soon be able to confidently drag the leash while he is heeling.

After two to four weeks of heeling your pup with his leash dragging behind him, you can unsnap the leash and maintain the same control you had when the leash was attached to his collar. For a stubborn pup that is having trouble making the transition to heeling off lead, you can attach an eighteen-inch street lead to his collar. Even though the leash is short, the pup will still know he's on lead and therefore under your control.

As well as heeling off lead, your pup can go off lead during his Sit- and Down-stays. When you began your pup's basic obedience training, you taught him to stay at a distance of six feet. In time, you gradually increased the distance to fifty feet, but the leash was still attached to his collar. Now you can unsnap the lead and proof your pup to stay off lead. Should he stand up during an off-lead Stay, you should posture with your body and bark a verbal correction. If he corrects himself by sitting, you should praise him and remind him to stay. If he doesn't correct himself following the verbal correction, you can repeat the Sit command; if your command is ignored, you should give him another verbal correction before returning to him and repeating the exercise.

Most pack-trained dogs prefer working off lead, and many of these work better off lead. The will of pack members is to please their pack leaders, and this is confirmed each time a pack-trained dog works off lead. Are there some breeds that cannot work off lead? While some breeds are more adept than others, all dogs can learn to work off lead. But what about wolf hybrids—can they be trained to work off lead? According to conventional wisdom, wolf hybrids, or wolf dogs, cannot be trained like a dog. Many experts claim that wolf dogs are "essentially wild animals."

Until I got Cheyenne, a seventy-percent wolf dog, I had never trained a wolf dog. In her litter of five, Cheyenne was not the biggest pup, but she was definitely the alpha pup. There were five wolf dogs at the breeder's home, and they all got to socialize with the pups. At six weeks of age, Cheyenne was demonstrating her dominance to her littermates, but she was also showing discretion when it came to the adult wolf dogs. She knew when submission should be expressed and when boldness could be entertained, but there was no doubt she was the alpha pup.

In 1996 I experienced the same dilemma I faced in 1964—either I follow conventional wisdom or I strike out on my own. Even though most of the information on wolf dogs was extremely negative, I knew that Cheyenne's parents were special dogs. That knowledge gave me the confidence I needed to put my pack-training techniques to the test. Her parents, Micmac (Mac) and Seneca (owned by Candace Hoffman) were extraordinary wolf dogs in every aspect.

Much of what is commonly believed about wolves, wolf hybrids, and dogs is illogical, vague, or incorrect. On the one hand, we are told that the wolves and dogs are genetically indistinguishable; yet many experts profess that wolves and wolf hybrids are inherently dangerous, unstable, and unpredictable. Wolves, however, usually live in harmony with one another in the wild, while dogs are traumatizing millions of children every year. According to many animal behaviorists, wolf dogs do not make safe family pets because of their innate "wildness." Some wolf dog breeders believe that they are too intelligent to train. I've heard my father say many times: "In order to train an animal, you have to be smarter than the animal." In other words, you must know more about the animal than he does about you, if you expect to train him.

Wolf dogs are highly intelligent and cunning animals, but they acquiesce only to a pack leader. If you don't know how a pack leader leads a pack of wolves, you will not be able to do much with one of these creatures. A dog can be loosely compared to a wolf dog as a Ford can be compared to a Ferrari. A Ford and a Ferrari are both cars, but one is much quicker and spirited. While an experienced driver can safely get behind the wheel of a Ferrari, a novice would have difficulty keeping the car on the road,

Those who believe the myths about wolf dogs have a hard time explaining why some wolf dogs do not fit the mold. After winning our wolf dog club's top prize—which only required a wolf dog to heel on lead, a three-minute Sit-stay on lead, an eight-minute Down-stay on lead, and various tests for socialization—I asked the club organizers if I could give an obedience demonstration with Cheyenne. She had just won their highest award of Champion Socialized Wolf Dog, but Cheyenne was working at that level when she was five months old. My intention was to show them that they too were underestimating the potential of these animals; so I gave an off-lead demonstration with Cheyenne heeling, standing for examination, recalling and finishing from a hundred feet away, dropping on recall, and retrieving over a high jump. In the club's following newsletter, the editor wrote: "No matter what you hear or see, you cannot make a safe family pet out of a high-percentage wolf hybrid. Those who believe otherwise are living in a fantasy world. Wolf dogs are essentially wild animals and quite unpredictable."

What does it mean when people use the expression "wild animal?" We know that dogs will return to a wild, feral state when they are separated from civilization—but do dogs suddenly become feral in our backyards? Of course they don't! Dogs remain domesticated until their domestic life ends; so, in reality, wild animals are animals living in the wild, but it does not suggest that they are unstable. Unstable behavior is commonly observed when wolves are caged, but not so in their natural habitat.

Since Cheyenne came into my life, I have trained dozens of wolf dogs, including two of her littermates with similar success. Had this not been the case, I might think Cheyenne was just a special dog. Cheyenne's sister lives with a disabled woman with absolutely no discipline problems, and the other wolf dogs have also become quality pets.

Cheyenne is not a fluke. Wolf dogs and dogs are both pack animals. They respond to leadership in a predictable and customary manner. When your dog accepts your alpha status, you will have authority. Where there is a belief in authority, there will be obedience—and you will have voice control with your dog.

Begin heeling off lead by allowing the pup to drag the leash behind him.
In the top photo, Lucky is heeling nicely for his owner, Carla Adcock.
In the bottom photo, Lucky is beginning to forge,
which is the handler's cue to make a quick left turn.

Cheyenne, like most pack-trained dogs, enjoys working off lead

Roxanne, a boxer-mix owned by Robert and Silvia Byrd,
was willing and able to work off lead following six weeks of training.

14

Training Equipment and Schedule

There are many choices of dog training equipment to consider. There are enough choices to cause some confusion, if we don't understand what we are trying to do when we train our dogs. Force trainers use prong collars (pinch collars), remote electronic collars, and heavy-handed discipline. Positive-reinforcement trainers use harnesses, buckled collars, and buckets of treats. From time to time, someone tries to reinvent the wheel or resurrect an old device. You may have seen the "Halti-Headcover" and "Gentle Leader" leashes that are designed to give handlers more control with their dogs. We also see a lot of trainers using clicker devices to gain and hold their dogs' attention. Some trainers believe that getting a dog excited with a game of tug-of-war will give them an edge in the obedience ring, while others rub the scent of food on their hands or clothes, thinking this will keep their dogs attentive. These are some of the tactics that trainers must utilize when they haven't established social order with their dogs. Few dogs can be champions, but no dog needs to be traumatized, coerced, or bribed to be a sound working dog or a great family pet.

The only equipment that is needed to train your dog is a choke collar and a six-foot nylon leash. Lightweight, metal choke collars give better corrections than nylon choke collars or metal choke collars with large links. During leash training, a longer leash may be needed for large pups, but no other training equipment is necessary. While I use metal choke collars for most pups, nylon choke collars are often preferable for toy breeds and omega pups. The weight and sound of a metal collar may intimidate an extremely submissive or small pup.

The term "choke collar" is a misnomer. Its function is to discipline a dog, not to choke him. During a correction a choke chain will quickly tighten around the pup's neck, and once it tightens, it will quickly release its pressure. When the collar is placed on a pup correctly, and the leash is attached to the free-hanging ring, the free ring will be hanging down on the right side of his neck. When the free ring extends upward on the right side of his neck, the collar will tend to keep pressure on the pup's neck following a correction.

Walking a dog on a harness will encourage him to pull. Harnesses are used to train tracking dogs and weight-pulling sled dogs. Keeping tension on a dog's lead and harness will stimulate him to pull against the restraint. When you use this approach during leash training, you will usually wind up with a sled dog pulling you down the street.

Buckled collars are not safe to use with pulling dogs. When a dog pulls on lead, the pressure of the collar is concentrated on the dog's throat. The effect of this pressure, in time, can cause injuries to a dog's larynx and trachea. A dog that pulls on lead wearing a choke collar would not be so affected because the pressure would be distributed around the dog's entire neck.

Prong collars inflict pain as a consequence for pulling on lead. When they are used during obedience training, corrections are usually traumatic experiences for shy and timid pups. While many dog trainers promote their use, many amateurs misuse or overuse them to the point their dogs become extremely anxious when they are working on lead.

The Halti-Headcover, or Gentle Leader, is designed to give a person more control with a pulling dog. The device works on the same principle as a horse halter. A strap encompasses the dog's muzzle and attaches to a leash. This enables the handler to control the dog by being able to pull the dog's head down. Because one cannot correct a dog wearing a Gentle Leader, a handler must teach the obedience commands by using food rewards.

Some of the newest gadgets seem more like medieval torture devices than training equipment. For example, there is a leash and harness assembly called a "Control Harness." According to its manufacturer: "Its special design converts forward movement into upward lift around the thorax." When a dog pulls with a control harness, he will have considerable pressure exerted on his chest. There are other devices that emit a high-pitch sound when a dog pulls on lead or hog-ties the dog's front legs so he can't pull.

After a long absence, clicker training has again emerged as an alternative form of dog training for those who reject the belief that dogs are intelligent and cunning animals. Clicker trainers use the sound of a clicking device to hold their dogs' attention. Obviously, if you have a hard time holding your dog's attention, you must not be his pack leader. It's not that clicker training doesn't work for some dogs; it's the way it works. Conditioned reflex training may be challenging for labs rats, but dogs are capable of much more than simply responding to a stimulus.

A remote electronic (shock) collar can be a useful tool in certain training applications, but not obedience training. Giving a pup a shock when he disobeys will not create an atmosphere of fun or leadership. For most dogs trained in this manner, obedience training will become a dreaded chore. I occasionally use these collars for stubborn dogs learning to range at an acceptable distance. They can also be used to poison proof dogs.

Poison Proofing

The crime of poisoning dogs occurs in many neighborhoods. Giving poison-laced meat to a dog is likely the cowardly act of someone with a fear of dogs. What we fear, we destroy. A shock collar can be used to poison proof a dog. You can teach a dog not to eat food he finds on the ground by placing a meatball of ground beef on the ground and releasing the dog into the yard. When the dog locates the meat and tries to pick it up, tell him, "No!" and give him a shock with the remote control. Each time he tries to take the bait, you should give him another shock. By doing this each day for a week or two, your dog will learn to move away from the meat in order to avoid the shocking surprise. However, as with prong collars, amateurs tend to overuse shock collars to the point their dogs become nervous wrecks. Only those who have the ability to read a dog should use them. In other words, shock collars can cause more problems than they solve for novice trainers.

When used correctly, a choke collar is the most humane training collar.

Training Schedule

Some dogs learn quickly because of their desire to please; some take longer to learn because of their stubbornness; some are too nervous to learn quickly; and others will start slow and pick up speed toward the end of the course. Therefore, you should use this training schedule as a general outline for achieving the different levels of obedience training.

I recommend training a pup five days a week. It will also be helpful if you are not tired or stressed when it's time to train your pup. And if you miss an occasional lesson, you cannot make it up by working the pup twice as long the following day. It doesn't work that way. By extending the time of the next lesson, you will likely only bore your pup.

Week One and Two

The first two weeks of training classes should be held in quiet, familiar locations. This quality time will enable you to strengthen your bond with your pup by projecting your alpha status. One of the best ways to strengthen the bond with your pup is to take him for additional hikes off lead. Before you turn him loose, you should give your pup a refresher lesson in leash training. After fifteen minutes of leash training, he will be more focused on his obedience lesson. Following his obedience lesson you can reward him with an off lead run.

For pups that need a lot of exercise, I will usually run them for a few minutes before their obedience lesson. Following a short run off lead, an energy-depleted "ball of energy" will be more focused on the task at hand. From the standpoint that obedience training should be fun and relatively lighthearted, we should always be taking note of our pup's attitude and responding accordingly. He should be enthusiastic and attentive, so use these indicators to decide if more encouragement or discipline is needed. Stubborn hardheads will need more discipline, and shy pups will need more encouragement and praise. In order to bring a shy pup out of his shell, I recommend making his obedience training a lighthearted activity.

Week Three

By the end of the second week, most pups will have learned Heel, Sit, and Stay, and they will also be learning Down-stay and Stand. Now you can begin training your pup in unfamiliar locations. By the end of a pup's third week of training, he will have a clear understanding of these five commands.

Week Four to Week Six

The final three weeks should be spent with your dog in a public place with increasing levels of distraction, such as parks, strip malls, and different neighborhoods. In addition to practicing the other commands, you will be teaching the Recall and Finish. The Recall part of this exercise is usually a no-brainer for pack-trained pups. By this time they will already be coming when you call. The Finish command, however, is more complicated and requires extra time for pups to learn.

When your pup is working confidently and efficiently on lead, you can begin his off-lead training. All pups can learn this basic obedience course in six to eight weeks, and many will be working off lead. This will depend both on your teaching ability and the cunning and work ethic of your pup. Once your pup has completed his basic obedience course, occasional refresher lessons will keep him working at a high level. Because most dogs enjoy working for their leaders, we should incorporate the obedience commands into their day-to-day life. For example, following an off lead run, you can heel your pup back to your car. Before you feed your pup or treat him to a snack or offer playtime, you can have him execute an obedience command before rewarding him. While a pup is learning his obedience commands, you can communicate and reinforce the meanings of the commands by praising the pup, "Good Sit", "Good Down", or "Good Come" when your pup sits, downs, or comes on his own volition.

Some breeds are usually more proficient than others in technical merit, but this is not the purpose of a pup's obedience training. A pup doesn't have to heel with perfection to be a wonderful family pet. Perfect heeling technique is a laudable goal, but it is not the purpose of this pack-training course.

Dogs and their owners are both creatures of habit. Anything a dog or a human does routinely will become a habit. And it is equally hard for humans and dogs to break a bad habit. Many dog owners and some dog trainers allow their pups to dominate them in obvious and subtle ways without realizing their mistakes.

Common Beginner Mistakes
- Heeling with a tight lead: as if they are trying to hold their pups in position.
- Failing to praise: Failing to praise a pup will make his training experience a dreaded chore.
- Following their dogs' lead: Instead of leading, handlers follow the lead of their pups whenever they change their pace or direction
- Walking on eggshells: Handlers move tentatively when their pups are on a "Stay," as though they might cause them to make a mistake.
- Coaxing a dog to stay: Some people try to mentally hold their pups in position, and others try to coax their pups to stay by repeating the command over and over.
- Bribing a dog with treats.
- Striking a dog for misbehavior.
- Inconsistent handling: A consistent training regimen is the trademark of a good dog trainer.
- The silent treatment: It is important to communicate with our pups. Don't neglect to tell your pup how you are feeling about him. A smile works for him, too!
- Drill instructor syndrome: Pups aren't looking for a drill instructor, so there is no need to bark commands at your pup. When you shout your commands, the barking tone of your voice sounds like discipline to your pup. The tone of your commands should sound more like requests than demands.

I teach people how they can have the best possible relationship with their dogs. It's not about heel, sit, and stay; it's about who's the leader of the pack. In order to have a positive relationship with your pup, your pup must see you as his alpha leader. When you are perceived as a strong, loving leader, your pup will always be willing and eager to win your favor.

Alpha leaders are not just about the rule of law. They also express their love and playfulness to their pack members, so fun-and-games should be part of every pup's education. It is no great accomplishment to teach a pup a few commands. The real accomplishment is having a pup that works with a joyful and eager attitude.

What exactly are we doing when we train our dogs? Are dogs learning because of the techniques or equipment we are using, or is something else taking place? When dogs are trained to track, what are their trainers teaching them? We know next to nothing about tracking—so what exactly are we teaching these dogs? We give tracking dogs an outlet to use their instinctive ability and the encouragement to follow a trail to its logical conclusion, but we cannot teach dogs how to track. Dogs know more about tracking than we will ever know. So, in a real sense, we are more like an activity director than a teacher.

The purpose of obedience training is not to teach pups the meanings of various obedience commands. Most pups know the meanings of most of the obedience commands long before we begin training them. When you train your pup, you are strengthening his desire to obey your commands. In order for your pup to want to please you, he must see you as a leader, worthy of his respect.

For this reason, hiring someone to train your dog for you is not recommended. No one can train your dog to respect you. A professional dog trainer can give you back a dog that is easier to handle and more willing to follow a leader, but you must duplicate what the trainer has done, if you expect to maintain a leadership position with your trained dog.

Pack training is a natural way of gaining a dog's respect. You will be gaining your dog's respect the same way other dogs gain the allegiance of their canine friends. When your dog sees you as his pack leader, he will be a respectful and loyal pet. Pack training is the process of making this pack connection with a dog, and it begins the day your pup comes home with you.

For pups and dogs to feel connected, they must bond with their families. You cannot expect your pup to accept your alpha status when you isolate him in a kennel or the back yard. Dogs living in solitude will not feel connected to their families. Solitary dogs are usually so grieved for companionship that they become extremely excited and out of control when they are with their families. This hyperactive behavior is characteristic of hunting dogs that live the majority of their lives in kennels. When released, their pent-up energy is expressed as a hyperactive hunting drive. In the field, this behavior is welcomed; in the home, it is not.

If for some reason your pup cannot be with you when you are home, he will need daily runs and long walks even more than pups that live freely with their families. Bonding with a pup is the first step in training a dog, and there are no substitutions for this effort. As a pack trainer, you will log many miles with each pup that comes into your life, but the rewards will far outweigh the effort. Frequent runs and hikes will only be necessary during his puppy development. By the time your dog is two years old, he will need only occasional runs for exercise and enjoyment.

Dogs are like people in regard to their aptitudes. Some dogs are easily amused and love repetition. Labrador and golden retrievers can often work for thirty minutes or longer without getting bored. On the other hand, hounds and terriers will lose interest after only a few minutes of training. Their independent nature and stubbornness get most of the credit. This doesn't mean they are simple-minded, just easily bored. Fifteen-minute obedience training classes will usually suffice for hounds, terriers, and Arctic breeds, such as malamute and Siberian husky.

While obedience training only takes a few minutes of your time each day, you will be spending many hours shaping your pup's intellect and instincts. A key component of training a dog is how you are using your time. If you are spending time with your pup as his pack leader, you and your pup will be on the right track.

15

The Health of Your Dog

We shop at grocery stores because we believe we are buying quality food. Most of us also believe that dog food companies are using quality ingredients in the production of their dog food. After all, their commercials are so well done. And what about the veterinarian and celebrity endorsements—could they all be duped?

If you want to know if you are feeding a quality diet to your dog, one that will give him the nutrition he needs to preserve his health, look at the ingredient list on the back of your dog food bag or can. Can you identify these ingredients? Do you know which foods are the best sources of protein, carbohydrates, and fats?

Many dog owners assume they are feeding a quality food to their dogs. Dog food companies are banking on consumer ignorance by spending millions of dollars on advertising while they minimize their production costs. Advertising executives are always trying to stay one step ahead of the consumer with their terminologies and deceptions.

Consider the inexpensive brand names of dog food: If a retailer charges you $10 for a forty-pound bag of dog food, it stands to reason that the manufacturer spent a lot less to produce the product; yet when you read the ingredient list, you might think the food has a good percentage of protein, carbohydrates, and fats. But again, if you can buy the dog food for pennies per pound, how much did they spend to make the stuff? What kind of protein can you buy for pennies per pound?

Theoretically, a dog could survive on vitamin-enriched sawdust, but it doesn't mean his health won't prematurely fail. Dogs that eat cheap dog foods look like dogs that have been eating sawdust: they are weak, fat, and lethargic; their coats are dry, dull, and brittle; and they shed year round. They usually have a short life span and are often plagued with chronic ailments and diseases.

Feeding a dog an expensive dog food does not necessarily mean you are getting your money's worth. One of the most expensive dog foods, Hill's Science Diet, has a similar ingredient list as the medium-grade supermarket brands, but it costs twice as much as Purina and Pedigree.

How can you get "the most bang for your buck?" Inexpensive dog food is junk food; mid-price supermarket brands are only marginally better than the inexpensive brands; and some of the most expensive dog foods use similar ingredients as the mid-priced supermarket brands. In order to make an informed decision about your dog's diet, you must learn how to read an ingredient list. Let's look at some of the ingredients being used in the production of commercial dog foods and learn what the FDA animal-feed governing body (AAFCO) and animal nutritionists have to say about them.

Corn

Because dogs cannot fully digest corn, they cannot utilize all of the nutrients contained in the grain. In spite of this fact, corn is the main ingredient in most of the brand name supermarket dog foods and some of the premium dog foods. Animal-feed nutritionists have determined that corn's absorption rate is only 54% for dogs, so the undigested corn is eliminated in the dog's feces. This is why a dog eating a corn diet will have large, soft, yellowish stools.

There is something else that bothers me about a corn diet for dogs. Undigested food in humans can produce allergic reactions—so why couldn't this be the case with our dogs? Could a corn diet be a contributing factor for dogs with chronic allergies? Many animal nutritionists believe that corn is the major contributor to allergies in dogs.

Animal nutritionists have determined that the nutrients needed for a healthy coat are the Omega-3 Essential Fatty Acids that are found abundantly in chicken fat, menhaden herring, salmon, and sunflower seed oil. Corn does not have these nutrients; as a result, corn-fed dogs have dry, flaky skin and dull, shedding coats. They are usually overweight, and they always seem to be hungry. Their ravenous appetites may be the effect of not being nutritionally satisfied, somewhat like a pregnant woman with food cravings.

When speaking of corn, I am referring to the whole grain. Corn gluten meal is the digestible, high-protein portion of the corn grain and is considered by some nutritionists, but not all, to be a quality ingredient.

Soybean meal

Soybean meal is a common but controversial dog food ingredient. Some breeds seem to be able to digest soybean better than others. Indigestion can result in bloating and intestinal problems. Many animal nutritionists believe that soybean can cause allergies in dogs.

By-products and meat products

The term "by-products" does not refer to meat of any kind. A by-product can be any part of the animal except its flesh. Hair, horn, teeth, and hooves are found in beef by-products. If the label lists chicken by-products, you are feeding guts, feet, heads, and feathers to your dog. If the label lists "meat products," the meat can be from any source, including diseased animals, spoiled supermarket meat, zoo animals, and dogs.

Animal fat

When a label lists "animal fat" this can mean just about anything, including discarded restaurant grease.

Sugar

Do you know if your dog food is laced with sugar? Look for corn syrup, sucrose, ammoniated glycyrrhizin, sorbitol, and sugar on your dog food's ingredients list. Sugar is added as a flavor enhancer and perhaps for its addictive property. Some dog food companies disguise the sugar content in their food by using different sugar sources and listing them separately. Sugar is also found in many dog treats as well.

Food Fragments

"Food fragments" are the by-products that result from the processing of human foods. Brewers rice is a food fragment found in many brands of dog food, even though it is a by-product of milling rice and contains minimal B-vitamins. Beet pulp is a by-product of the sugar industry. Wheat bran, the indigestible, fibrous hull of the wheat grain, can also produce allergic reactions in dogs. The pet food industry uses these ingredients because of their lower cost.

Artificial Ingredients: chemical additives and dyes

Chemical additives include the following: BHT, sodium nitrite, ethoxyquin, propyl gallate, ammoniated glycyrrhizin, potassium sorbate, and propyl glycol. They are used as preservatives and softening agents. Artificial coloring additives do not require a listing on ingredient lists, even though these dyes have been banned from human food production.

Is there any reason to subject our dogs to these chemicals and coal tar products?

Beef Tallow

The dictionary defines tallow as "a mixture of the whitish, tasteless, solid or hard fat used to make candles, leather dressings, soap, lubricants, and foodstuffs." Beef tallow is found in many cheap and mid-priced dog foods, even though beef tallow will break down only in a digestive tract with a temperature of 109 degrees or higher. (That's a little warmer than I like to keep my dogs!)

Ascorbic acid

There is a difference of opinion concerning the use of ascorbic acid in dog food production. Some veterinarians and nutritionists recommend supplementing vitamin C for the prevention of bladder problems. Some premium dog food companies are using vitamin C as a preservative.

The Food and Drug Administration has issued a health alert concerning the use of ascorbic acid as a preservative in dog food. Dogs make their own vitamin C, but when ascorbic acid is added to a dog's diet, it can cause kidney failure, according to this FDA report.

Animal Digest

As a flavor enhancer, "animal digest" is sprayed on the extruded kibble at the end of its production. Animal digest is a waste product from animal rendering plants.

Wheat middlings

Wheat middlings are wheat products that are intermediate in quality, price, size, or grade.

Propylene Glycol

A colorless, viscous, hygroscopic liquid used in the production of antifreeze solutions, hydraulic fluids, and solvents, propylene glycol is used to tie up the water content in the kibble, thus inhibiting bacterial growth.

Synthetic Flavorings

Synthetic flavorings are listed as "natural flavoring" and "natural flavor." Little is known about these mysterious additives.

Rating Commercial Dog Foods

Supermarket and discount store dog food will not satisfy your dog's nutritional needs. In the vast majority of these products, corn and by-products are the main ingredients. Soybean meal, beef tallow, animal fat, animal digest, and food fragments are also found on most of their ingredient lists.

That leaves us with the premium dog foods that are sold in pet stores, health food stores, and veterinarian clinics. While premium dog food is generally of a higher quality than supermarket brand names, there is much to be desired in some of these products.

Science Diet's main ingredients in most of its dog food are corn and by-products. Some of their prescription diets even contain peanut hulls. Even though it is one of the most expensive dog foods, it would be my last choice of a premium dog food. At the end of the chapter is a comparison of ingredient lists of some of the popular brands of dog food.

Poisonous Plants
(Source: ASPCA Animal Poison Control Center)

Following is a list of toxic and poisonous plants:
- SHRUBS: Azalea, Boxwood, Holly berries, Hydrangea, Oleander
- FLOWERS: Amaryllis, Autumn Crocus, Buttercup, Calia Lilly, Christmas rose, Chrysanthemum, Daffodil bulb, Easter lily, Foxglove, Hyacinth bulb, Iris root, Jessamine, Jonquil, Narcissus, Morning glory, Peony, Periwinkle, Poinsettia, Primrose, Tulip bulb
- GROUND COVER: Devil's Ivy (Philodendron), English ivy, Jasmine, Matrimony vine, Virginia creeper
- ORNAMENTALS: Asparagus Fern, Caladium, Elephant's Ear, Dumb Cane, Philodendron Saddle Leaf, Split Leaf, Poinsettia, Pot Mum, Spider Mum, Umbrella Plant, Holly berries
- TREES: Apple leaves and stems, American yew, Cuban Laurel (Ficus), Fiddle-Leaf Fig, Oak acorns, English yew, Apricot, Almond, Peach, Cherry leaves and stems, Wild Cherry, Japanese Plum, Balsam Pear
- FRUITS AND VEGETABLES: Apple seed, Apricot seed, Avocado seed, Cornstalk, Eggplant leaves and stems, Onion, Peach seed

- OTHER DANGERS: Aloe Vera, Mistletoe, Granular pesticides and herbicides, Mushrooms, bakers chocolate, antifreeze, dental floss, electrical cords, small objects that can be swallowed

Home Remedies

Activated charcoal can save your dog's life when a veterinarian is not readily available. Dogs will try to eat a lot of stuff they shouldn't, and pups will try to eat almost everything. I have listed many of the poisonous plants and foods that pups should not consume, but there is also the problem of people deliberately poisoning dogs.

If you know your dog has eaten a poisonous or toxic substance, you can treat him with activated charcoal before you take him to a veterinarian. The dose recommended for poisoned dogs is 3-6 ml of activated charcoal suspension per pound of dog, and it can be repeated in one-hour intervals. Activated charcoal will absorb the poison before it gets into the dog's bloodstream. Activated carbon can either be purchased from your veterinarian or health food store. You should consult with your vet before using this product.

Aspirin is an effective painkiller, but you should give only the buffered or baby aspirin to your dogs because of their sensitive stomachs. Give 10 mg per pound of your dog's body weight every eight hours. Do not give aspirin to your dog if he is on cortisone (steroids) or as a long-term treatment for arthritis, because it can cause stomach irritation and bleeding.

Benadryl should be in everyone's car because it could save your dog's life. If a poisonous snake or spider bites your dog, you can pill him before you take him to the veterinarian. Benadryl will help neutralize the effect of the venom. Give your dog 1 to 2 mg per pound of your dog's body weight.

Glucosamine sulfate is a nutrient that is often effective in relieving the pain associated with arthritis in older dogs. Some nutritionists claim the nutrient is utilized to grow new cartilage in arthritic joints. I use it for my knees, and it works for many dogs with similar needs. Give 1000 grams a day to a fifty-pound dog and add 500 grams for each additional fifty pounds of weight.

MSN and flaxseed oil are also recommended for dogs suffering from arthritis.

Kaopectate and Pepto Bismol are excellent remedies for diarrhea and vomiting. Give 1 ml per pound of dog and repeat every two to four hours, until the symptoms dissipate. (1 tsp = 5 ml   1 tbsp = 15 ml)

Gatorade can also be used to treat dogs for chronic vomiting and diarrhea, given in one-cup doses every thirty minutes.

Probiotics are the beneficial bacteria that all healthy animals have in their gut. After a dog has completed a round of antibiotics, which kills all the bacteria (good and bad), you should supplement your dogs' diet for two to four weeks with Acidophilus. In between meals, the dose for small dogs is one capsule, two capsules for medium dogs, and three capsules for large and giant dogs. Probiotics can be purchased in health food stores. Plain yogurt can also be used for this purpose.

Lecithin can be used to treat dogs with weak bladders or urinary tract problems. Lecithin can help strengthen the sphincter muscle in the dog's bladder. A twenty-pound dog can be given one-quarter of an adult daily dosage. A forty-pound dog can take half of an adult dose.

Metamucil is a good laxative for dogs given in one-quarter adult dosages for small dogs. Give half of an adult dose to a fifty-pound dog.

Enzymes will help dogs utilize the food they are eating. Evidence of indigestion can be bloating and flatulence. Dogs that are eating a cooked diet need to be supplemented with enzymes. If you cook for your dog, you are serving up meals devoid of digestive enzymes. Enzymes are killed at temperatures over 120 degrees F. As well, dogs that are eating commercial dog foods are not getting the enzymes they need to digest their food properly. All dogs should be giving enzymes as a daily supplements with their meals, because all commercial dog food is cooked at temperatures that kill the natural enzymes.

Garlic, or as I like to call it, "vitamin G," is a powerful herbal medicine. It can be used to boost a compromised immune system and to repel fleas, ticks, and intestinal worms. It also has antiviral and antibiotic properties. I give garlic to my family, including my dogs, whenever they are lethargic or off their feed. You can purchase garlic pills or raw garlic, and give one half of an adult dose or one clove of raw garlic per day to a fifty-pound dog. I also recommend garlic oil as a topical antibiotic.

Natural Flea Shampoo can be made from orange peelings: blend or puree the peelings of two oranges in a quart of water, strain the mixture through cheesecloth or a coffee filter, and add the filtered liquid to a half-full bottle of regular shampoo. Orange-peel shampoo will not only kill fleas but also keeps your dog smelling fresh for up to two weeks.

Bladder Problems such as cystitis are not common, but when a dog suffers from the inflammation of the bladder lining and the resulting mineral deposits and stones that become lodged in the urethra or penis, he really suffers. Symptoms include frequent urination, with only a small amount of urine being voided, and blood in the urine. If the dog's condition is chronic, there may be a complete blockage of the urethra with no urine being voided. In both cases, surgery will be required ASAP.

Dr. Pitcairn's Natural Health for Dogs and Cats suggests that some commercial dog foods may be responsible for the animal's urine becoming too alkaline, thus causing the cystitis. Allowing a dog to feed-on-demand can also result in the urine become alkaline. Feeding dogs organ meats (by-products) and meat meal (pesticide-laced) can also be a contributing factor, according to this homeopathic veterinarian. He recommends supplementing a dog's diet with vitamin C to prevent the blood from becoming too alkaline. Small dogs can be given 250 mg twice daily; medium dog can take 500mg twice daily; and large dogs can take 500 mg three times a day.

Once a dog has had stones removed from his urinary tract, it is likely he will need surgery again in the future. For this reason, I would consider using a vitamin C regimen to prevent the stones from returning. If your dog is healthy and eating a typical American dog diet of corn and by-products, I would recommend feeding a quality diet to your dog and supplementing his diet with enzymes, but I would not recommend supplementing vitamin C into his diet, until more is known of the effects of ascorbic acid.

Dog Food Ingredient Lists
(Upper case bold words indicate suspect ingredients)

Solid Gold: Hund-n-Flocken Adult Dog Food:
Lamb, ground millet, ground brown rice, ground barley, menhaden fish meal, canola oil, flaxseed oil, rice bran, garlic, amaranth (a grain from Central America), blueberries, yucca schidigera extract, taurine, carotene, choline chloride, calcium carbonate, vitamin E supplement, iron proteinate, vitamin A supplement, zinc proteinate, niacin supplement folic acid thiamine, pyridoxine hydrochloride, manganese proteinate

Nutro Natural Choice: Chicken Meal and Rice Formula:
Chicken meal, ground rice, rice bran, rice flour, oatmeal, sunflower oil preserved with mixed tocopherals, a source of natural Vitamin E, dried egg product, **NATURAL FLAVORS**, monosodium phosphate, dried kelp.

Flint River Ranch:
Chicken meal, whole wheat flour, ground rice, lamb meal, poultry fat, ground wheat, flax seed, dried whole egg, ascorbic acid as a preservative

Eukanuba Adult:
CHICKEN BY-PRODUCT MEAL, GROUND CORN, rice flour, chicken, chicken fat (preserved with BHA), dried beet pulp, **CHICKEN DIGEST**, dried whole egg, **ETHOXYQUIN** (Chicken digest comes from poultry rendering plants and is sprayed on the extruded kibble at the end of production.)

Iams Adult:
Chicken, **CORN MEAL**, ground whole grain sorghum, **CHICKEN BY-PRODUCT MEAL**, ground whole grain barley, fish meal, chicken fat

Pro Plan Adult:
Chicken, **BREWERS GROUND RICE**, ground wheat, **POULTRY BY-PRODUCT MEAL, GROUND YELLOW CORN, BEEF TALLOW**, corn gluten meal, **CORN BRAN**

Science Diet Maintenance:
GROUND YELLOW CORN, POULTRY BY-PRODUCT MEAL, PROPYL GALLATE, SOYBEAN MEAL, ANIMAL FAT preserved with BHA, dried whole egg, vegetable oil

Purina Dog Chow:
GROUND YELLOW CORN, CHICKEN BY-PRODUCT MEAL, corn gluten meal, **SOYBEAN MEAL, BREWERS RICE, BEEF TALLOW**

Purina One:
Chicken, corn gluten meal, **BREWERS RICE, POULTRY BY-PRODUCT MEAL**, whole grain wheat, **WHOLE GRAIN CORN, BEEF TALLOW**, pea bran, fish meal, **NATURAL FLAVORS**

Pedigree Healthy Start:
GROUND YELLOW CORN, CHICKEN BY-PRODUCT MEAL, corn gluten meal, **ANIMAL FAT**

Purina Beneful:
GROUND YELLOW CORN, CHICKEN BY-PRODUCT MEAL, corn gluten meal, **SOYBEAN HULLS**, whole wheat flour, rice flour, chicken, **SOY FLOUR, BEEF TALLOW, SUGAR, ANIMAL DIGEST**

Kibbles 'n Bits:
CORN, SOYBEAN MEAL, ground wheat flour, **BEEF AND BONE MEAL, ANIMAL FAT, CORN SYRUP, WHEAT MIDDLINGS, ANIMAL DIGEST, HYDROCLORIC ACID**

Old Roy:
GROUND YELLOW CORN, MEAT AND BONE MEAL, SOYBEAN MEAL, WHEAT MIDDLINGS, ANIMAL FAT, CHICKEN DIGEST, BREWERS RICE, ANIMAL DIGEST

16

When Dogs Attack

There are a lot of contradictory and questionable beliefs about dog behavior, especially aggressive dog behavior. The majority of dog trainers and animal behaviorists would agree that there isn't much hope of rehabilitating a dog with a history of biting people, but their explanations for dog bites are widely varied. Explanations for dog bite include a dog's prey drive, the owners' handling of their dogs, an agitating stimulus that evokes protective behavior, and abusive children. Many animal behaviorists assert that a dog's prey drive is what triggers a dog to bite. In other words, a dog sometimes mistakes a running child for a prey animal. Some believe that people make their dogs aggressive, and others maintain that children were teasing or threatening the dogs that bit them.

These explanations range from ludicrous to half-truths. Dogs do not mistake children for rabbits or any other animal, and I find it hard to believe that there are three million "mean little kids" in the United States causing their dogs to bite. The same goes for people training their dogs to be aggressive. While some people do encourage their dogs to bite, and some kids are abusive to their dogs, it doesn't explain why the number of dog-bite cases has dramatically increased every year since 1970.

When a dog bites an innocent bystander, he is demonstrating his dominance, not his protective nature. The dog-bite problem is more neglect and effect than cause and effect. People aren't training their dogs to bite; they are allowing their dogs to become pack leaders. Many of these alpha dogs become the disciplinarians of their pack-families. A pack member would not feel the need to discipline an unruly or teasing child. Pack members will move out of harm's way, but pack leaders will often discipline their misbehaving subordinates.

Two recent court cases illustrate the misconceptions being touted as explanations for the dog-bite epidemic. In 2001, two dogs fatally attacked a collegiate lacrosse player in California. While this case was atypically violent, we can still understand the motives of unprovoked and brutal attacks. The dogs were Presa Canarios, a giant dog-fighting breed from the Canary Islands. They attacked and killed the young lady in their shared hallway of an apartment building in San Francisco. The owners' lawyers argued that the victim triggered the attack, either with her behavior, perfume, or some other odor producing substance, such as anabolic steroids.

The media coverage of this fatal dog attack centered on the legal question of responsibility, but it was never determined what triggered the attack. Were the dogs being protective? Did the owners teach the dogs to behave in such a way, or did the dogs act on their own initiative? And why was the attack so brutal? The fact that such questions have to be asked suggests that we do not truly understand dog behavior.

The following year, two bull terriers bit two children in a park in London, England. The defendants, Princess Ann's pair of bull terriers, were charged with biting two cycling children in the local park. The Royals' barrister argued that the dogs were agitated by the sound of the bicycle chains as the children rode past the dogs. Animal behaviorists also testified that the dogs were stable-tempered animals. With no objections or dissenting expert witnesses called to testify, the judge ruled in the defendant's favor that the dogs were well behaved and not at fault. As ludicrous as this should sound, it is a commonly held belief that stable dogs can be agitated to bite innocent bystanders.

To see the difference between these two dog-bite cases, we need an understanding of pack-animal behavior. We know that dogs are pack animals. While all pack animals seek order, they usually live in harmony with one another. So why do some dogs attack strangers for no apparent reason?

Pack leaders are driven to maintain order within the pack. The pack social order is a simple hierarchy with each member occupying his or her own distinct level of authority. Those below a particular wolf's level of authority, he can discipline; from those above him, he must accept discipline. Social order is what allows pack animals to live in harmony. Without social order, there would be anarchy and chaos. However, social order is normally maintained without the need for traumatizing discipline or physical injury. But there are exceptions to the rule. Do you remember Adolph Murie's observation about wolf dictators? While they are not the norm, they do exist. A dictatorial wolf's behavior will appear ruthless to any casual observer. When a wolf challenges a dictator or break his laws, the subordinate will be severely punished, banished from the pack, or even killed.

In the case of the "Killer Presa Canarios," they weren't merely disciplining the young lady or being protective—they were punishing her and trying to kill her. The initial bite was to the girl's throat, causing her quick and merciful death; but even after her demise, they continued to bite and pull at her. These dogs were dominant-aggressive alpha dogs that were trained to attack by prison convicts. As a result, they became alpha dictators. By allowing their dominant-aggressive alpha dogs to be trained to attack, the owners had given their alpha dogs the green light to attack at will. They had literally embedded canine terrorists in their apartment building.

Because it was the male dog that initiated the attack, he was the alpha male. Because the female was allowed to join in, she was his alpha female. It must have been a horrible scene. This is why I refuse to give protection training to alpha dogs. Teaching a pack leader to bite is reckless and dangerous.

Princess Ann's bull terriers, on the other hand, were not trying to harm the children; they were disciplining the kids for riding past them in a dominant manner. When a subordinate or stranger runs past a pack leader, the behavior is often interpreted as an expression of dominance, and it will elicit a disciplinary response. When the bull terriers bit the boys, they gripped their legs with their front teeth, not their canines. Their bites were acts of discipline, not aggression. Although the dogs' intention was not malicious, they were disciplining the children for not respecting their authority in the park. When they disciplined the children, the dogs were demonstrating their alpha status.

The vast majority of dog-bite cases involve an alpha dog biting a child or a visitor to the home. The same parallel is found in wolf packs. Wolf pups and strange wolves also receive the bulk of the discipline. Alpha wolves and alpha dogs discipline by gripping a subordinate's head or neck. 77 percent of the children victimized by dogs will be bitten on the head, neck, or face; and typically, the gripping will be a single bite (Kidsource.com). When we understand dog behavior, we will know the truth about the dog bite conundrum: 90 percent of dog-bite cases are evidently alpha dogs giving discipline to family members and visitors to their homes. If your dog sees himself as the pack leader, he will rule as he sees fit. Some reign by being aloof, grumpy, and standoffish; others are more dominant with their behavior and attitude; and a few will rule with an iron hand.

Alpha dictators are the despots of the canine world. Thankfully, most alpha dogs do not become dictators, but some breeds are more likely to follow this path than others (e.g., pit bull, Rottweiler, Presa Canario, and some of the mastiff breeds).

When the news media investigate the dog-bite problem, the pit bull often gets the bulk of their coverage. With this breed, you will find a legion of people who profess that pit bulls are no different than other breeds. They believe that aggressive pit bull behavior is the fault of the owners, not the breed. You will also find a strong, opposite viewpoint that pit bulls are dangerous and sometimes vicious, because of the high incidence of fatalities attributed to pit bull attacks.

In order to understand the behavior of pit bulls, and dog behavior in general, it helps to understand how a dog's behavior is influenced. While your input certainly has a lot to do with how your dog behaves, genetics also plays a role. If a pup comes to your home with a dominant-aggressive temperament and a predisposition for fighting dogs, he will likely have serious problems with discipline and aggression. Dominant-aggressive pit bulls produce more pups with dominant temperaments and aggressive dispositions than stable pit bulls with good dispositions.

Russian fox breeders in Siberia provided us with evidence of the importance of genetics when it comes to animal disposition. By breeding their foxes with good dispositions, they were able to produce foxes that would socialize with humans in a friendly manner. Surprisingly, it only took twenty generations of selective breeding to produce a domesticated fox.

No matter which breed you select, whether you are looking for a pet or a working dog, stable dogs produce more stable pups, and unstable dogs produce more of their kind. A pup's family history, temperament, and disposition will determine his positive potential as well as the likelihood of problem behavior. If you choose a dominant-aggressive pup, you can expect to be frequently tested. After all, for the first eight weeks of his life, he was the alpha pup; so you shouldn't expect him to readily accept your leadership without a lot of testing.

Pups also inherit prey drive, i.e., the drive to chase and capture prey. Prey drive can also be called a strong work ethic. Some dogs have a strong prey drive and some don't. A strong work ethic is found in hunting dogs, guide dogs, search dogs, and guard dogs.

Schutzhund, which means "protection dog" in German, is a sport that tests and evaluates dogs in obedience, tracking, and protection. Schutzhund is the most popular method of protection training in Europe and the United States. If you buy a pup from Schutzhund-titled dogs, you will likely get a pup with a strong prey drive. The pup will be genetically predisposed to want a job, and he will more likely be dominant-tempered as well. He will also test you throughout his development.

If you select the dominant-aggressive pup from a litter of guard-dog pups, you will be severely challenged to maintain order with such a dog. Top police and military dogs are commonly dominant-aggressive dogs. Because guard dogs and police K-9 dogs are conditioned to be suspicious of all strangers, these working dogs cannot turn off this training when they are in public. They have not been taught to discriminate between innocent physical contact and threatening behavior. Police and military security dogs are weapons, and they must be handled differently than other dogs. Most guard dogs cannot be safe family pets.

Dogs are the product of their heritage and life experience. They come into our homes with instincts, temperaments, and dispositions that produce testing behavior to one degree or another. How you respond to these puppy tests will determine how your pup behaves as an adult. If your pup believes that you are a pack member, he will likely try to attain the alpha position for himself. However, if you respond to his puppy tests with discipline that he understands, he will mature knowing that you are his alpha leader.

Dominant biting dogs are pack leaders. In order for an alpha dog to stop biting, he must be demoted to pack member. When a demotion of rank is made, a dog's demeanor and behavior will immediately change. Prior to his demotion, a stranger could not approach one of these dogs without being warned or threatened. Following the demotion, a dominant dog's response to strangers will be entirely different. Instead of communicating his authority, he will exhibit a relaxed or disinterested demeanor. Instead of taking charge, he will defer to the authority of his leader. His body language will communicate this by moving alongside or behind his owner in a submissive manner.

When an alpha leader accepts his demotion to pack member, he will no longer have the stressful responsibility of disciplining subordinates and outsiders. His personality will therefore change from tense and threatening to laid-back and tolerant. This would make sense to anyone with an understanding of pack-animal behavior. Pack leaders are always on the job. Pack members are always on holiday, but they will be there when we need them. Even though a pack member's demeanor will be relaxed, happy, and tolerant, this doesn't mean he won't defend his family.

The following breeds of dogs were involved in the most dog-bite fatalities between the years of 1979 and 1998, according to Dr. Jeffrey Sacks – Centers for Disease Control and Prevention:

Pit bull	- 76
Rottweiler	- 44
German shepherd	- 27
Siberian Husky	- 21
Malamute	- 15
Wolf-hybrid	- 14
Mixed breed	- 12
Chow-chow	- 11
Doberman pinscher	– 9
Great Dane	– 8
St. Bernard	– 8

17

Protection Training for Pack Members

The term "guard dog" means different things to different people. When I use the term, I am referring to security dogs or police K-9 dogs. When I speak of protection dogs, I am referring to a totally different animal. Protection dogs are family dogs that will protect their families in a crisis situation. It is fairly easy to teach a dominant dog to be aggressive. It is not a simple matter to teach a dog to be protective at the appropriate times.

Because everyone they meet in their communities is a potential adversary, police dogs must always be on alert. For this reason, a police dog would be stressed at family gatherings and social events. Because of his training, a police dog would likely respond defensively should someone give his handler a hug or a slap on the back. Guard dogs are trained to respond to sudden movements and aggressive physical behavior. Needless to say, you wouldn't want a police dog at a New Year's Eve party, but you could have a family protection dog at the party without a problem. Giving guard dog training to a family pet is therefore inappropriate, for there is no need for a dog to be on guard duty round the clock.

The purpose of training a family pet to be protective is to produce a confident and courageous dog, not an aggressive dog. Pack training begins this process by establishing social order and creating a bond of friendship with a pup. Pack training also indirectly engages a dog's natural protective instinct. By making a dog a full member of your family, you will gain the loyalty needed in this regard. By establishing social order and teaching a pup to trust the world around him, you will produce a stable pack member. Because of his trust of strangers, protection training will not change his outlook. He will remain a safe and loving family pet, but he will also have the courage to protect his family during a crisis.

Many untrained dogs have come to the rescue of their families. These are the dogs that are running into burning homes to save their families and defending their owners from the criminal element. Protection training does not teach a dog to be protective; it stimulates a dog's natural protective instinct in an orderly manner. However, if your dog is not a stable pack member, protection training should not be undertaken. There are no short cuts.

Protection training is a series of staged confrontations with a mugger. In order for your dog to experience criminal behavior, he must have contact with criminals, so you will need to recruit someone who can play the role of a cowardly mugger. Successful protection training depends on this person's ability. He must be able to project his emotions and read the emotions of your dog. A young dog can easily be overpowered in stressful situations; therefore the mugger, or agitator, must be able to read the same emotions he will be projecting to the dog: fear and anger.

A pack member being trained (encouraged) to be protective must always feel victorious following each of his encounters with the "bad guy." Once his courage is sufficient to stand up to an aggressive threat, you can then build the dog's confidence to the point he will resist a violent attack.

Before I can begin protection training, I must evaluate and validate the dog's natural courage and socialization. The dog must be able to demonstrate his social skills when experiencing the real world. He must be confident in crowds of people and relaxed when strangers approach him. A passing grade will be given to a calm, confident dog; however, an anxious or aggressive dog will not qualify for protection training. An anxious dog does not have the natural courage needed for protection training, but when a dog expresses dominance or aggression in public, he is posturing his authority as the alpha dog. If we encourage an alpha dog to protect his family from the criminal element, we will also be encouraging him to discipline his family members.

Protection training should only be offered to stable pack members with natural courage. If a pack member has been socialized, and has the courage to stand his ground during an aggressive encounter with a stranger, we can begin the process of building his confidence. For a young dog to respond defensively to a threatening encounter with a stranger, he must make the psychological transition from flight to fight. Most pups and young adult dogs will instinctively run away from a threatening encounter with a stranger. This is especially true for young dogs that are pack members. After all, pack members don't have the responsibility of defending the pack--that is the responsibility of the pack leader. Most young dogs in good pack-member standing will not understand that it is ever permissible to use force against a stranger. Our job is to overcome this aversion by gradually building his confidence with progressive levels of agitation. This confidence building will be a gradual process over a fairly lengthy period of time. Few dogs "come out" (become defensive) early on in their protection training.

In addition to qualifying a dog for protection training, the owner must be able to demonstrate his leadership and off lead control with his dog. If a dog is not a pack member in the owner's family, and we encourage him to make a bite, he will become a liability in his home. An alpha dog's first victim will likely be a family member who tries to discipline him or breaks one of his rules. As you might expect, some people only want a big, bad dog they can use as a weapon or a status symbol, but they never meet my qualifications. On the other hand, a person who has taken the responsibility of being his dog's leader has already demonstrated the maturity and character needed to own a protection dog.

In order for a young dog to stand his ground during a threatening encounter with a stranger, he must have natural courage. A young dog's courage is manifested when he discovers a new creature or explores a nature trail for the first time. A confident dog with natural courage will appear more curious than cautious when exploring new territory. Confidence is also witnessed when a dog is in the company of other dogs and strangers. Most one-year-old dogs will have the confidence needed to take the test for courage; the rest will be mentally mature when they are a little older, around eighteen months old.

Testing for Courage

The person used to test a dog's courage must be a stranger to the dog. He will be holed up in a secluded location as I approach with the dog on lead. The agitator will come out of hiding when we are a hundred feet away. As he shouts and jumps from his cover, his demeanor will be confrontational but cowardly. He should not overpower the dog by approaching any closer than twenty feet or showing a great deal of dominance. At long range, he can be verbally abusive, but his body language will appear cowardly as he nervously circles the dog.

He will be armed with a burlap bag and a bite tube, or bite tug. A burlap bag is less intimidating to a dog, so I like to begin protection training with a burlap bag and work up to a bite tube when the dog's confidence is stronger. Both are used to agitate the dog in an underhanded, flicking manner, but they are not meant to be offensive weapons. The agitator's role during the test for courage is to play a deranged coward, not a formidable foe. Protection training equipment can be bought at www.bridgeportequipment.com.

Following the sixty-second test, the agitator should run away, expressing as much fear as he can. Should the dog exhibit any protective behavior during the test (e.g., barking, lunging, or growling at the agitator), the agitator must run away as soon as the dog postures his dominance. Few dogs react defensively during these tests, but occasionally you meet a dog prodigy.

My two-year-old Doberman pinscher, Rocky, was a dog that "came out" on his first encounter with the criminal element. A friend, who had trained military guard dogs in the Philippines, offered to help with Rocky's protection training. After parking his car down the street, he began sneaking up to my property. Meanwhile, I was waiting in the yard with Rocky on lead.

I had no reason to think Rocky would respond defensively during his test for courage. He was a social dog that had never met a stranger—that is, until he saw the strange man coming down the street. The moment he saw Steve doing his imitation of a sneak thief slithering from tree to tree, Rocky alerted to the strange behavior in an unusual manner. His body language resembled a playful invitation, with his front end lowered to the ground and his head positioned between his front paws, but then a sound emanated from Rocky that could only be described as a deranged Swiss bear – it was part roar and part yodel. And then, like a coiled spring, Rocky lunged against the lead, pulling me awkwardly forward. After regaining my footing, I motioned for Steve to come inside the fence. Steve shook his head. I asked him again, but I couldn't convince him that I had control of the beast, so Rocky had to settle for a bite as Steve held his padded arm over the fence.

Rocky was a natural. He didn't need to learn how to protect his family—that was part of his instinctive make-up. His natural protective instinct had been engaged and nurtured during his pack training. Because he felt connected to my family, Rocky was more than willing to protect me.

Six protection-training classes were all that Rocky needed. He made full bites from the start and would release his bite on command. As a pack member protecting his family, Rocky's intention was to discipline the aggressive stranger. When you witness a dog defending his family without malice, you will be impressed with his professional demeanor.

Finding a qualified person to agitate your dog is critical. Successful protection training depends on the ability of this individual. If he is not up to the task, he will adversely affect the outcome. If he is not able to read a dog's emotions and take direction from you, he should not be considered for the job. Before you begin your dog's protection training, the agitator must have a clear understanding of his role. In addition to reading this chapter, some rehearsal time without the dog will be beneficial for both you and your assistant.

During the test for courage and protection training, the agitator's behavior will be erratic and exaggerated, both physically and emotionally. His exaggerated body language will draw attention to his agitated emotional state. During the commission of a violent crime, the brain triggers an adrenalin rush for the criminal. Dogs can readily detect the subtle changes in body chemistry and body language that occur when a person is extremely agitated and submissive. For this reason, the agitator must be able to project appropriate fear, anger, cowardice, and dominance to the dog. While he is projecting his arsenal of emotions, he must also be responding to the dog's emotions. In order to grow the dog's confidence, the agitator must fearfully retreat whenever the dog responds with dominance or submission.

Following the test, a failing grade will be given to the dog that expresses fear or tries to run away. A passing grade will be given to the dog that stands his ground or moves closer to me. Should the dog exhibit any defensive posturing, such as raising his hackles, barking, growling, or lunging at the attacker, he will get a high mark for natural courage. However, if the dog tries to run away or responds with any fearful expression, he will fail the test for courage. Without natural courage, a dog cannot usually learn to be courageous.

Pack Protection Training

I will give the same test for courage the following day, and if the dog passes that one as well, we can begin his protection training. The cardinal rule for protection training is as follows: The agitator must not overpower the dog or cause him to shy away during his agitation. The dog must always feel confident during and victorious following each of these confrontations. If the dog responds in any anxious manner, the agitator must make a fearful retreat and become less threatening with his agitation. With any confident or defensive behavior, he should also make a quick retreat before returning for another encounter.

During early protection training, the agitator's body language will alternate between fear and cowardice to anger and dominance, as he agitates the dog from long range. Meanwhile, I will maintain my position behind the dog as the agitator circles our position. If the dog backs against my legs, he is using me for emotional support—so I will be supportive by holding my position.

As the cowardly mugger nervously creeps along, he can use the burlap bag to flick in the dog's direction in a teasing manner. Should the dog turn away during his agitation, the agitator should slap the ground with the bag. As soon as the dog turns his attention to the sound of the bag slapping the ground, the agitator should express fear and retreat a few steps. As subtle as the dog's behavior will be when he turns to look at the agitator, it will be a positive, defensive response; therefore the agitator should respond with a fearful retreat. The dog will be encouraged to "play the game" each time the agitator makes a fearful retreat. I will praise the dog heartily when he responds with any confident behavior, and encourage him during each encounter with the agitator.

Whether or not the dog responds defensively to the agitation, the agitator will make a fearful retreat at the end of each lesson. I will then praise the dog enthusiastically, as though he snatched me from the jaws of death.

When you recruit an agitator who can read a dog's body language and respond appropriately, your dog will gain confidence with each encounter with his nemesis. As the dog's confidence grows, the agitator will be responding with closer and stronger agitation. Stronger agitation includes more threatening advances, agitation with the bite tube, and fixed stares. When giving a fixed stare, the agitator can either stand motionless or advance slowly toward the dog.

Your objective is to build the dog's confidence a little each day. This gradual progression of confidence building usually begins slowly and picks up steam along the way. For this reason, an awareness of your dog's emotional state during his agitation is necessary so you can end the lesson when the dog is showing increased courage. During the first week of protection training, lessons may only last for a couple of minutes; but when a dog realizes his defensive behavior produces a positive effect, his courage will be tapped, and his confidence will grow rapidly. For example, I will end the first protection lesson should the dog simply take a step toward the agitator. The following day I would expect the dog to display a little more confidence before ending the class.

The Bite

Following four to six weeks of protection training, most dogs will have dramatically grown in confidence. They will also be expressing their courage by standing up to the agitator. They will either be showing teeth and barking or lunging at the attacker and biting the bite tube. When your dog is confidently lunging against the lead, you can prepare him for a sleeve bite by allowing him to take out his frustration on the bite tube.

The bite tube, or bite tug, is used to agitate, but it should only be flicked underhanded at the dog's legs and face. Each time the tube is flicked against the dog, he will become increasingly agitated. When he bites the tube, the agitator can resist for a few seconds before dropping his weapon and retreating. Your dog may want to bite and shake the tube as a means of venting his agitation.

The agitator will make three or four threatening advances with the goal of ending each lesson on a high note—that is, when the dog is showing more courage than the day before. Should there be any expression of apprehension, the agitator should retreat in a fearful manner and become less confrontational, until the dog's anxiety is replaced with confidence.

If your dog is not progressing by the end of the fourth week, you should end his protection training. While most stable, young adult dogs are mature enough to handle this stressful activity, not every dog will want to participate. If your dog is taking no interest in his protection training, you should postpone his protection training for a few months. Some dogs mature slower than others.

Dogs can sense our emotions, so the agitator must remain in character and be able to express his emotions at a moment's notice. Stable dogs know when someone is mentally unstable. They can also distinguish between friendly roughhousing and aggressive threats. For the dog's benefit, you will need to impress the importance of staying in character to your assistant. You don't want your dog to think that stable and friendly people can suddenly become a threat.

When you give protection training to a pack member, it will not change the dog's demeanor or personality. He will remain your stable pack member, but he will also be courageous and protective. Because you have spent countless hours socializing your dog to all the "good guys" in the world, he will not suddenly become distrustful of strangers. In between protection training classes, you can continue your normal daily routine with your dog, but, following each protection-training workout, you should give your dog some downtime to relax and take a nap.

Stable pack members instinctively protect their loved ones. We engage these protective instincts during pack training and reinforce them during protection training. Your leadership and pack training has instilled confidence and courage in your young dog. As a result, he will not be distressed by normal human activity; he will trust friends and strangers alike; and he will now protect his family at the appropriate time. It's a natural progression, but it must progress with your full understanding of pack-animal behavior and diligent management. By following a pack-training regimen throughout a pup's development, you can begin his protection training when he reaches maturity.

When your dog is offering strong resistance to the agitator, he will be ready to make a bite on a padded sleeve. His frustration, combined with his increasing confidence, will make it possible for him to do the unthinkable—to bite a human.

An appropriate sleeve for a first bite is a soft, adolescent (beginner) sleeve (www.leerburg.com). A soft sleeve will make it easier for him to hold his bite. Before using the sleeve to agitate the dog, you should allow the dog to see the sleeve on the agitator's arm for a few lessons. In the meantime, the agitator will continue teasing the dog with his weapon of choice and resisting the dog when he makes a bite, but the dog must win all the tugs-of-war and be allowed to possess the bite tube when the agitator retreats.

When the dog's confidence and courage has peaked, the agitator should give the dog the opportunity to make a bite by moving the sleeve closer to his mouth. When the dog is lunging against the lead, the agitator should lean forward and offer the sleeve. The act of moving the sleeved arm toward the dog will produce a bite reflex. The agitator should cry out when the dog bites the sleeve. This submissive outcry will be conducive to a young dog's growing confidence. As soon as the dog makes a bite, the agitator should drop the sleeve and run away, allowing the dog to possess his new prize. Your dog may feel the need to bite and shake the sleeve, which is natural and permissible.

If the dog's first bite is a solid bite, you should allow him two or three more encounters before ending the class, but the agitator should offer the sleeve only when the dog is fully agitated. If he is apprehensive with his bite, you should continue to build his confidence for a few days before giving him the opportunity to make another bite. The ability to read a dog is crucial because of the necessity of your dog to feel confident during his workouts. You should always keep this in mind during his training.

Working five days a week, your confident dog should be making hard bites on the sleeve by the end of the eighth week of protection training. With your dog's newfound confidence, you can condition him to resist an adversary who fights back. The agitator can stimulate the dog's courage by resisting his defensive behavior for longer periods of time. Instead of dropping the sleeve and retreating following a bite, he can resist the dog's effort to drive him away. The sleeve can be used to lift and pull against the dog's bite in a tug-of-war, but as before, the agitator will end each battle by dropping the sleeve and retreating.

When the dog is making consistent, hard bites and resisting the agitator's assault, you can teach him to release his bite on command. Following a battle on the sleeve, the agitator should stop resisting the dog's defensive effort. Instead of dropping the sleeve and running away, the agitator should stand upright and motionless. If the dog releases his bite before you instruct him to do so, the agitator should resume his assault. The dog should hold his grip until he is told to "Out". When the agitator has surrendered, and the dog is holding onto the sleeve, you can teach your dog to release his bite. You should give the Out command while pulling back on the leash. If you cannot coax the dog to release the sleeve, you can repeat the command in a firm tone, "That's enough…out." If your dog still doesn't comply, you can make the dog let go of the sleeve by pushing quickly against his throat with your open, free hand. This will cause him to open his mouth and release his bite. When he releases his bite, you should congratulate your dog and allow him to escort the prisoner back to his car. As the agitator drives away, you can celebrate your dog's courageous and defensive behavior.

Protection training will take ten to twelve weeks to achieve what I have described, but this is only a general guideline and not meant to be strictly followed. Your dog's growing confidence, courage, and enthusiasm is more important than a rigid schedule. Through controlled and progressive agitation, most pack-trained dogs will enjoy this activity as a game of disciplining-the-bad-guy. Once he is making consistent bites and releasing on command, you should end the daily lessons. Excessive training (i.e., continuing daily workouts after the dog has proved himself) can make a dog feel anxious, as though he is always expecting to be attacked by every stranger he meets. Excessive training can also make a dog bite-happy (i.e., a dog that is too eager to make a bite).

When your dog has completed his protection training, you will not see a change in his temperament or disposition. He will still be a stable pack member and your loving family pet, but he will also have the confidence to defend his family at the appropriate time.

Pack-trained dogs make wonderful family protectors. Not only is it possible to have a protective family dog, it is a natural progression for stable pack members.

18

Which Breeds Make the Best Protection Dogs?

German Shepherd

The German shepherd is a medium to large dog that is highly adaptable and impressive, both in the working arena and at home. Males weigh 75 to 100 pounds at a height of 23 to 26 inches at the withers. Females are somewhat smaller at 22 to 24 inches. As pack protectors, quality German shepherds are highly regarded. Their alertness, courage, and loyalty, combined with high intelligence, cunning, and a love of children, make them the total package. The only problem is finding a quality German shepherd.

German shepherds were historically bred to be herders, and they were second to none in courage and devotion to their livestock and owners. German shepherds are presently being employed as police and military K-9 dogs, guide dogs, search dogs, and guard dogs. A superior sense of smell also makes them proficient in bomb and drug detection.

The German shepherds' courage is legendary in the dog world. A German shepherd will routinely stand his ground against an angry mob or rush into a burning building to save his family. The courage, devotion, and intelligence of the German shepherd make them highly regarded by law enforcement agencies throughout the world.

Doberman Pinscher

Another German breed to consider is the Doberman pinscher. Males stand 25 to 27 inches and weigh 65 to 90 pounds. Females are somewhat smaller. Doberman pinschers most obvious trait is their attentiveness, which is often mistaken for aggressiveness, but it's their alertness that makes them watch people so intently. The cropping of their ears only adds to the menacing illusion. The custom of cropping Doberman's ears began during the Second World War to protect their dropped ears from being torn as they ran through heavy brush. Today it is done for cosmetic reasons.

As a protection dog, a stable Doberman pinscher is an excellent choice. The only drawback is their need for extensive exercise. If not given frequent opportunities to exercise, they will usually devise their own means of expelling their nervous energy—and that doesn't bode well for your home and yard. The end result of not being exercised can be destructive behavior or aggressive, barking behavior. Doberman pinschers make wonderful pack members and awesome protection dogs, when they receive leadership and ample exercise. My advice for Doberman owners is to schedule their pups thirty to sixty minutes of off lead exercise every other day.

Rottweiler

The history of this German breed goes back to the days of Roman Empire. Over the last twenty years, the Rottweiler's popularity as a family pet has grown rapidly. Male Rottweilers should be 25 to 27 inches in height and weigh 100 to 120 pounds—females, 23 to 25 inches and 90 to 110 pounds.

Throughout ancient history, Rottweilers were used as boar hunters and cattle guards for marching armies. Their devotion and courage made them highly regarded in their work and legendary in their contributions. Marching armies would sometimes hang their money purses around their dogs' necks as a security measure.

Rottweilers are well known in Europe and the United States for their strong protective instincts. Their demeanor is usually low-key around the home, and they do not require rigorous physical exercise. While all pups test their owners, Rottweiler pups often take it to a higher level. These pups need pack training, and obedience training can begin as early as three months if the pup is displaying dominant and aggressive behavior.

When I am asked to evaluate a litter of Rottweiler pups for a client wanting a protective family dog, I will first evaluate the pup's parents. If they prove to be stable pack members, I will give their pups my consideration. I would not, however, recommend a Rottweiler pup unless I could evaluate both the pup and the parents. When a Rottweiler becomes a pack leader, the consequences can be tragic for its owners. On the current top-10 list of biting dogs, the Rottweiler is now the most likely breed to kill a human, according to the CDC.

English Mastiff

English Mastiffs are physical giants. The AKC Standard sets the minimum height for males at 30 inches, females, 27 ½ inches. Males weigh 130 pounds or more, and two-hundred-pound English Mastiffs are not uncommon. In ancient times, mastiffs were ferocious war dogs in the Roman army. For centuries English mastiffs have been working as sentry dogs in Europe. As a sentry—a dog that announces the arrival of strangers—his massive size alone will discourage all trespassers. Personally, I have never trained an English mastiff to be protective, but this is not to suggest it could not or is not being done. But as sentries, they are historically acclaimed as staunch defenders of their territory. They do not require a lot of exercise, but they usually prefer being outdoors. As with other mastiff breeds, stubbornness is a common trait of English mastiffs.

Boxer

Often overlooked by those considering a family protection dog, boxers are deserving of consideration. The height of a male will be 22 to 25 inches, females, 21 to 23 inches. A quality boxer is cunning, loyal, courageous, compactly muscular, and extremely athletic. They do require rigorous exercise, but as protection dogs, these wonderful dogs would rank high on my protection-dog wish list. Max, the boxer, is a dog that possesses the extraordinary ability of discernment when it comes to reading the character of people. Being a social creature, Max loves his friends and enjoys having contact with strangers, but there was one man that he took exception to. Whenever this man would pass Max and his owner, in their condominium, Max would go on the alert by posturing in a defensive manner. If they encountered the man on the elevator, Max would refuse to allow his owner to enter. It was learned at a later time that the strange man had a history of sex crimes.

Other Possibilities

As a rule, the working breeds are preferable protection dogs; but other breeds, as well as mixed breeds, can be considered for protection training, as long as the dog is a stable pack member and has natural courage. Pack training indirectly activates a dog's natural protective instinct. This occurs when you bond with your pup and establish social order. During protection training, you are simply reaping the harvest that results when a pack connection is made with a dog.

The only breeds that I would not recommend for protection training are the dog-aggressive breeds, such as pit bulls, Presa Canario, chow, and Akita. Not that a stable-tempered dog of one of these breeds could not participate in this training, but the odds are stacked against you because of the genetic dog-aggressive predisposition. Neither would I recommend purchasing a trained protection dog, for a number of reasons: These dogs are raised in kennels and have had little or no experience living in a family environment; commonly, they are hyperactive dogs with a strong prey drive; and bonding with an adult dog is not a simple undertaking.

My recommendation is to adopt a quality, dominant-submissive pup from stable, well-mannered parents and become the pup's pack trainer. The instinct to protect their families is intact in all higher animals. While these instincts can become perverted (dictators and fear-biters), a stable dog can be protective without becoming a liability.

When considering a litter of pups, consider more than the price of the pup. Paying a high price for a pup doesn't mean you are getting what you want. If you are looking for a working dog or wish to participate with your dog in competition, look for a pup that has competitive protection dogs (Schutzhund- and Sieger-titled dogs) in his pedigree. If you are looking for a protective family pet, you should locate a mated pair of stable, well-mannered family dogs and select one of their dominant-submissive pups. If the pups' parents are friendly, stable dogs, you can validate your pup's evaluation by checking the pup's pedigree. Obedience-titled dogs and champion show dogs in the bloodline would give more credence to the pup's character and potential.

As you can see, this protection-training course is an eighteen-month regimen, and it began the day your pup came home with you. Protection training should not be offered to a dog that has not been socialized and pack trained. Your dog must first and foremost be your stable pack member. Teaching an alpha dog to bite will only put you and your family at risk, but teaching a stable pack member to be protective is one of the most rewarding experiences a dog owner can have.

19

Myth or Reality

The sensory abilities of dogs often defy our understanding. Which of their senses are dogs using when they travel hundreds of miles to reunite with their families? We know that dogs can detect our emotional state through their sense of smell, but they even seem to know what we are thinking. Consider these examples: What are dogs sensing when they know we are preparing to take them for a walk, even before we reach for the leash? And why do hunting dogs get excited when their owners walk past the gun cabinet on opening day of hunting season?

In England, animal behaviorists have tested the extrasensory abilities of dogs. A certain behaviorist noticed that her dog was always waiting by the front door when she returned home from work. Her mother had also noticed the dog approaching the front door well prior to her daughter's arrival. Curiously, the time spent waiting at the door was the same time it took his owner to drive home. The dog's owner wondered if her dog was only remembering or anticipating the time of day she returned home each day. To determine this, she returned home from work at different times each day, recording the time she decided to leave and the time she actually left her office. At home, her mother was noting the time the dog went to the front door each day. As it turned out, the dog was going to the front door when his owner made her decision to leave work.

Certain words and phrases are easier for dogs to comprehend. When a barking tone is used, the word "no" is readily understood. This is why I recommend using "no" as your primary verbal correction. The phrase "cut it out" also has a dominant tone, and the word "okay" is usually interpreted in the literal sense

Because dogs are emotion detectors, they respond favorably to those who can express their emotions. It's no secret that the best trainers are expressive with their dogs. Dogs express their emotions in a wide variety of ways. We know that dogs grieve for their loved ones when they are sick or pass away; and they also express their joy when their family members return home each day. When a dog is filled with joy, he will often shake his head and body. You may notice this when you ask your dog if he wants to go for a walk or if he wants a treat. He will smile and shake his head. Sometimes his whole body will shake, as though he is trying to shake water off his back.

Something that intrigues me is how dogs behave around babies. Dogs often become paternal caretakers around babies, as though the babies were their concern and responsibility. Hyperactive dogs will usually be on their best behavior when a baby is present, as though they understand the baby could be hurt should they become too excited.

I also see this attitude in dogs that live with disabled people. A former student was a schnauzer that lived with an invalid lady. Because of her immobility, she could not give the dog proper exercise, so the dog burned off his nervous energy by running laps inside the house. When the owner walked through the house during one of her dog's marathons, he would continue to run, but he would avoid bumping into her as he ran past. It was quite a feat, considering there were only a few inches on either side of the lady for the dog to pass in the hallway. The dog either knew she would likely be injured if he collided with her or she was in pain and didn't want to add to her misery.

Not only can dogs detect human emotion, they seem to be able to discern good and evil. It has been reported that dogs become frantic to the point of hysteria when they witness supernatural phenomena. It is commonly reported that UFOs terrify dogs. Chained dogs have choked themselves to death trying to escape from nearby UFOs. Dogs will also be terrified during satanic rituals, and tracking dogs will not track Bigfoot (Sasquatch). This is truly puzzling because Bigfoot is known to have awful body odor. The odor is often compared to rotting garbage, but tracking dogs become extremely fearful when they encounter the beast's pungent scent. No one knows why these courageous bloodhounds tuck their tails and refuse to follow the trail.

Many dogs can discern a person's character and intent. Two of my dogs have demonstrated this ability. One dog came to the rescue of my wife in a parking lot. The other dog alerted to an ill-natured neighbor when they met for the first time. As soon as my surly neighbor entered my home, Rocky, a three-year-old Doberman, instantly fixated on this man. Rocky was a trained protection dog, but there was not an aggressive bone in his body. He liked everyone, but when this man entered his home, Rocky immediately began posturing and staring at him.

If a dog has a stable temperament, and has been socialized to strangers, he will enjoy being included at social gatherings. However, when one of these dogs appears concerned or anxious around an individual, there is usually a reason for the dog's reaction. If the person has a fear of dogs, you will sometimes get this response from a stable dog. Fear produces subtle changes in our body scent and body language. This disparity will make a dog curious and somewhat cautious. (This is why a dog will want to sniff and follow a frightened child.) However, if the person does not fit this profile, your dog may be sensing something you should.

The dog that came to the rescue of my wife was a six-month-old Doberman pinscher. He had accompanied my wife to a grocery store, and when she returned to the car with her midnight snack, a stranger approached her and tried to make conversation. When he asked if Ace were friendly, she replied that he was and opened the car door. Without hesitation, Ace jumped from the car, approached the stranger, and began growling and baring his teeth. That was the first and only person that Ace took exception to. He was extremely social, but that night he was sensing something he had never experienced. Even though he was only a pup, he was more than willing to protect his family.

A stable dog's ability to read human emotion and character makes him a wonderful companion and a valuable security asset. Combining deductive reasoning with a keen sense of hearing makes a pack-trained dog one of the most dependable security systems. They hear everything, including sounds you miss; and they will respond to anything out of the ordinary, like a door opening late at night or a sound outside a window. Even if you haven't trained your dog to be protective, that doesn't necessarily mean he won't protect you.

I have seen this natural protective instinct many times and have read countless stories of family pets rescuing and protecting their families—so keep this in mind when you think that your dog's training takes up a lot of your time. The time invested in your pup's development will be repaid with years of friendship, companionship, and family security. Criminals have been polled about their opinions concerning home security. The vast majority of convicts believe that the best deterrent to burglary and home invasions is a dog in the home.

Dogs even seem to understand the motives of their owners' behavior. During her formative years, my wolf dog had a history of being spiteful. Even though Cheyenne had been conditioned to be self-reliant when she was home alone, she occasionally copped an attitude and looked for something to steal or shred when I left her behind. I would occasionally find my reading glasses, a shoe, or a hat in the yard. Her first spiteful deed was shredding a phonebook. Twice she took loaves of bread from the kitchen counter and played shred-the-bread in the living room. On another occasion she stole a plate of oatmeal cookies and carried it into the living room. After unwrapping it carefully, she ate what she wanted before stashing the remaining cookies between the couch cushions, in my bed, the closet, and a box in the storage room.

My solution was to set a trap for my spiteful, thieving wolf by placing a set mousetrap in the center of the kitchen table with three pieces of cheese leading up to it. The third piece of cheese was butted against the base of the trap. After turning on the video camera, I drove around the block. When I returned home, the sprung mousetrap was on the floor, the cheese was gone, and Cheyenne came slinking from the bedroom. When I viewed the videotape, I saw something I had not expected.

As I backed the truck down the driveway, Cheyenne was spying from the living room window. When I drove away, her tail began to wag. Then she walked over to the video camera, looking into the lens, and yodeled, "Aa-ooo-wa." After circling the kitchen table twice, she jumped up and carefully took the piece of cheese adjacent to the mousetrap. Then she returned for the remaining cheese. Following her morning snack, as she licked the taste from her lips, her attention turned to the trap—and it didn't take long for her curiosity to pique her interest. With her front paws on the table, she lifted the trap from the table by its wooden base—and then it sprung in her mouth. The total surprise and pure fright caused her to jump back about six feet. After taking a long look at the trap on the floor, she sheepishly trotted off to the safety of the bedroom. If I had thought she might try to pick up the trap, I would not have used the mousetrap in this manner. I would have placed a sheet of newspaper over the trap. Thankfully, no harm was done.

A week later, I gave her another opportunity to be tempted. However, this time I didn't set the trap. I hoped she wouldn't make the same mistake twice, but I didn't want to take the chance. I did, however, want to know if she had learned her lesson. On the film, she looked at the bait and the trap, and then made a conscious effort to avoid the kitchen table.

Dogs are cunning and discerning animals, but I wonder what she was saying when she yodeled at the video camera. Did she know I was setting a trap for her?

Max, the boxer, also has demonstrated his ability as a problem solver. His owner bought a "scat mat" for her antique loveseat, with the idea of keeping Max off the furniture. After placing the dog-repelling device on the couch, Max checked it out, only to receive a buzzing sensation on his nose. His solution was to carry the device into the back yard and bury it.

Another example of canine cunning is the dog that can slip out of his buckled collar at will. A dog that is walked on lead with a loose fitting collar often knows he can escape from his owner's control by twisting his neck so the collar slips off. This talent will usually be reserved for times when a dog is stimulated to be free of his owner.

Many people believe you cannot correct a dog for misbehavior after the fact. This suggests that a dog has no short-term memory and no sense of right and wrong. There are many examples of why this is a misconception, but here is one of my favorites. My stepmother had left two frozen steaks on the kitchen counter to thaw while the family went water skiing. Upon arriving home, Betsy, our six-year-old golden retriever did not greet us at the front door in her customary manner. Instead, she slinked to the far end of the living room where she began expressing passive submission. Her guilty expression was made before we had discovered that she had eaten one of the steaks.

A dog's ability to track cannot be measured in terms we understand. A good example of this was a bloodhound that was called to help with a missing-child case. There were no witnesses to the child's disappearance from her home, so the officers called for their tracking dog. Upon arriving at the home of the missing girl, the handler allowed his dog to become acquainted with the child's scent. From her bedroom, the dog followed her scent into the front yard. After sniffing excitedly at the end of the driveway, the dog began coursing down the street in a S-pattern. The handler informed the missing girl's family that the dog was following the kidnapper's car.

The bloodhound eventually led them to a freeway entrance several miles away, so they transported the dog in a police cruiser to the next freeway exit and walked the dog past the exit ramp. When the dog walked past the exit, they loaded up and drove to the next exit. This procedure was repeated numerous times before the dog led them down a particular off ramp. The girl's body was found a short distance from the freeway—thirty miles from her home.

The bloodhound had followed the scent of the girl deposited on the roads and freeway by the wind blowing through the kidnapper's car. They believed the child was taken from the end of her driveway because of the dog's particular interest at that spot. The girl's sudden fear had produced a different scent on that spot. The dog had detected the change in the girl's scent and recognized it as the smell of fear.

After four decades of training dogs, what impresses me most about dogs is their friendly attitude toward the ones they love. Such a nurturing spirit is not always evident in other members of the animal kingdom. Adolph Murie said it was the wolf's friendliness that stood out from their other traits. However, Murie's research did little to change public opinion or the decisions to wipe the wolf from the face of the earth. Mankind has been hell-bent for the extermination of the wolf for many centuries.

Have you ever wondered about the inspiration that created the villainous character, "the big, bad wolf?" Throughout most of their history, Europeans have believed that wolves were evil creatures. The werewolf legend and the portrayal of the wolf as an evil character in their fables were likely spawned from this erroneous belief. From the resulting trumped-up fear came the decisions to exterminate the wolves. These fables of the big, bad wolf may also be influencing the psychology of people who are currently protesting the introduction of wolves on federal lands.

Few words trigger as much emotion as the word "wolf." At a local television station, I was waiting to be interviewed by the news anchor. Cheyenne and I had arrived a half hour before we were scheduled to go on the air, and during that time, a particular station employee stopped to pet Cheyenne each time he walked past. She was enjoying his attention until he asked, "What kind of dog is she?" "Wolf and malamute," I answered. At that moment, his expression changed from a smile to a grimace, as he jumped back with his hands in the air and cried out, "Wolf!"

Throughout centuries of persecution, wolves always found a way to survive. And today we are still struggling with whether or not wolves have the right to exist in the wild. Once we hold a belief, we will resist anyone who contradicts our belief system. We have all experienced this truism at work, and at home, when someone has a new idea about how a job could be done differently. The longer the company or person has been doing a particular task, the harder they will resist change. World-renowned animal trainers, Gunther Gable-Williams, Tom Dorrance, and Ray Hunt challenged the status quo throughout their lives, and they never wavered in their belief that intelligent animals respond best to love, leadership, and communication.

Another example of an established idea that resists change is the belief that Doberman pinschers are inherently dangerous dogs. Many people have an irrational fear of this breed. When I was a child, someone brought a beautiful and well-trained Doberman pinscher to our family reunion. Upon their arrival, the guests began sharing stories of Doberman pinschers attacking their owners and killing children. Some even called them "devil dogs." Throughout my life, I have heard incredible stories about Doberman pinschers. Some people believe that a Doberman's brain actually outgrows its skull, and this is why they go insane and attack their owners. Of course this urban myth is almost laughable—but why are these stories so long-lived?

The Doberman is a relatively new breed, so tracing their history is easier than the older breeds. It was during the Second World War that the U.S. government began to seriously consider using dogs in the military. When the war broke out, the German military had 200,000 trained dogs in service. The United States military had a few sled dogs in Alaska. To correct the disadvantage, the military began the Dogs for Defense program. In this government program, American citizens donated their family dogs to the military to help with the war effort. The athleticism and work ethic of Doberman pinschers made them well suited for military life. And with a little genetic manipulation, these military Doberman pinschers became legendary war dogs.

During the war, Doberman breeders began breeding their dominant-aggressive dogs and bitches. From the resulting litters, they selected the dominant-aggressive pups and bred them to each other at maturity. This breeding practice produced Doberman pinschers with extremely dominant-aggressive temperaments and a higher percentage of dominant pups in each litter. When this procedure was done in successive generations, the military produced a bloodline of bloodthirsty Dobermans. The German troops were reportedly more afraid of those wild-eyed Doberman patrols than they were the advancing Allied army.

WWII Doberman pinscher military K-9 units were well known for their ferociousness, and it may be this perception that remains with us today. This perception flies in the face of the reality that Dobermans are statistically one of the safest working breeds. The unpopularity of the breed and the American Kennel Club (AKC) share most of the credit for the transformation of the Doberman temperament. For a dog to compete in AKC sanctioned bench shows, he must be good-natured and social when a judge inspects him during a competition. As a result, modern Doberman pinscher breeders have bred the aggressiveness out of the breed. However, these stories of crazed Dobermans turning on their owners are still being told. Ignorance, when it comes to dog behavior, fuels this urban legend.

When a breed of dog becomes popular, it usually sounds the death knell for the breed. When there is a demand for a particular breed, backyard breeders, with no regard for the integrity of the breed, will breed these dogs at every opportunity. As a result, the popular breeds are often the most affected breeds.

Your pup's gene pool has more to do with his potential than public opinion. Labrador retriever field trial champions produce more pups with strong prey drive than Labrador retriever champion bench dogs. Gun-shy dogs produce a higher percentage of pups with this fault. Dogs with stable temperaments and friendly dispositions produce more pups with those traits. And dogs with less than stable tempers will produce more of their kind.

This is why I advise people, who are looking for a family pet, to choose a breed that fits their lifestyle, whether active or sedentary, and then adopt a pup from stable, well-mannered family pets. If you want a hunting dog that can also be a family pet, you should locate a mated pair of stable hunting dogs with good dispositions and choose one of their dominant-submissive pups. The pup's parents should be verified as stable pack members, and they should be responsive to their owner in the field. If only the dam is on site, you should insist on meeting the sire. If possible, meeting the grandparents would give you a better indication of your pup's potential.

In every litter, there will be one dominant-aggressive pup. Unless you are looking for a challenge, I would not recommend adopting one of these pups. As well, I would not recommend an omega pup for a family with small children. An omega pup is the most submissive pup in the litter and may be intimidated by young children or an extremely active lifestyle.

After discounting the alpha and omega pup, the remaining pups can be tested for various positive traits. Unlike the alpha and omega pup, they will neither be totally dominant nor totally submissive; and each pup will be submissive to those above him in the pack hierarchy. In effect, dominant-submissive pups will be trained to submit to your authority. By being able to evaluate the temperament, disposition, and social status of a pup, you can improve your chances of choosing the best pup for your family.

We see the effects of bad genetics in many dog breeds. The most popular breeds are also the most affected. The Labrador retriever has been one of the most popular breeds in the U.S. for many decades. As a consequence of their popularity, the integrity of the breed has been compromised. Over the last forty years, I have trained hundreds of Labrador retrievers. Labs with stable temperaments and strong prey drive were once the norm—today they are the exception.

Stable-tempered dogs are able to focus on the task at hand. This positive trait can be witnessed by observing a dog during routine activities. Dogs with focus are purposeful during their activities, whether it's scouting a trail or socializing with people or dogs. Unstable-tempered dogs are all over the map with their behavior, and everything distracts them. They are often highly excitable and hyperactive dogs.

My father used to breed and train golden retrievers, Labrador retrievers, pointers and English setters. Of those breeds, the Labs and golden retrievers have become popular family pets during my lifetime; the pointers and English setters have not. The English setters and pointers that I meet today are much the same as the ones I trained forty years ago. The golden retrievers and Labs have not been so fortunate. The resulting fault, stemming from indiscriminate breeding, is similar in effect and appearance to attention-deficit disorder (ADD) in children. Dogs with this disorder are somewhat scatterbrained and unable to focus on an activity for more than a few seconds at a time. When you meet a dog like this, you can suspect that one (or both) of the pup's parents suffers from the same fault.

In years past, dog breeders had a better grasp on the importance of genetics. They knew that special dogs produced better pups than inferior dogs. Through this simple philosophy, purebred dogs remained sound for many generations. Yet today, after only two generations, breeders have done tremendous damage to the integrity of many breeds of dogs. Labrador retrievers, golden retrievers, German shepherds, cocker spaniels, poodles, Dalmatians, Rottweilers, and pit bulls are now demonstrating unstable temperaments at an alarming rate.

We have seen the dog-bite problem dramatically increase over the last thirty years—from less than one million dog bites in 1970 to nearly five million dog bites in 2003. We also see a correlation between the list of biting dogs and the most popular breeds. In the '80s the cocker spaniel was the most popular dog—and the most likely dog to bite. Over the last thirty years, Rottweilers and pit bulls have become popular family pets. They have also become the two most likely breeds to bite—and the most likely to kill: 50 percent of fatal dog attacks are attributed to these two breeds (U. S. Humane Society).

When considering a pup for your family, his genetics should influence your decision more than public opinion. If his parents are stable and loving pets, your pup will likely have the same potential. Once you have decided on a compatible breed, and have evaluated and chosen an appropriate pup, your first order of business is pack training. By socializing your pup to the outside world and establishing social order, you will prevent the common behavioral problems that result from neglect.

What all pups are looking for is someone to lead them. Along the way, you will be learning how to read your dog. Learning to read a dog cannot be gleaned entirely from books, even though this is the best place to start. The only question is, which books? *National Geographic* has published many excellent articles on wolves and dogs. Adolph Murie, J.P. Scott, L. David Mech, Michael W. Fox, and R. D. Lawrence are respected in their field and informative authors on wolf and dog behavior.

By studying wolves in their natural habitat, we can understand our dog's behavior and communication. This is not possible when wolves are confined. Determining the nature of the wolf by observing wolves in zoos is analogous to determining the nature of man by studying convicts. You will never see wolves pacing in the wild, yet when they are caged, this is a common behavior. Wild wolves are not a threat to humans, but caged wolves have attacked and killed their caretakers.

Unstable temperaments and dispositions are more common today than in years past. When I am asked to solve a dog's behavioral problem, I must first determine what the problem behavior is communicating. In order to understand the behavior, I must determine the dog's temperament and disposition. If the dog is anxious or neurotic, this may well be the cause of his problem behavior. If he is mentally and physically stable, the problem behavior is likely a testing behavior or a demonstration of authority. Thankfully, most dogs are not unstable or neurotic.

An extreme example of a neurotic dog is the fear-biter. These are not outwardly aggressive dogs, but they will sometimes bite when someone tries to pet them or walks past. Failing to socialize pups to strangers and traumatic events during their development can produce this abnormal behavior.

Another example of an abnormal disposition is the dog that becomes frantic following a sudden noise, such as thunder, gunfire, or motorcycles. When triggered, these dogs experience an adrenalin rush, making it impossible for them to remain under control. All they want to do is run away and hide.

Separation anxiety is the most common psychological problem for dogs and the most difficult to solve. Ironically, an ounce of prevention could have prevented the need for a pound of cure. Solving the problem of separation anxiety is always an uphill battle, but there is always hope for rehabilitating an anxious dog when patience and understanding are factored into his behavior modification.

Failing to socialize a pup to the outside world can produce a dog that appears secure at home but extremely stressed in new environments. While these dogs may not become panicky, they will be distressed when subjected to new environments. No quick or certain cures can be prescribed for this condition. Some anxious dogs can recover from their disorder, but many will not be able to overcome their distrust of strangers and strange environments. Whereas socialization is a simple and natural process for young pups, it is a tedious undertaking to teach an older dog to trust the world around him.

Everyone can have a great dog, if they know how to communicate with their dogs and have the time and diligence to implement a training regimen. Dogs are extremely intelligent and resilient animals, and even though they sometimes act the fool, they will always be loyal and devoted to their pack-families.

There is a great dog inside your pet, waiting to surface. He will materialize when he has a strong, loving, and active pack leader. If you can be that leader, your dog will want to be your pack member. He won't even care if you lose all your possessions and friends, as long as he can be with you. What better friend could anyone have!

20

Can you Read These Dogs?

Visualize these examples and determine what the dog is thinking or saying.

1. The dog that ignores an exuberant dog's attempts to engage him in play is saying: A. I'll play with you when I am ready. B. I don't understand what you want. C. I'm not feeling well.
2. The dog that stands with his mouth open and his tongue hanging, as his tail wags slowly and methodically is saying: A. Warning, stay away! B. Whassup? C. I'm dazed and confused.
3. The dog that greets another dog by standing erect and sniffing the dog's anal area is saying: A. I'm in charge here. B. I'll submit to you by sniffing your butt. C. Just checking to see what you had for dinner.
4. The dog that raises the hackles on his shoulders and back, as another dog approaches is saying: A. I'm scared of you. B. I'm agitated. C. I'll be submissive if you want.
5. The dog that raises his hackles at the base of his spine and lowers his head when approached by another dog is saying: A. I'm more than just a little nervous about you. B. I'm dominant. C. I think I have a flea.
6. A dog that stands motionless with his mouth closed, his head and ears pushed forward, and his tail wagging excitedly over his back is saying: A. Let's play! B. I'm too shy to play with you. C. Submit, or else I will discipline you.

7. The dog that places his feet on another dog's back is saying: A. Let's play. B. Tag, you're it. C. Tag, I win.

8. The pup that bites at your feet, hands, or clothing is saying: A. Oops! I thought it was a toy. B. I decide what I play with. C. I need a teething toy.

9. The pup that ignores his owner's call by walking away is saying: A. I'll come when I'm ready. B. Let's take a hike. C. I didn't hear you.

10. The pup that growls from his possession when someone approaches is saying: A. Don't steal my stuff. B. It's fun playing the tough guy. C. Let's just see how much authority I have around here.

11. The dog that nudges your arm with his head or prompts you with a paw is communicating: A. Pet me, now! B. I'm depressed. C. How can you resist all this cuteness?

12. The dog that lowers his tail and head but remains upright when another dog approaches in a dominant fashion is saying: A. I respectfully acknowledge you. B. You better submit to me. C. Please don't hurt me.

13. The dog that tucks his tail tightly and crouches to the ground when another dog approaches is saying: A. This is the big one Elizabeth—I'll be the one that's all chewed up! B. Scratch my belly. C. Let's wrestle.

14. The dog that tries to initiate a game of chase with other dogs is saying: A. Let's race. B. Chase me. C. Let's hunt.

15. The dog that gazes into your eyes with his mouth open and his ears cupped together and held out to the side is saying: A. It's good to be your pack member. B. You want to keep that face? C. Feed me.

16. The dog that stands erect with a closed mouth and his tail held over his back is saying: A. I'm dominant. B. How's this for a bird dog imitation? C. Let's play.

17. The dog that stares at another dog, with a closed mouth and a horizontal tail, as his ears push forward is saying: A. Prepare to be disciplined. B. Prepare to be licked. C. Prepare for some roughhousing.

18. A dog uses his body in a blocking manner against another dog or person is demonstrating: A. Dominance. B. Clumsiness. C. Playfulness.

19. A dominant dog that growls at you from your bed is saying: A. Sleep somewhere else. B. Just practicing being protective. C. Thought you were someone else.

20. The dog that growls softly when you bump him in bed but is not considered a testing dog is demonstrating: A. A grumpy disposition. B. Dominant-aggressive behavior. C. Playfulness.

21. The misbehaving dog that lowers his body, head, and tail when you approach is saying: A. Please don't beat me. B. Forgive me. C. Let's play.

22. The misbehaving dog that stands tall when you approach, with his head and tail held high is demonstrating: A. Pride. B. Dominance. C. Confusion.

23. The misbehaving dog that acts like nothing happened following a correction is demonstrating: A. Submission. B. Stubbornness. C. Confidence.

24. The dog that acts like he saw a ghost following a correction is expressing: A. Active submission. B. Extremely passive submission. C. A hallucination.

25. The dog that lowers his head a little and licks his mouth, following a correction, as he looks up at you is saying: A. Let's eat. B. Let's play. C. I submit to your authority.

26. The dog that urinates on your leg is saying: A. I thought you were a tree. B. When nature calls, you answer. C. I'll do with you as I please.

27. The dog that humps your leg is saying: A. Love is in the air. B. I need to have my vision checked. C. I'll do with you as I please.

28. The dog that urinates when you pet him is evidence of: A. A bladder problem or a passive-submission display. B. Tap water consumption. C. A testing behavior.

29. The house-trained dog that soils your house is demonstrating: A. Dominance. B. Forgetfulness. C. Neurotic behavior.

30. The dog that moves his head from side to side as you communicate with him is saying: A. It's hard to concentrate with all the distractions. B. Let me think this over. C. The answer is No.

31. The dog that chases its tail excessively is demonstrating: A. Playfulness. B. Dominance. C. Neurotic behavior.

32. The dog that bites at invisible flies is demonstrating: A. Superior vision. B. Dominance. C. Neurotic behavior.

33. The dog that shakes uncontrollably in social situations is experiencing: A. A climate change response. B. High anxiety. C. Active submission.

34. The dog that jumps onto you when you arrive home is usually saying: A. It's great to see you. B. Tag, you're it. C. I'm dominant.

35. The dog that routinely jumps onto you is saying: A. Let's play. B. I can dominate you. C. I'm glad to see you all the time.

36. The dog that tries to stand across a resting dog is demonstrating: A. Submission. B. Dominance. C. Playfulness.

37. The dog that tries to get between you and another dog or person is saying: A. Let's share the good times. B. I get first dibs on petting. C. I'll protect you.

38. The dog that pulls its owner down the street on lead is saying: A. Try and keep up—I'm taking the lead. B. I'm on a hot trail. C. Can we go home?

39. The dog that loves to play tug-of-war with you or other dogs: A. Is just having fun. B. Is getting good exercise. C. Is competing for power.

40. When a dog's tail begins to rise from its relaxed, hanging position, he is expressing: A. Arousal. B. Gas. C. Dominance.

41. When a dog's ears are cupped and his mouth is open, he is communicating: A. Joy. B. Dominance. C. Submission.

42. A dominant-aggressive male dog would best be companioned with: A. A dominant-submissive female. B. An omega female. C. His clone.

43. How much discipline should we give a pup? A. As much as you can bear. B. As much as the dog can bear. C. Only as much as needed to produce a submissive response.

ANSWERS:

1-A	8-B	15-A	22-B	29-A	36-B
2-B	9-A	16-A	23-B	30-B	37-B
3-A	10-C	17-A	24-B	31-C	38-A
4-B	11-A	18-A	25-C	32-C	39-C
5-A	12-A	19-A	26-C	33-B	40-A
6-C	13-A	20-A	27-C	34-A	41-A
7-C	14-B	21-B	28-A	35-B	42-A
					43-C

YOUR PACK RATING

Correct answers:

     40-43 ---------------------------------Congratulations, alpha pack leader.
     30-39-----------------------------Keep trying, Beta: second-in-command.
     16-29-------------------------------------Go to the back of the line, Omega.
      0-15-------------------------------------You may be better suited for a cat.

21

Dogs I Have Known and Love

Buster and Hansel

On my fifth birthday, I remember going to a kennel to pick out my first pup. Buster came home with me that day, but our time together was cut short by the distemper virus. Soon thereafter, my grandmother and Aunt Elizabeth gave me a Welch corgi. Hansel was a smart and extremely courageous dog. He saw himself as my personal bodyguard, but he also had his own agenda. Our neighbor, Addie Davis—who had taken a liking to Hansel—would offer him something tasty to eat whenever he came to visit. In short order, it became his habit to visit her each day for his five-o'clock snack. On many occasions Hansel demonstrated his courage and protective instinct as well as his cunning, memory, and sense of time.

Wink

I have heard it said that a dog trainer is someone who has owned a special dog— a dog that epitomizes intelligence, courage, loyalty, and friendship. Wink was such a dog. He was also the first dog I attempted to train. I don't think any of us appreciated how unique he was, even though everyone agreed that Wink was the best example of a golden retriever they had ever seen. On one occasion, Wink and I were playing in the front yard when a car with Georgia plates pulled off the highway. After taking a long look at Wink, the driver offered me $500 for the dog. Even though my summer job as a farm laborer earned me fifty cents an hour, I declined his offer, feeling offended and proud at the same time. Wink was much more than a beautiful dog. He also possessed a wonderful temperament and disposition.

When it came time to train Wink, I faced a dilemma. In 1964 most dog trainers were using force-training techniques, and stubborn and testing dogs would often be beaten into submission. While beating a dog wasn't an option, I knew of no other method of training a dog—so I struck out on my own. Having spent the previous summer hiking the trails behind our home, I had already formed a bond of friendship and leadership with Wink. As an eight-week-old pup, he had been eager to follow me down the trail, but when his stamina increased, so did his confidence and curiosity. When his curiosity led him down the trail without me, I used those opportunities to play hide-and-seek.

With each hike it became more evident that his behavior and attitude were changing. Instead of me watching him explore his world, Wink was now paying closer attention to me. After a couple of hikes and a few games of hide-and-seek, I found it difficult to hide without being seen. In order for Wink to know when I was attempting to hide, he had to voluntarily range within fifty yards of me. In short order this became his natural range.

Not only was he following my lead, his attitude was changing as well. I had become more than just a friend – I had become his pack leader. When it came time to teach Wink his obedience commands, I found him to be an enthusiastic student. In the summer of '64, I had stumbled onto something I call pack training. And after forty years of training dogs, I can report that pack training works with every breed of dog.

If your dog sees you as the pack leader, he will want to please you more than he'll want to test your authority. Training dogs has been my passion for most of my life, and I will be forever grateful to Wink, the greatest golden retriever I have ever known.

Ace

Ace was an eight-week-old Doberman pinscher that I adopted under less than ideal circumstances, knowing nothing of his family history. When he was five months old, he contracted red mange and was misdiagnosed until the parasites had covered his body. A year later the mange was somewhat under control, but Ace was losing the battle internally. The toxins in the mange dip were destroying his nervous system. He ultimately had to be destroyed once his nervous system began to shut down. He only lived for two years.

Ace was a social dog that loved everyone, but he instinctively knew when danger was present. This was demonstrated when Ace came to the rescue when my wife was approached by a suspicious stranger late at night in a parking lot. He alone had detected the threat. Even though he was only a six-month-old pup, Ace had demonstrated his willingness to defend his family by putting himself between my wife and danger.

Ace was a loving dog and a wonderful friend. We spent countless hours running and hiking in the Pacific Northwest. Even though his life caused him a lot of stress and pain, he never complained when I poured the burning mange dip on his raw skin. To their credit, dogs do not hold grudges, and they are always willing to forgive our shortcomings.

Kolohe

As a three-year-old German shepherd with no training, Kolohe was donated to the guard dog kennel where I worked in Hawaii. His stable temperament and his love for work made Kolohe a truly special dog. He was what dog trainers would call a natural. A natural is a dog with a strong desire to please his owner and an eagerness to perform some function, whether it's babysitting kids, hunting game, or protecting his family. Kolohe learned his obedience training in two weeks, and became a formidable family protection dog soon thereafter. Kolohe taught me that it is never too late to train a dog.

Dogs that are saved from an animal shelter or a chain in the yard, as was the case with Kolohe, will often show tremendous devotion to their liberators.

Rocky

Rocky was my thrice-adopted Doberman pinscher. His second owner had thought he could leave Rocky home alone while he was at work. His belief was short-lived. Upon arriving home to find his home in shambles, I received his phone call.

Dobermans have always been one of my favorite breeds because of their athleticism and exuberant dispositions. And being the outdoors type, Dobermans fit easily into my lifestyle. It will always be a special pleasure to watch a Doberman running at top speed. Physical exercise is a must, if you want a calm Doberman around the house. Giving regular exercise during their puppy development makes life much easier for these athletic dogs.

Rocky, like most stable dogs, could read a person's character and intent. This was demonstrated when Rocky alerted to the troublemaker in my home. Without any coaxing on my part, he either sensed that the man was a threat or I was not pleased having him in our home.

Max

Max is a true representative of the boxer breed that became my student and friend when he was five months old. He has a dominant-submissive temperament and an exuberant disposition. This combination of traits usually produces a versatile dog. For Max, it produced a gifted athlete who loves to compete, whether it's racing another dog or running down a retrieve; yet he never loses his temper, even when competing with other intact, dominant male dogs.

Once Max and his owner, Joanne McCormick, were taking Clancy, their thirteen-year-old blind Boston terrier, for a bathroom break behind their condominium. Clancy was dragging his leash behind him while he sniffed for a good place "to go." Before Joanne realized it, Clancy was walking toward the seawall edging the bay. When Joanne cried out, "No, Clancy," Max ran to his old friend, picked up the leash with his teeth, and led Clancy away from the drop-off.

A loyal, gentle, cunning, and naturally protective dog with a tremendous character and work ethic—that's Max.

Angel

Angel, a female German shepherd security dog, patrolled commercial buildings in Dothan, Alabama after business hours. Following one of her night shifts, I returned to pick her up. As a rule, she would be waiting by the front door when I arrived; but on this occasion, she was nowhere to be seen. As I walked to the back of the building, I found a blood trail that led me to Angel straddling a man on the floor. He told me that each time he tried to move from underneath her, she gripped him by the neck and growled until he became still. This was especially impressive because the thief had shot her in the shoulder during her attack. What determination we see in dogs—that never-say-die attitude, no matter what.

Frodo

When I met Frodo in 1976, he was a seven-year-old Schutzhund III Doberman pinscher. He was also a happy-go-lucky dog. This is not a contradiction because stable dogs can be good-natured and protective. Their participation in protection training is not a stressful or emotional experience. Frodo's protection work was a job he performed with confidence and cunning. Like most intelligent dogs, he loved to solve problems, and protection training served him well.

On one occasion, following my agitation, I ran behind some cover at the back of the property. When Frodo was released, he began tracking me through the woods. Because he was off lead, I had to make sure he made a solid bite on the padded sleeve in order to keep him off my legs. As the ninety-pound Doberman bounded through the brush, I braced myself, hoping I could maintain my balance and he would make a full bite—but Frodo had other plans. Instead of making a full bite, Frodo made a "pinch bite"—that is, he had only the leading edge of the sleeve between his front teeth. In protection training, this is a dangerous situation. Without a firm hold on the sleeve, a dog can lose his grip in close proximity to the agitator's legs. My defensive response was to lean forward so he could make a full bite, but when I did, I placed myself in a vulnerable position. My forward center of gravity made it impossible for me to move. Frodo realized my mistake before I did and took advantage of my disability. Instantly, he released his bite on the sleeve and made a bite on my inner thigh.

At that moment, his owner had run to the back of the property and saw my predicament. He quickly gave the command, "Out," which was the dog's cue to release his bite. When Frodo heard the command, he pulled his fangs from my leg, sat down, and looked up at me with the biggest, bloody smile I ever saw. With no tearing whatsoever, my only wounds were two puncture holes. It was obvious that Frodo was proud of his achievement, but there was no malice in his attitude. He was simply doing his job. And my future children were grateful for his professional work ethic.

Kodi

Kodi is a wonderful example of a quality German shepherd. His owner's job required him to travel much of Kodi's first two years of life, so Kodi came to live with me and Cheyenne. Kodi is a classic dominant-submissive dog with an exuberant disposition. At my home, I keep former students when their owners are out of town. Max, the boxer, has been one of my frequent boarders. Like Max, Kodi is an intact dog with a dominant temperament and an exuberant disposition. Even though both dogs are dominant males and my dog is a dominant-aggressive female wolf dog, there was never a serious quarrel. Because social order was well established, no matter how exuberant Kodi's play became, he would always submit when he was corrected for his dominant attitude. Comically, Kodi would submit to discipline by lowering his head until the disciplinary stare was completed, and then he would resume his play as though he had a clean slate.

Kodi was perhaps the strongest dog in my extended pack-family, yet he was the youngest member and the lowest-ranking subordinate in the pecking order. Even after completing his protection training, his temperament and disposition did not change. Protection training was just a game he enjoyed, while his position in the pack order remained the same.

Cheyenne

If a dog trainer is someone who has owned a special dog, then I have been truly blessed because I have owned two of these remarkable creatures. Cheyenne is a high-percentage fourth-generation wolf dog. On the wolf side of her family tree, there are five species of wolves, including three extinct species; on the dog side, malamute and German shepherd.

There were five pups in her litter, but there was no doubt Cheyenne was the alpha pup. In many of her puppy pictures, Cheyenne is facing the camera, standing apart from her littermates and posturing her authority. Even though she was the dominant-aggressive pup in a litter of high-percentage wolf dogs, I decided to put my pack-training techniques to the test.

I brought Cheyenne home when she was ten weeks old. Before arriving home, we stopped for her first trail hike. Being a dominant tempered pup, I wasn't surprised when she confidently sniffed her way down the trail. Upon arriving at her new home, she was initially apprehensive, choosing to hide behind the couch. I gave her the time she needed to acclimate to her new environment from the security of her makeshift den, for there was no reason to force her to come to me until she wanted to. After fifteen minutes in hiding, she had gained enough confidence to come out from behind the couch. An hour later, she had checked out her new home and was sleeping peacefully on the floor.

The following morning, we went for our second hike and her first swim. I had hoped she would continue to show her stable temperament by being curious and cautious when she discovered the bay—and she didn't disappoint. She walked cautiously to the edge of the water; she sniffed and tasted the water; and then she walked into the water and began swimming like it was her second nature. Following her swim, I discovered that I had lost my truck keys in the bay. To make matters worse, my wallet and her leash were locked inside the truck. After considering my options, I decided to walk home by crossing the half-mile span of the Hathaway Bridge, so we began walking across the bridge at the peak of tourist season using my belt for a leash. As a ten-week-old pup, Cheyenne was experiencing heavy traffic for the first time, yet she maintained her composure as the cars rumbled past—and I knew I had a special dog. There aren't many pups that could handle that kind of stress.

Cheyenne is my first wolf dog. Before adopting her, I had read everything I could about these animals. It was not encouraging. According to most authorities on the subject, wolf dogs cannot be trained like other dogs because of their "innate wildness." According to many animal behaviorists, wolf hybrids can't go off lead in the woods or in public; they are not social with other dogs or children; they can't be house-trained; and they won't come when called. If the "experts" were right, and her socialization and training were predestined to end in failure, I decided it wouldn't be for a lack of effort on my part. During her first year, I exercised her daily and socialized her to the world we lived in. At three months old, she was running free in the woods and making strides with her socialization. She would take a step back when a stranger reached down to pet her, but this is not a fault. When a stranger reaches down to pet a dog, he is posturing dominance to the dog. I often wonder if these people also try to touch people they don't know.

By the time she was five months old, Cheyenne had learned her basic obedience commands. At six months of age, she could have earned her AKC Companion Dog Title. Tracking, however, may be her strong suit. In fact, she amazes me with her tracking skills. Even when I hide downwind of her, she locates me in a calm and methodical manner. She doesn't frantically search for my track or sniff the air to find me—it's not like that at all. On one occasion, Cheyenne and I were hiking on the beach with a warm morning sea breeze. Fifty yards ahead, she was hunting for fiddler crabs when she passed behind a sand dune near the water. As she slipped out of sight, I ran to another sand dune a hundred yards away. After climbing to the top of the dune, I hid behind a cluster of sea oats. For a minute or two, Cheyenne remained unaware of my deception, and then she checked on my whereabouts. For a few seconds she stood motionless, staring in my direction, and then she nonchalantly trotted to my hiding spot with a big grin on her face.

Dogs are near sighted. They can detect motion but cannot clearly distinguish distant forms. And I was a hundred yards away, flat on my belly on top of a fifty-foot sand dune. For Cheyenne, and many other dogs, this mysterious sense is still functioning as it has for eons.

Cheyenne's loyalty, intelligence, cunning, temper, and disposition are all strong and pronounced. She is the star of my obedience training classes, and has participated in training seminars, television spots, and school and nursing home programs throughout her life. Cheyenne won her Wolf Dog Championship when she was two years old. In addition to her other virtues, she has a strong maternal instinct. Although never bred, she has had extensive contact with my clients' pups. What intrigues me is her ability to instantly read a pup. From the moment she makes visual contact, she knows which pups will be calm and respectful, and which will try to roughhouse or challenge her authority. If the pup is respectful of her social status, they will enjoy their time together from the start. But should submission not be expressed, Cheyenne's first order of business will be to establish order. She begins by giving a fixed stare and raising her hackles. If her warning is ignored, she will escalate the discipline by gripping the pup or restraining him on the ground.

Cheyenne has met hundreds of pups, yet she has never injured one of them. Many of my clients believe otherwise when Cheyenne pins their pup on the ground and wraps her mouth around his neck. As soon as the pup submits, Cheyenne will release her hold and forgive the transgression. While her corrections would seem harsh to unknowing eyes, the pups instantly change their attitude and respect her authority. In fact, pups will want to be with the dog that disciplines them. This is verified each time a disciplined pup eagerly follows Cheyenne down the trail. At moments like these, you are witnessing the dominance order in action and seeing pure instinctive behavior.

Max and Kodi

Cheyenne, Rocky, and my son, Seth

22

Walk On the Wild Side

"The presence of the wolf adds immeasurable richness and a wilderness spirit to the landscape. One need not see a wolf to benefit from his presence; it is enough to know that there is the possibility of discovering one on some distant ridge."
                                                    -- Adolph Murie, *A Naturalist in Alaska*, 1961.

To my grandchildren: Kodi, Erik, Karly, Logan, and Conner

Ravens…there! Two green eyes focused on the distant ridge that buffered a wide glacial valley. Standing erect and motionless, the guard hairs of his three-year-old body danced to the soothing music of the autumn breeze. Beyond the snow-dusted trees and high above the crest, three ravens were sounding the alarm for the upcoming feast. Caribou, heading south, were moving as though the trail would never end, as their ancestors have done since the beginning of time.

Gray signaled with a quick glance that it was time to go. The two leaders and their six-month-old pups were sensing the excitement on different levels. As the pack trotted down the sloping trail, the pups began jockeying for position and whimpering with all the joy they could muster. White glared at her boisterous pups with a quick movement of her head, and in unison, they silently fell into a single file behind their parents. Both alpha leaders knew they must keep an eye on their pups so they wouldn't spoil the day.

Following a thirty-minute trot through stands of black spruce and around several tamarack bogs, the trail brought them to the base of the ridge. Gray knew the north wind had already announced their arrival, so he and his mate would have to use their cunning to overcome their handicap. They would need to find a straggler or a cripple, and use the element of surprise, if this hunt were to end with a meal.

Gray and White were an experienced hunting team, but this would be their pups' first hunt where they were the underdog. The black male was the alpha pup and heir apparent to his father's title. While he wasn't the largest of the four pups, his cunning and determination worked to his advantage—and today he would prove his merit. Desire and anticipation were burning through his amber eyes.

After leading the pack to the top of the narrow ridge overlooking the spruce flats that peppered the subarctic landscape, the leader stopped in his tracks. His body language told his hunting party to be on alert and to follow his lead. His head was held high with each ear independently targeting the familiar sounds, as the alpha female moved alongside her mate. From underneath an ailing alder, with the sun breaking from its cover, twelve ears and eyes began scanning the migrating herd.

Suddenly and stealthily, the alpha male led the pack down the steep slope and around the Precambrian outcropping at the base of the ridge. Meanwhile the caribou were picking up speed and moving closer together, as this instinctual game of survival and sacrifice took center stage. From their vantage point behind the massive granite bedrock, the alpha leaders were hoping that an opportunity would materialize. If a calf strayed from the herd, Gray's job would be a simple task, but he knew the risk of bringing down a bull or a defensive maternal caribou. He had lost a tooth to the hoof of a caribou during his first hunt.

It was then that Gray and White's appetites were whetted. Heading their way, a hundred yards away, were a pair of calves and a cow using the cover along the base of the ridge. Although on alert, the cow was not aware of the ambush until the ravens entered the mix. Gray looked up to see a dozen or more frenetic ravens filling the sky with their noisy anticipation of a wolf kill to scavenge.

Seeing the excited behavior of the ravens, the cow realized her mistake and the imminent danger. With a snort, the maternal cow and the calves broke into a full run toward the safety of the herd. In the same moment, the pack leaders bolted from their cover, leading the way for their pups. With streamlined bodies, pinned-back ears, and streaming tongues, six gray wolves sprinted after the panicking caribou. Although somewhat anxious from all the commotion, the pups were being compensated by the excitement and the desire to participate, as they followed closely behind their leaders.

Using her greater speed, White was hoping to intersect the stragglers before they reached the herd. If she could turn her prey, they would fall into the trap being set by her mate. As the pack splashed across one of many rivulets that weaved their way through a sea of cottongrass, their plan began to take shape. The caribou were turning away from White's advance and their only hope. Gray Leader quickly closed the gap, coming alongside the maternal adult and tearing at her neck with a quick, slashing bite. The desired effect was realized when she spun around, turning on a dime and facing the onrush of White. The alpha female quickly gripped the cow by the nose and pulled her head to the ground, while Gray severed a tendon in the cow's hind leg, causing her quick collapse. The remaining struggle would last for only a few seconds, once both wolves converged on the animal's throat. As the cow exhaled her final breath, six panting wolves stood listening to the sound of caribou hooves beating their retreat to the raucous clamor of hungry ravens.

After catching their breath, the pups began sniffing their fallen prey. While Black pulled at the ear of the carcass, the leaders took inventory of their kill. Gray initiated the feast by tearing open the belly and pulling out a large portion of steaming liver. After swallowing the delicacy, the alpha male suddenly stood erect and stepped away from the kill. A fox was scurrying from bush to bush a hundred yards away, but there were no thieving bears that he could detect. Sensing the freedom from danger, Gray moved back to the feast as the pups were gorging the organs and intestines provided by their alpha leader.

Following their feeding, the pups were playing a game of catch-me-if-you can with their red brother when their parents lifted their heads to sing their ancestral song. The pups quickly called the game off and joined in with delight, as their cracking howls tried to harmonize with their beloved leaders. It had been a good day, and following a short celebration and a long rest, they would feed again on their kill before returning home. Then the ravens, foxes, marmots, and voles would claim their share, leaving little more than bone and hide.

Meanwhile the pups would sleep off their swollen bellies and relive the excitement of the hunt in their dreams. They had followed their leaders' instructions and had not put themselves in danger or jeopardized the hunt with foolish independence. By following their leaders, they had been protected from the sharp edges of the caribou hooves. Injuries were not acceptable in their world, where only the strong have the opportunity to survive.

As the pack drifted off to sleep, the dominant black pup was recalling the events of the day. He was also remembering an earlier hunt for summer rabbits when success was spoiled by his inexperience and exuberance. His mother had been on the track of a rabbit in high grass when he trotted alongside and ahead of her. He still remembered how she gripped him by the shoulder and slammed him to the ground. He remembered that lesson, and after comparing the two hunts, drifted off to sleep knowing he had learned a valuable lesson. And he would never forget.

The orange sun was low in the afternoon sky when the triumphant pack returned to their den. While the leaders checked for the possibility of trespassers, the pups began tracking the mice that scavenged their den in their absence. With Black taking the lead in the hunt and his red brother following closely behind, the cream-colored omega female observed from her customary safe distance. Their tawny brother, however, had opted for his own adventure.

Tawny had wandered far away from his pack, nibbling on berries and grasshoppers along the way, when he discovered something that caused him great concern. He had never seen one of these creatures and wasn't sure how to respond to his discovery. Had his independence doomed him? Could he investigate? Should he retreat to the safety of his pack? As the pup stared at the ominous creature, both wonder and peril entered the mix of thoughts now racing through his mind. While his curiosity and the excitement encouraged him to take a step closer, his cautious nature made for a tentative advance. Fifty feet away, a wolverine was glaring menacingly from the hole he was excavating. And when the creature hissed, Tawny jumped back with his tail tucked tightly between his legs and again considered the option of retreat. Tawny, however, held his ground until curiosity overcame his fear, and then he took a few more steps, with quivering and twitching muscles and a lowered body posture. But when the creature charged the intruder, the brave, bloodstained young hunter yelped and retreated to the security of his pack, as the setting sun bade him farewell.

With winter's approach, the wolves' coats had filled, and their guard hairs were at their greatest length. And they would soon be well fattened for the coming winter. The female leader moved over to nuzzle the neck of her mate. It had been a good year. All four of their pups were healthy, and each possessed a strong prey drive. Their pack was well on its way to becoming a stable and formidable force in their world. There was also an air of friendliness among their pack members that promoted civility and social order. The tranquility was a welcomed change from the previous summer, when their social order had been threatened following the appearance of a reddish, lone wolf.

The chance encounter occurred as Gray and White were returning home from another unsuccessful hunt. As they climbed the trail leading to their den, in the distance stood a thin and bony male wolf. Gray began sniffing the air-born scent, and both wolves focused as well as they could on the strange wolf. The stranger's body language and behavior would determine the outcome of this meeting. As Gray and White deliberated, the lone wolf stood motionless and erect as he stared back.

For a closer inspection, Gray and White raced down the side of the sloping trail to the center of the grassy clearing where the trespasser awaited them. With his tail, head, and hackles raised to their highest position, Gray Leader took charge by circling the strange wolf. While the newcomer wasn't expressing a great amount of dominance, he was neither expressing submission to the satisfaction of Gray. Even though his body posture was somewhat lowered, his ears were erect and independently focusing on Gray and White, as they circled his position. As Gray approached the animal's hind end, he was hoping to engage the newcomer to join his pack, but the outsider must first submit to his close inspection. His first attempt to inspect the wolf's anal area caused the outsider to lower his hind end and move away. The second attempt, however, would be successful, with Red submitting to his inspection. As Gray performed the ceremonial inspection, he was detecting the emotional state of his new pack member and expressing his authority.

The alpha leaders had lost their first litter of pups to marauding, den-robbing bears; and currently, they had four pups that were too young to hunt for themselves. Even though the incentive of increasing their pack size was strong, Gray has some misgivings for this wolf.

Red had become a lone wolf following his banishment from his natal pack. Being both stubborn and aggressive, discipline had little effect on his antisocial attitude. And when he ultimately challenged the authority of his alpha leader, he was defeated in battle by the alpha male and ostracized from the pack. For a week, he lingered in the periphery, grieving over his banishment and hoping for a reunion with his family. But that day never came.

After being accepted into Gray's pack, the two-year-old male responded by lifting his leg on one of the leader's scent posts. Gray realized the day would come when his authority would be challenged, as he trotted over to cover the dominant wolf's scent with his urine. Afterwards, as he scratched the ground with all four feet, Gray glared at the offender. Red lowered his head but returned the stare before turning away from the piercing stare. Hardly a satisfactory response, yet the alpha leader allowed it to pass.

The following afternoon found the three adults dozing in the warm sun and the pups playing a game of tug-of-war with a sun-bleached bone. When the game brought the pups near the newcomer, Red sprang to his feet and postured his dominance to the lead pup. Black reacted with surprise and submission to the show of dominance but held his ground. With raised hackles, Red quickly moved alongside the pup. His intention was as clear as the growls emanating from his throat. With a quick movement, the adult male rode up onto the pup's back. Black yelped and dropped to the ground, offering as much submission as he could, but instead of accepting the pup's apology, the dominant adult wolf stood across the recumbent pup with his tail held high over his back and his teeth bared.

As the pup cried for forgiveness, and before any retribution could be administered, Red was suddenly slammed from behind. In a flashing moment, the red and gray bodies were a rolling blur. And then, before Red could regain his footing, Gray pinned his adversary to the ground. The wolves were face to face, with their lips drawn back, but Gray maintained his position on top, growling through his exposed teeth. The only remaining question was whether or not order would be restored. Gray would decide whether or not the subordinate's pack membership would be revoked—and that decision hinged upon Red's response. Due to his stubbornness, however, submission to authority was not a viable option, so Red attempted to free himself from Gray's restraint by kicking and pushing with his hind legs.

It would be a short, one-sided battle once the leader's mate entered the fray. Having crossed the line of tolerance, Red scrambled to his feet, tucked his tail, and made a full retreat with the entire pack participating in his expulsion. Red was once again a lone wolf; but he would live for only one more season, surviving on meals of mice, rabbit, and carrion—hardly a proper diet for the likes of one of these creatures.

With the changing of the seasons, the wolves would soon leave their summer den and follow their caribou meal ticket all the way to the coast. By the time they returned next spring, the pack would include six adult wolves and perhaps a new litter as well. The likelihood of the pack remaining intact was strong. The friendly dispositions of the pack leaders promoted civility among their pack members, and the dominant-aggressive male pup displayed the same attitude toward his brothers and sister.

On the morning of their departure, there was a sense of excitement and fulfillment as the pack headed southwest on their yearly migration to their coastal mountain range. Once there, they would return to their mountain lake and refurbish their den for the winter. The caribou would continue southward, but the wolves would remain behind, not wanting to compete with the resident bears on the coast.

Along the lakeshore, the bearberry and dogwood bushes had provided good cover for stalking moose. Gray was remembering one moose hunt in particular. He and his mate had been hiding behind the bushes and listening to the familiar sounds of breaking ice and sloshing water. As the sounds moved closer and a form took shape, their excitement quickly turned to disappointment. A bull moose was not what they wanted, and this was an extremely large and dangerous animal. Both wolves knew that a bull moose was anything but defenseless when it came to two wolves.

On this morning, however, the hungry wolves decided that the reward outweighed the risk. With their bodies pressed close to the frozen shoreline, they moved into position, flanking the moose on both sides. Fifty yards away, the towering bull raised his head from the icy water with a bawl and faced the advance of the stalking wolves. Having lost the element of surprise, Gray and White were left with only a frontal attack; but if they could frighten the bull and cause him to panic, they could attack his hind legs when he climbed onshore. With this in mind, each wolf independently began charging the bull. But this strategy also failed, for the bull did not panic. Instead, he confronted the wolves with his threatening rack as he backed into deeper water.

For several minutes the wolves held their ground in shallow water while the bull snorted his discontent. Having reached another stalemate, the wolves were forced again to improvise. If they couldn't cause the bull to panic, perhaps they could make him angry enough to charge. As Gray's hackles stood on end from the base of his neck to the base of his tail, and from a stalking position at the water's edge, the alpha male suddenly charged dangerously close to the bull's rack before splashing away. This was repeated several times before the agitated bull took the bait.

As Gray provided a diversion, White was moving into position off to one side. When the bull finally lunged at Gray, White took advantage of the moment by rushing in and making a hard, gripping bite to the side of the beast's neck. But when the bull lowered his massive head, White's legs became entwined with the antlers; and when the bull raised his head and gave a quick shake, White was thrown high into the air. When she splashed down on her back, the infuriated bull frantically charged her as she swam to shore. Sensing the danger, Gray charged the bull and made a hard bite to the animal's hind leg. But he also lost his grip, leaving him to take a kick to the head.

And such would be the outcome of many days like this. The bull would not leave the lake, and the wolves would not change his mind; so after a lengthy standoff, the bruised and disappointed wolves returned to their den, exhausted and hungry. Later they could dig out a few muskrats, but it would not be the same. And tomorrow would be another day—one that promised the opportunity for survival but never the outcome.

Gray remembered that day and believed he could produce a different ending when he returned to his mountain lake with a pack of six experienced hunters. Until then, the moose could swim without fear and feed on the aquatic plants in peace, and the lynx could stalk their prey by moonlight without interruption. But when Gray exercised his right of return, the lynx would gravitate deeper into the forest, and the moose would be on constant alert. And time would continue as it has forever, with harmony and order in this corner of the universe.

"The caribou feed the wolf, but it is the wolf who keeps the caribou strong."
(Keewatin Eskimo saying)

Seacrest Wolf Preserve, Inc. (seacrestwolfpreserve.org) is located
in the Florida panhandle. Owners: Wayne and Cynthia Watkins.
Captive wolves have the ability to form
deep bonds with their human caretakers.

Seacrest Wolf Preserve's Chinook, a two-year-old British Columbian male wolf, gives ten-year-old Kaylea Danielle an affectionate greeting. Wolves love young children and are normally at ease around them.

Wolf Heart Caiozzo, an American Indian from the Apache Nation, gives Kiowa a big hug. Kiowa, a three-year-old male British Columbian wolf, is social to visitors and relates to humans in a positive and profound way.

Chumani, a three-year-old female, gives Rick Burr
and daughter Trina a warm greeting
(photography by Wayne Watkins, Seacrest Wolf Preserve)

23

Q & A

What is the fastest and easiest way to house-train a puppy?

The fastest and easiest way to house-train a puppy is to keep him on a schedule during the house-training process. This means we should take our pups outside at the same times each day and feed them at the same times. Free feeding throughout the day is not recommended. Nibblers will produce a larger number of stools each day. Pups have an internal clock and remember past events if their timing is predictable; so if they go outside at the same times each day, pups will be expecting to go outside at the appropriate times.

As well as taking your pup outside every two to four hours, you should be aware of the times a pup will be most likely to have an accident in the house: following playtime, naps, and feedings; when he wakes up in the morning; before he retires at night; whenever you see the pup walking aimlessly with his nose sniffing the floor; and whenever the pup enters a strange home or building. Before taking your pup inside a home or a building he doesn't know, you should allow him to sniff around outside and relieve himself before taking him inside. Whenever a pup is excited, he will need to relieve himself.

Accidents should be disciplined with a gripping and banishment. When you witness an accident or your pup sniffing the floor as he walks aimlessly, call out, "No," grip him by the scruff, and transport him outside. When a pup walks aimlessly sniffing the floor, he is sniffing for his scent before eliminating. This behavior was learned from his mother between six and eight weeks of age.

Should you find the pup's wastes without witnessing the event, you can still correct the pup. He will not have forgotten the wastes are his. While there is no reason to rub his nose in it, you should place his nose near the soiled area as you verbally chastise the pup. Following the correction, the pup should be banished to the yard or his crate for a half hour, while you clean up the mess and neutralize the odor with a product designed for the job.

In addition to disciplining a pup for soiling the home, you should give your heartiest praise whenever the pup relieves himself outside. In addition to your praise, offering a treat when your pup relieves himself outside will be a positive stimulus.

Supervision will be necessary for the pup's first couple of weeks at your home. At times when you can't keep an eye on your pup, he should either be crated or left in the yard. Crates with enclosed sides provide more security for pups than open wire cages. A pet carrier with opaque sides simulates the security of a den.

All accidents must be cleaned with an odor neutralizer. Soap and water will cover the odor with perfume, but it will not mask the scent from your pup's nose. If a pup detects his scent in the home, he will be stimulated to eliminate on that spot.

If you buy a pup from a pet store, you may be buying a pup from a puppy mill. In puppy mills and pet stores, pups are usually forced to eliminate where they eat and sleep. This will often become a difficult habit to break.

Why did my dog react to a man wearing a clown suit? He is extremely social with my friends and strangers, but when he saw my friend entering my home dressed as a clown, I thought my dog had seen a ghost. Should I be concerned about his fearful reaction?

Social dogs are usually stable tempered, but that doesn't mean a dog won't respond erratically to unusual stimuli such as a clown in his living room. It is natural for a dog to respond with some anxiety when he encounters something extremely different from his life experience.

Cheyenne, my wolf dog, had a similar experience when she was a pup. Even though she was socialized extensively as a pup, I had overlooked some common visual experiences, namely, skaters and skateboarders. She was about five months old when she saw her first kid skating down the street. Her reaction could be described as someone seeing a ghost. Saying she had a fearful reaction would be a major understatement.

For Cheyenne to gain confidence in the presence of skateboarding kids, I had to expose her to the stressful stimulus a little at a time. We began by parking a block away from an outdoor skate park. As she grew in confidence at that distance, I walked her closer to the skaters. Even though she hasn't totally accepted the normality of skaters, no longer does she panic when she encounters a skateboarder.

Understanding a dog's perspective will explain your dog's behavior. Socialization means learning to trust the world. While Cheyenne had been socialized to children and bicycles, the movement of cycling kids is different from the movement of skaters and skateboarders who glide over the ground. Even though your dog had been socialized to your friends and strangers, he likely had never met a clown. This is what caused the fearful response. There is no reason to worry about your dog's behavior.

Can wolf hybrids be safely kept as pets?

While there are quality dogs and problem dogs found in all breeds, there are some breeds that present more problems than others. Wolf hybrids or wolf dogs would seem to fall into this category. On the one hand, wolf dogs and dogs are basically the same animal. Like all dogs, wolf dogs need love, discipline, leadership, and pack activities to be stable and well-mannered pets. On the other hand, many wolf dogs have extremely unstable temperaments and dispositions. The most common problems associated with wolf dogs are fearfulness in social situations and destructive behavior in and around the home.

I have noticed that first-generation wolf dogs (one parent is a wolf and the other is a dog) are more likely to be unstable than wolf dogs from wolf-dog stock. These dogs are classified as fifty percent wolf dogs. First-generation wolf dogs are often less stable than high-percentage wolf dogs that are designated second-, third-, or fourth-generation crosses. A second-generation wolf dog has wolf dogs for parents. Third-generation wolf dogs have parents and grandparents that are wolf dogs.

I do not recommend wolf dogs for the average American family. They require both diligence and a great amount of understanding. Wolf dogs must be allowed to bond with their families. You cannot leave a wolf dog in the back yard or a kennel the majority of the time and expect to have a positive relationship with one of these animals.

However, if you have a real desire, and the time, understanding, and dedication to give to a wolf dog, you can have a rewarding experience and a wonderful time in the process.

My one-year-old mixed-breed dog bit my three-year-old daughter when she approached the dog while he was eating. The bite was only a slight puncture to her chin. Was the dog being protective of his food?

Your dog's behavior was not expressing protectiveness. He was expressing his dominance. Some dog behaviorists would suggest the child was at fault for not respecting the dog's privacy. This was not the problem as far as the dog was concerned. When a dog bites a child in his family, or any child for that matter, it is not the child's fault for being in the wrong place at the wrong time. A pack member would not feel the need to discipline an unmannerly or unruly child, but a pack leader surely would. The problem will likely continue if you do not take control of the dog's behavior. Your job is to establish social order so he will not feel the need to discipline his family members.

When my pup was very young, she fell into the swimming pool and became panicked before I could pull her from the water. Now, as a ten-month-old pup, her fear of water remains. Is there anything that can be done to overcome her fear of water?

Dogs are intelligent creatures with incredible memories. This is why such a traumatic event as falling into deep water can be permanently debilitating. Dogs do not have short memories; in fact, they never forget. They are shaped by their negative and positive experiences during their development.

I knew a Labrador retriever that had the same experience as a pup. When he was five years old, I was asked to help him overcome his fear of water. I began by taking him for walks on a lakeshore. It took a couple of days for him to walk in the edge of the water without overreacting to his fear. By the third day, I was able to coax the dog into deeper water. As the water reached his chest, I noticed something unusual—the dog was standing on his tiptoes. With a little more coaxing, the dog's fear turned to joy when he finally took the leap of faith into deeper water.

The key to correcting a phobic behavior is desensitizing the dog to the stimulus that causes the anxiety. Forcing the issue should not come into play, if we want to build a dog's confidence. Perhaps a wading pool or walks in shallow water will help boost your dog's confidence enough to overcome her fear. When she is confidently walking on lead in shallow water, you can unsnap the leash and encourage her to follow you into deeper water.

If I allow my pup to socialize with my friends and strangers, will he still be protective as an adult?

Dogs are not simple creatures. If we fail to socialize our pups to friends and strangers, as adults, they will likely be terrified of people outside the immediate family. If your pup doesn't learn to trust people, he will not have the confidence to defend his family when he reaches adulthood. Stable dogs do not need to be trained to discern danger. They only need to learn to be confident in social situations. Protective instincts are intact in every healthy, stable dog.

My older dog is considered to be the bully on the block when it comes to other dogs. However, when my sister and her toy poodle visit my home, her poodle dominates my much larger dog. My five-year-old German shepherd even allows the poodle to bite him on the face. Why does he tolerate this?

I have seen this behavior under similar circumstances. Some dogs seem to think toy breeds are very young puppies. Because of this perception, they will not discipline them for rambunctious or testing behavior. On one occasion, Cheyenne, my adult wolf dog, was meeting a client's six-month-old miniature poodle when I noticed the same behavioral expression. The poodle was jumping onto her and biting her on the lip. Cheyenne's reaction was as any maternal dog tolerating a young pup's rowdy behavior.

My dog has the habit of running out the front door at every opportunity. How can I break her from running down the street when someone opens the door?

As for any behavior modification, I will devise a consequence for a bad behavior and be consistent in offering the consequence each time the dog behaves badly. While standing at the front door, I will tell the dog to stay as I open the door. I won't open the door all the way, however. Instead, I will open it just enough for a dog to squeeze through. Should he try to walk through the opening, I will gently close the door on the dog's head, holding it between the door and the doorjamb. When I feel the dog pulling back to free himself, I will release my hold and allow him to pull his head inside the house. Then I will offer the dog another chance to make the right decision about running out the door.

This training sequence should be repeated daily until you see a submissive willingness of your dog to change her behavior. When she makes the right decision, you should praise her behavior.

Why is trauma so devastating to pups?

I learned as a child that animals never forget. At my dad's home, we trained a variety of hunting dogs including golden and Labrador retrievers. In the summer of 1964, we lost one of our golden retrievers when he tried to retrieve a cottonmouth moccasin from our pond. To rid us of the problem, my father acquired two baby alligators from a wildlife officer. Alligators love to eat snakes, and it didn't take them long to do the job.

Early one morning, I was fishing in the pond when one of the baby gators climbed onto my kayak. I overreacted by swatting the gator from the bow with the paddle. Both gators made our pond their home for five years, feeding on fish, turtles, and our scrap meat, and they grew to over six feet in length. One gator was tame and would come when we grunted like a gator. The other gator—the one that I swatted with the paddle—would never come near me or anyone else. Even though he experienced only one traumatic event in his life, and even though alligators are extremely simple creatures, he never forgot. If gators never forget, dogs surely remember past events, especially if the memory is traumatic in nature.

How do you get a dog to stop raiding the litter box?

Many dogs love to eat "cat scat." One technique that can work, if we are persistent, is to pour a little aftershave lotion or cayenne pepper on the cat's feces and allow the dog to take a sniff. By consistently offering the repulsive smell over a period of time, a dog will likely change his attitude about the litter-box buffet.

Is it better to purchase one puppy or two? My husband thinks it would be better to have two, so the pups would have company. So far, I'm not convinced.

It would be beneficial to have a companion for your pup, especially if both of you work outside the home. However, while you will be satisfying his need for companionship, you will also have two pups bonding more to each other than to you and your husband. While a single pup will need to be exercised daily, you will be able to bond more easily with a pup when competition is absent.

My advice would be to acquire one pup. By the time you have completed his obedience training, you can then add another pup to your family. With a trained, older pup in the home, you will receive your trained pup's assistance with the pack training of the new pup.

Why does my dog try to fight the neighborhood dogs when we meet them on the street? Is he only being protective?

Being protective has nothing to do with your dog's behavior, unless the other dogs are trying to dominate him. If your dog is being the aggressor, he is expressing his dominance to the neighborhood dogs, but he is also expressing his authority to you as well. Alpha leaders look for opportunities to demonstrate their authority, and they will continue to do so until their owners take charge. You need to establish social order with your dog. By leash training in neighborhoods with barking dogs and producing a consequence each time your dog expresses his dominance to other dogs, you will begin his demotion from power.

For stubborn dogs, a snap correction will also be needed with your about-face corrections. To determine if your correction was consequential, judge by the dog's reaction to the correction. If he continues to focus on the other dogs following a correction, it wasn't considered a consequence. If he turns his attention back to you, it was adequate. In order to demote your alpha dog, you must become a consistent disciplinarian and be more aware of the dog's testing behavior.

My one-year-old dog sometimes growls and barks at family members and neighbors. If one year in dog years equals seven human years, isn't this unusually aggressive behavior for such a young dog?

The adage that one dog-year equals seven human years would apply better to adult dogs than pups in their first year of life. A six-month-old pup is comparable to a seven- to eight-year-old child. A year-old pup is more like a teenager than a seven-year-old child. Your "teenage" dog is testing your authority and the authority of your neighbors. Whenever a dog displays aggressive behavior to family members or innocent bystanders, he is in need of discipline and pack training.

When my husband leaves home, our three-year-old female Rottweiler seems agitated and on alert throughout the day and night. This is not the case when my husband is home. Why does she behave differently when my husband leaves home?

Your adult female dog is likely seeing your husband as the alpha male and herself as the alpha female. This would explain her demeanor when your husband is away. She is taking charge when her alpha is absent. These dogs are often referred to as "one man dogs," but in reality, these dogs are seeing themselves as second-in-command.

Recommended Reading

Davis, L. Wilson, 1974. *Go find!* Howell Book House, Inc. New York.

Fox, D. Michael W., 1972. *Understanding your dog*, Coward, McCann & Geoghegan, Inc. New York

Holaday, Bobbie, 2003. *The return of the gray wolf.* University of Arizona Press

Koehler, William R., 1984. *The Koehler method of training tracking dogs.* Howell Book House, Inc., New York.

Koehler, William R., 1982. *The Koehler method of dog training.* Howell Book House, Inc., New York.

Lawrence, R. D. 1980. *Secret go the wolves.* Holt, Reinhart and Winston. New York.

Lorenz, Konrad 1952. *King Solomon's ring.* Methuen & Co., Ltd., London.

Mech, L. D., 1970. *The wolf.* University of Minnesota Press, Minneapolis, Minnesota.

Mech, L. D., 1966. *The wolves of Isle Royale*, U. S. Nat. Park Serv. Fauna Ser. No. 7.

Mech, L.D., 1998, *The wolves of Denali*, University of Minnesota Press.

Mech, L.D. 1992. *Wolves of the high artic*, Voyageur Press, Stillwater, MN.

Murie, A. 1944. *The wolves of Mt. McKinley.* U. S. Nat. Park Serv. Fauna Ser No. 5., University of Washington Press.

Murie. A. 1963. *A naturalist in Alaska.* Doubleday Co., Inc. New York.

Peterson, Rolf; Vucerich, John. 2002-2003. *Ecological studies of wolves of Isle Royale*, Annual report. Michigan Technical University Houghton, Michigan.

Pitcairn, Richard H., D.V.M., Pitcairn, Susan Hubble, Ph.D., 1995. *Dr. Pitcairn's complete guide to natural health for dogs and cats.* Rodale Press, Inc., Emmaus, Pa.

Readers Digest, 1997. *Intelligence in animals.* The Reader's Digest Association, Inc. New York.

Saunders, Blanche, 1946. *Training you to train your dog*, Doubleday & Company, Inc., New York.

Scott, J. P., and J. L. Fuller. 1965. *Genetics and the social behavior of the dog.* University of Chicago Press, Chicago.

Steves, Dororthy, 1974. *Radar.* Pelham Books, London.

Walker, Joanna, 1977. *The new Doberman pinscher*, Howell Book House, Inc., New York.

Wolters, Richard A., 1961. *Gun dog.* Penguin Books USA Inc. New York.

Web pages:

Defenders of Wildlife: www.defenders.org
Seacrest Wolf Preserve: www.seacrestwolfpreserve.org
National Wildlife Federation: www.nwf.org
Sinapu: www.sinapu.org
Timber Wolf Alliance: www.northland.edu/soci/timber_wolf.html

ISBN 141201213-9

9 781412 012133

Made in the USA
Lexington, KY
13 January 2016